Office 97

FOR BUSY PEOPLE

Blueprints for Office 97

On the following pages, we provide blueprints for some of the best ways to use Office 97:

- Express Yourself with Word
- Plan Your Retirement with Excel
- Plot Your Profits in an Excel Chart
- Sell Your Ideas with PowerPoint
- Use PowerPoint to Become a Web Publisher
- Build Online Databases with Access
- Use Outlook to Correspond with Anyone on E-Mail
- Organize Your Life with Outlook
- Use Internet Explorer to Surf the Net
- Create a Winning Business Plan

Express Yourself with Word

Appearances are important if you want to get your message accross. Add special effects to make your documents more interesting and easier to read (pages 26-28).

Got a question? Turn to the Office Assistant for easy-to-use, online help (pages 33-35).

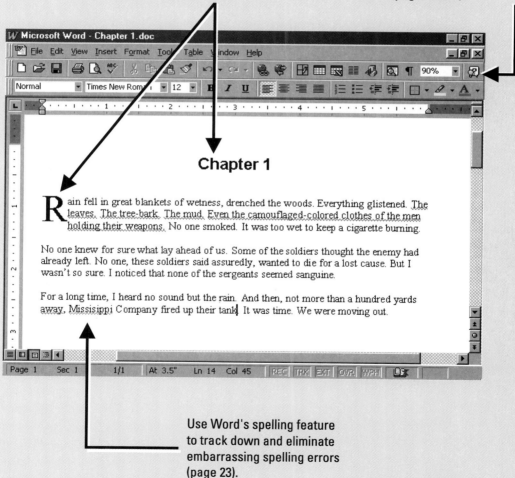

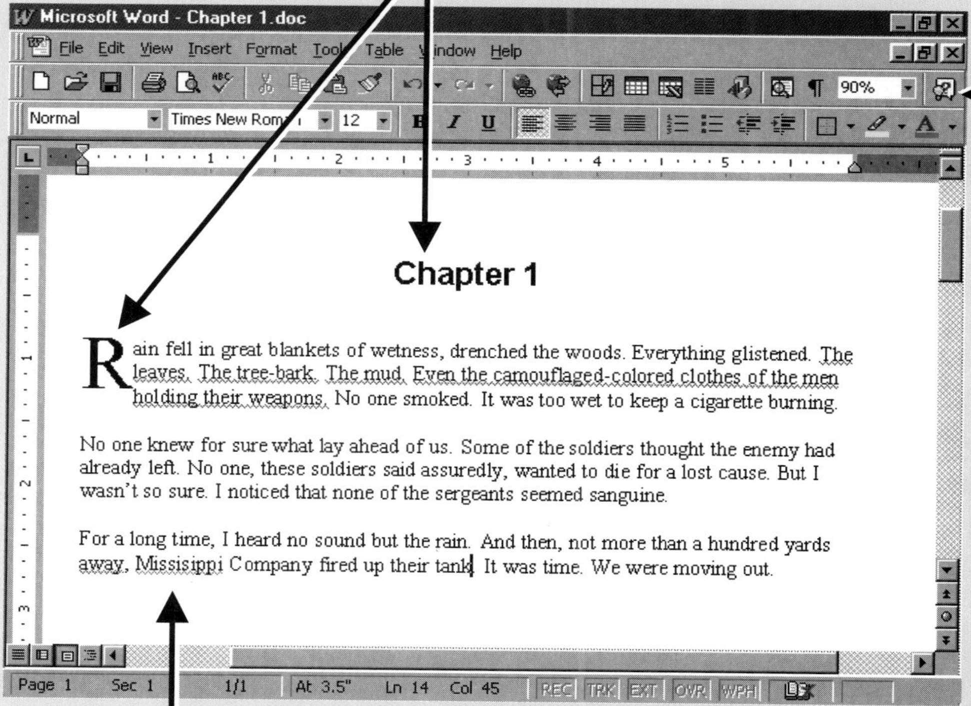

Use Word's spelling feature to track down and eliminate embarrassing spelling errors (page 23).

BLUEPRINT FOR BUSY PEOPLE™

Plan Your Retirement with Excel

Need to do some personal financial planning? Grab this workbook (and many others) from the Osborne web site (pages 257-262).

Make your plans confidential by using passwords for important workbooks (pages 146-148).

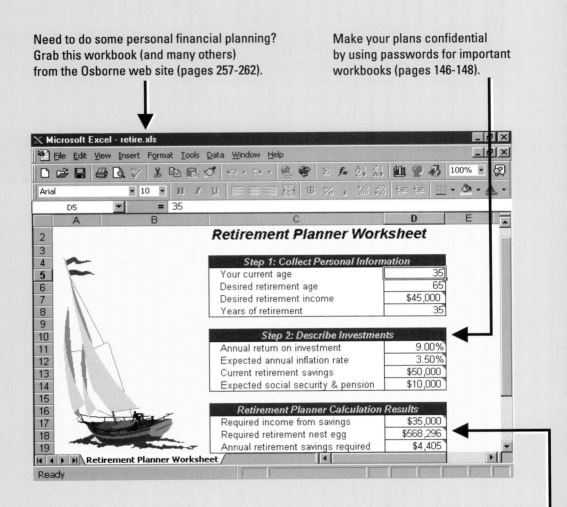

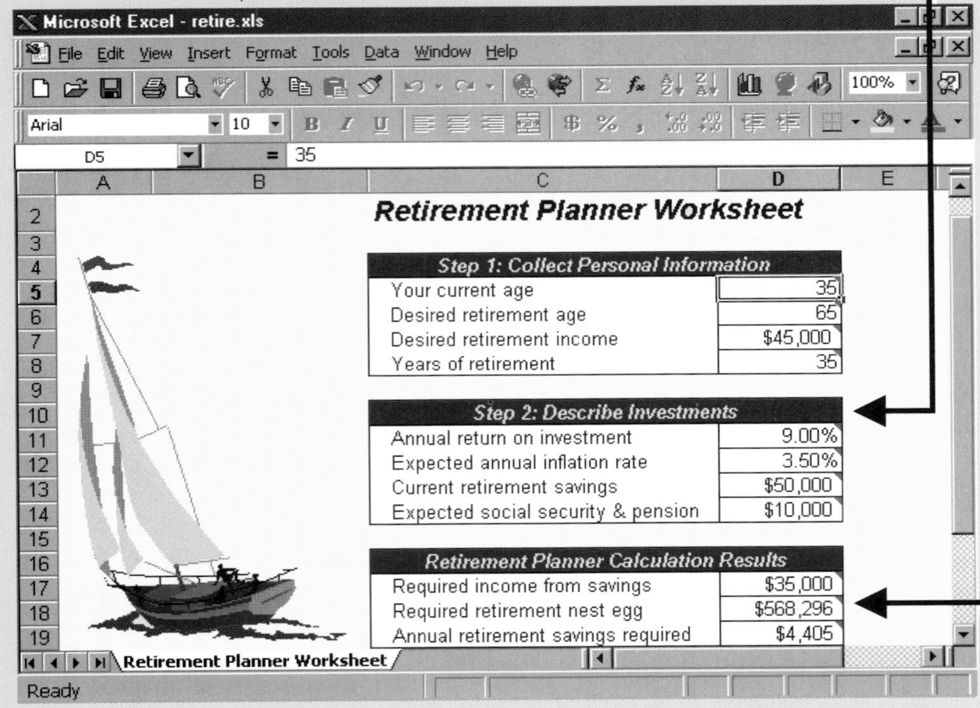

Don't worry about worksheet or formula complexity. Excel's functions let you easily make complicated calculations (pages 54-60).

BLUEPRINT FOR BUSY PEOPLE™ | Plot Your Profits in an Excel Chart

Use Excel charts in other Office applications. It's easy to copy and move charts from Excel to Word, PowerPoint, and even Access (pages 112-113).

Easily customize charts by adding titles and legends so that they send the right message (pages 102-103).

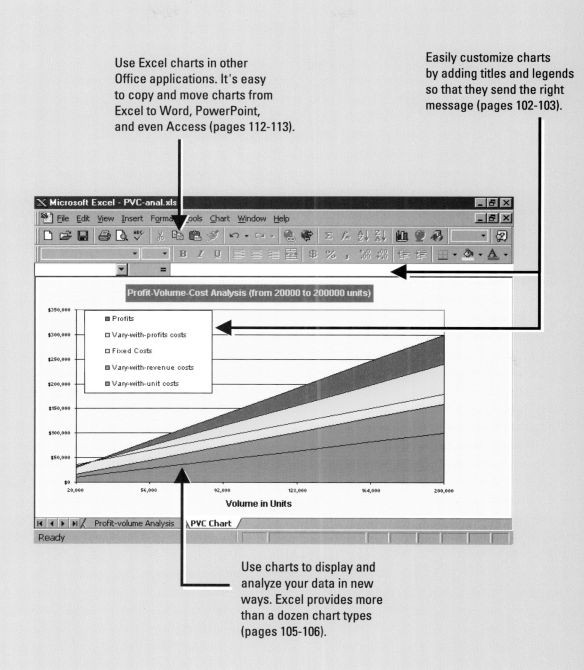

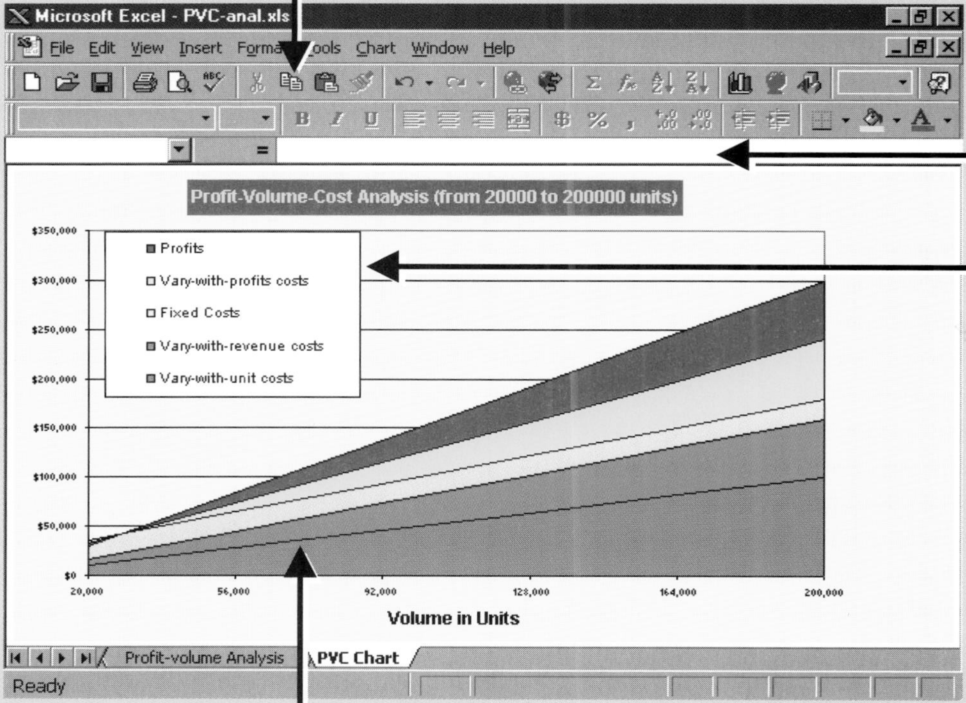

Use charts to display and analyze your data in new ways. Excel provides more than a dozen chart types (pages 105-106).

Why reinvent the wheel? Use PowerPoint's AutoContent wizard to create a first-cut rough-draft of your presentation (pages 73-77).

Make your presentation unique by adding charts, worksheets, clip art, and even animation (pages 82-84, 112-113).

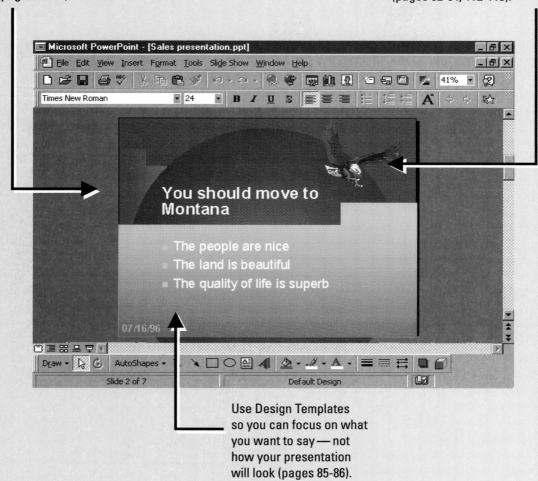

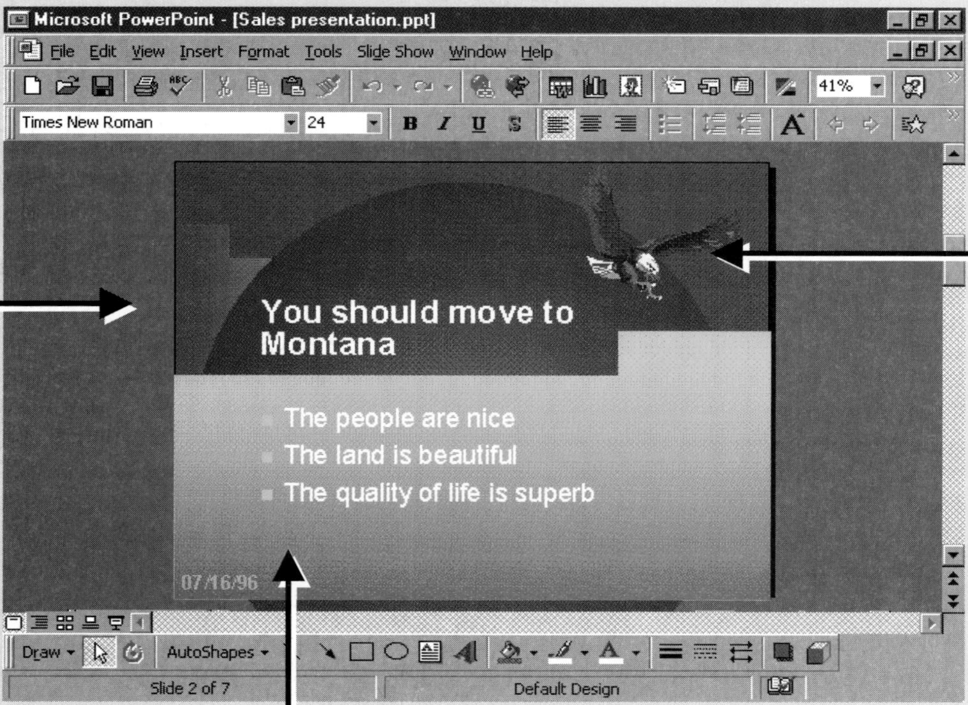

Use Design Templates so you can focus on what you want to say — not how your presentation will look (pages 85-86).

Use PowerPoint to Become a Web Publisher

Tap the power of Office's clip art, WordArt, and drawing tools to make your web pages more interesting and attractive (pages 124-135).

Don't get run off the Information Superhighway. Use PowerPoint to create HTML documents — even full web sites (pages 195-200).

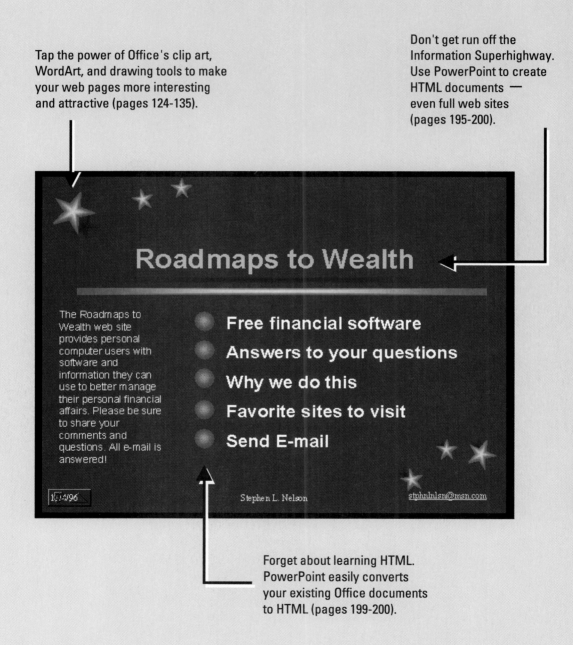

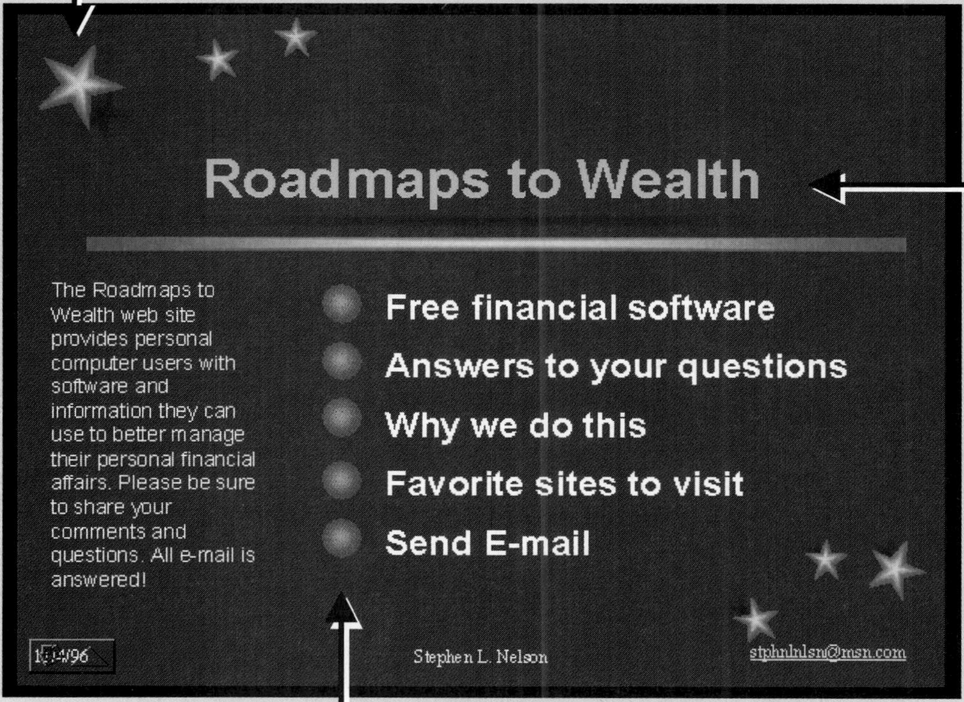

Forget about learning HTML. PowerPoint easily converts your existing Office documents to HTML (pages 199-200).

Afraid you need to be a database guru? You don't. Just take advantage of Access's powerful wizards to create the database you need (pages 243-245).

Gain new insights into your data by rearranging, sorting, and filtering it — all with just the clicks of your mouse (pages 249-251).

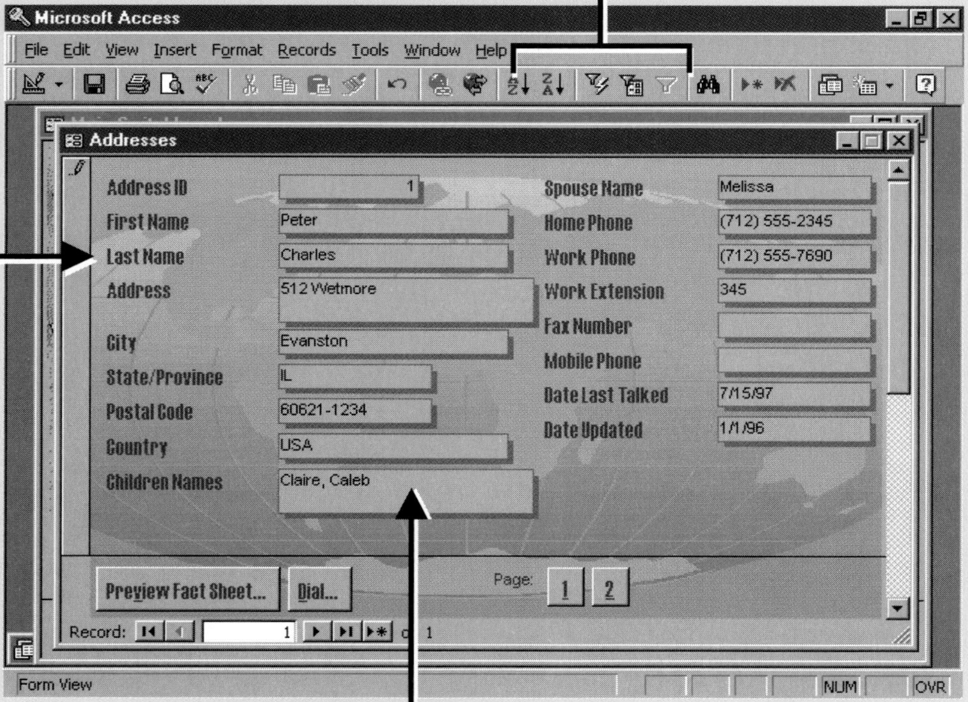

Use a query to ask any question you want about the information in your database (pages 238-239).

BLUEPRINT FOR BUSY PEOPLE™

Use Outlook to Correspond with Anyone on E-Mail

Share your information. With Outlook, you aren't limited to just textual messages; you can also attach files (pages 214-215).

Join the dialog. Use Outlook's e-mail client to correspond with anyone else connected to the Internet (pages 211-216).

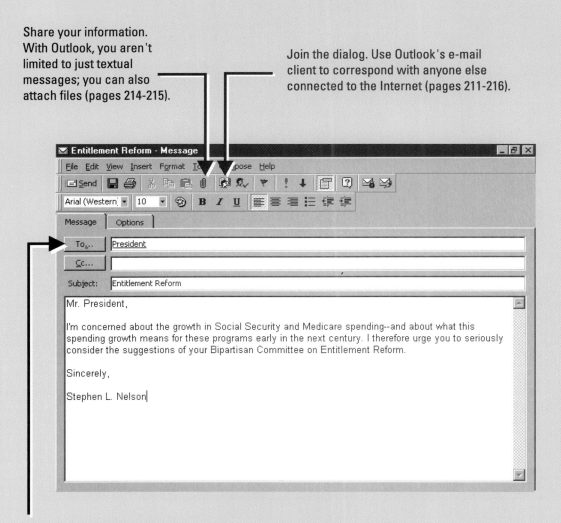

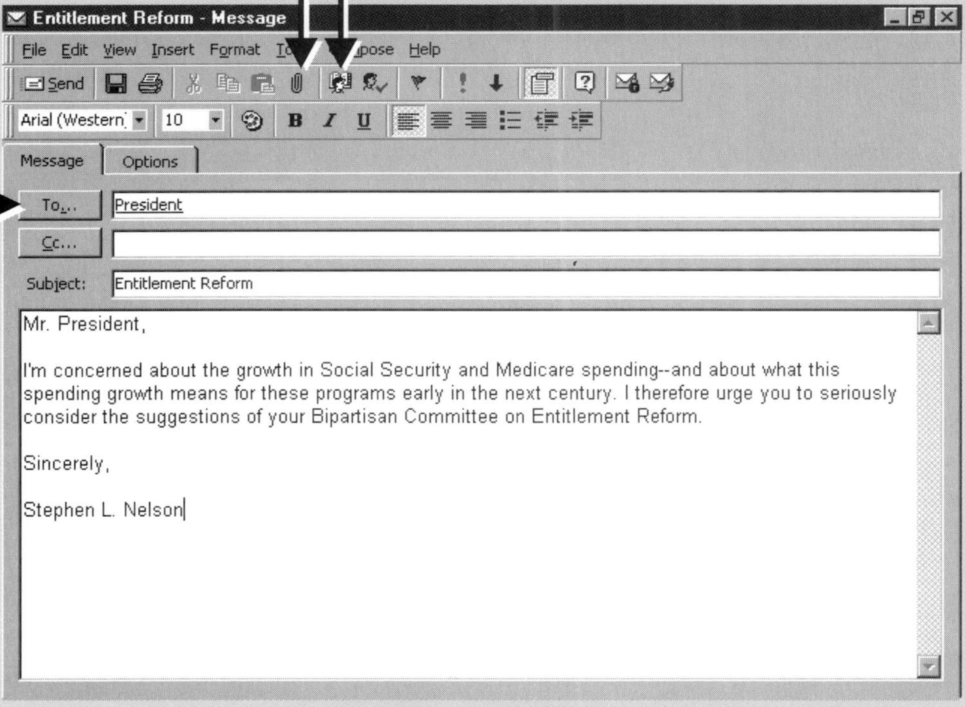

Build your own online address book for handy access to the names and addresses of those people you frequently correspond with (pages 218-220).

Become more productive. Use to-do lists to organize your time, track projects and your progress, and keep on top of your work. (pages 222-224).

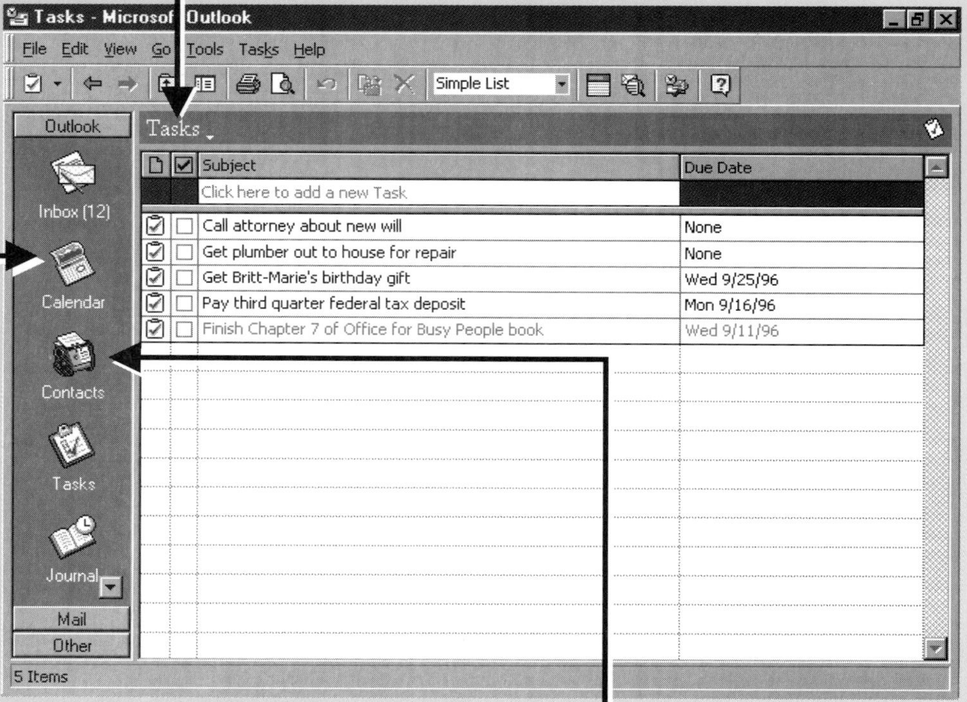

Coordinate your work. The online calendar lets you and your coworkers schedule appointments and meetings, and organize and plan events (pages 226-227).

Stay in touch by keeping a list of contacts with telephone numbers and addresses (pages 220-221).

Use Internet Explorer to Surf the Net

Discover what the Web is, what URLs are and how they work, and how you surf the Net (pages 187-189, 190).

Get wired. Use hyperlinks to connect your Office documents to the Internet (pages 189-195).

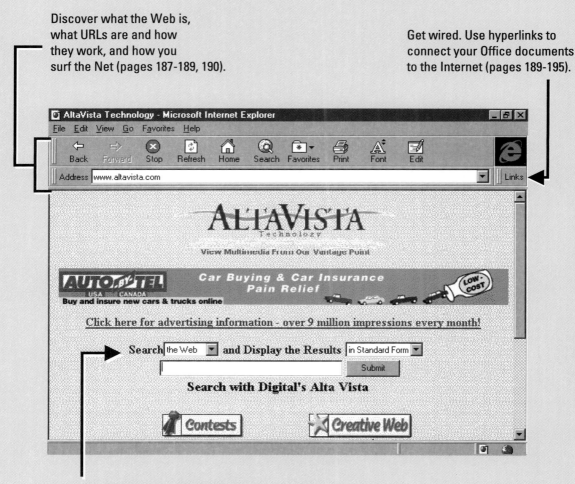

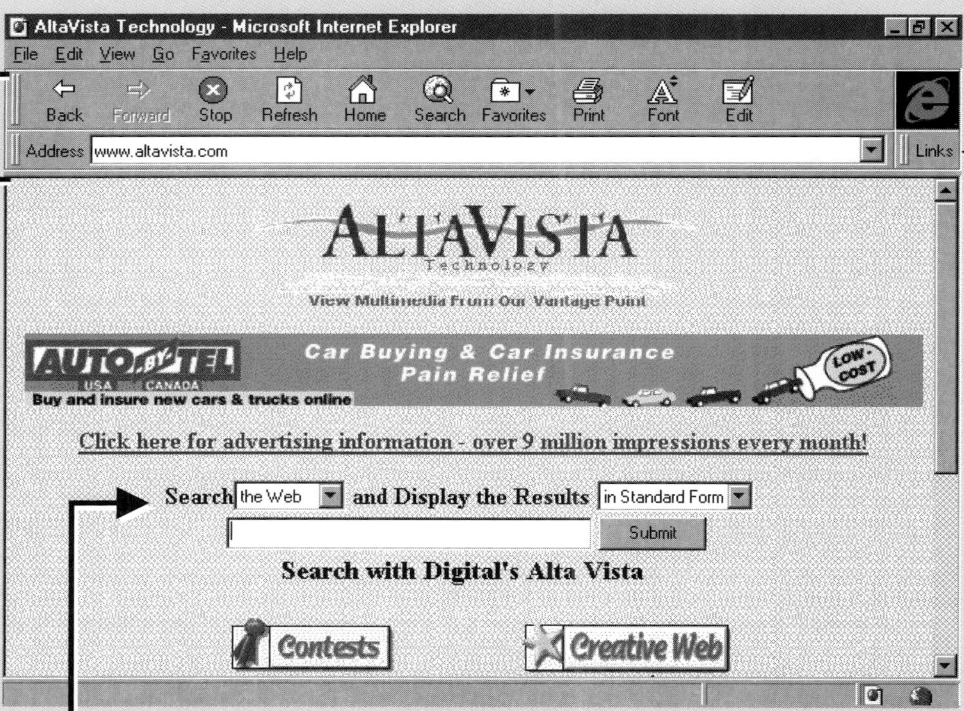

Need to find a needle in a haystack? Learn how to use powerful search services like AltaVista to locate just the information you want (pages 200-202).

BLUEPRINT
FOR BUSY PEOPLE™

Create a Winning Business Plan

Use Microsoft Binder to create compound documents that include text, numbers, or graphic images (pages 171-176).

Need to do some business planning? Grab this workbook (and many others) from the Osborne web site (pages 257-262).

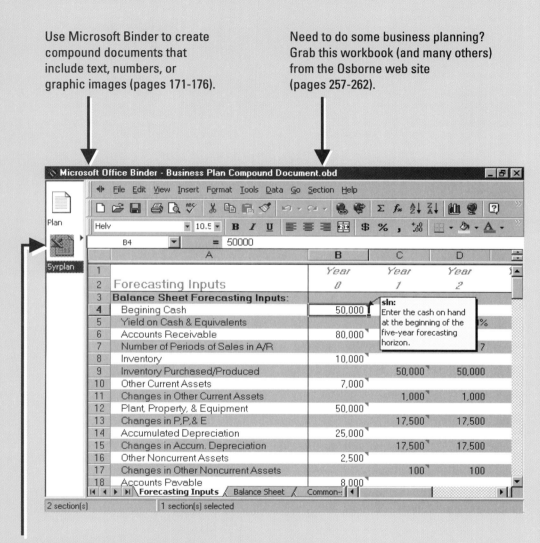

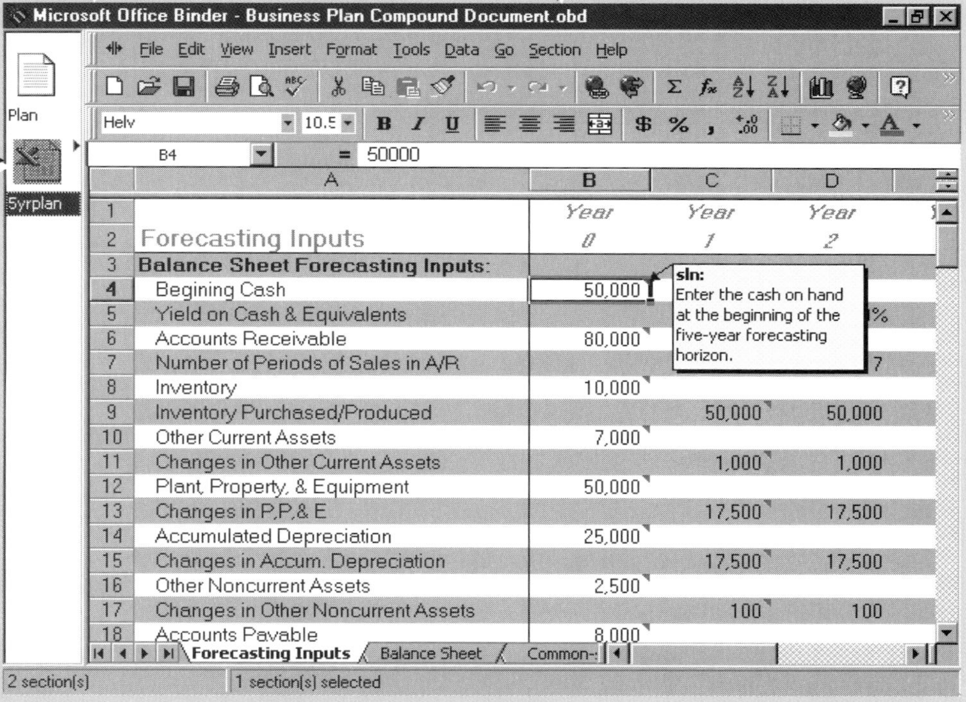

Don't get stuck in a rut, or with your data in the wrong application. Use ActiveX technology to easily share information between applications (pages 169-171).

Office 97

FOR BUSY PEOPLE

The Book to Use When There's No Time to Lose!

Stephen L. Nelson

OSBORNE

Osborne/**McGraw-Hill**

Berkeley / New York / St. Louis / San Francisco / Auckland / Bogotá

Hamburg / London / Madrid / Mexico City / Milan / Montreal / New Delhi

Panama City / Paris / São Paulo / Singapore / Sydney / Tokyo / Toronto

A Division of The **McGraw-Hill** *Companies*

Osborne/**McGraw-Hill**
2600 Tenth Street
Berkeley, California 94710
U.S.A.

For information on translations or book distributors outside the U.S.A., or to arrange bulk purchase discounts for sales promotions, premiums, or fundraisers, please contact Osborne/**McGraw-Hill** at the above address.

Office 97 for Busy People

1234567890 DOC 9987

ISBN 0-07-882280-7

Publisher Brandon A. Nordin
Editor in Chief: Scott Rogers
Acquisitions Editor: Joanne Cuthbertson
Project Editors: Janet Walden, Cynthia Douglas, Heidi Poulin
Editorial Assistant: Gordon Hurd
Technical Editor: Saul Candib
Copy Editor: Judy Ziajka
Indexer: David Heiret
Computer Designers: Roberta Steele, Leslee Bassin, Peter F. Hancik
Quality Control: Joe Scuderi
Series and Cover Designer: Ted Mader Associates
Series Illustrator: Daniel Barbeau

About the Author

Stephen L. Nelson, a best-selling author and consultant, has written more than 50 books and more than 100 articles on using computers for personal and business financial management. His books have sold more than one million copies in English and have been translated into 11 different languages.

furvehz

Contents at a glance

MAIL

Contents

ACKNOWLEDGMENTS

A book like this is really a group project. Lots of people contribute in all sorts of ways. So I want to thank them here right up front.

Thank you, Joanne Cuthbertson, acquisitions editor, for conceiving this book idea, organizing much of the material, and then (most of all) for letting me have the fun writing it. Thank you, Gordon Hurd, for playing the role of friendly traffic cop and thereby keeping contracts and chapters flying up and down the West Coast. Thank you, Janet Walden, project editor, and Cynthia Douglas and Heidi Poulin, associate project editors, for getting this book together in such a short time. Thank you, Judy Ziajka, copy editor, for a great job and pertinent suggestions. Last but not least, a special thank you to the folks in Osborne/McGraw-Hill's production department—Marcela Hancik, Roberta Steele, Leslee Bassin, Lance Ravella, Peter F. Hancik, and Joe Scuderi—you did a wonderful job at laying out the pages of this book.

Steve Nelson
December 12, 1996

PRIORITY!
MEMO:
FIRST CLASS OVERNIGHT
RUSH!

INTRODUCTION

The basic premise of this book is simple. You're a busy person. You don't want to or can't spend the time required to get the equivalent of a graduate degree in business application software. I hear you. And so does the publisher. For this reason, this book gives you the low-down on Microsoft Office 97 in as expeditious a fashion as it possibly can. Restated in a slightly different way, I respect your time. I know you have other things to do with your life. So this book amounts to a fast-paced romp through the information you'll need to become proficient using Microsoft Office 97.

I have to tell you one other thing, too, and I'm not just salving my own ego (or at least I don't think so). This book is fundamentally different from the other Microsoft Office 97 books you see or saw on the bookstore shelves. This book doesn't pretend that Microsoft Office is exactly what the Microsoft marketing people say it is. And this book doesn't bog you down with painfully detailed discussions of stuff you'll never need to know. Sadly, the other books on Microsoft Office (and I read most of them as part of doing my research for this book) don't do this. For the most part, they appear to take everything that Microsoft says about Office as the Gospel Truth. (It's not.) And they invariably drag you into lengthy discussions of all sorts of esoteric whistles and bells. I'm not going to waste your time with this stuff.

What Is Microsoft Office: A Quick Definition

For example—and I may as well broach this topic here—Office is not really what Microsoft often says it is. Office is *not* some tightly integrated software toolkit for creating complicated compound documents. No way. Office is a grab bag of software programs. To be fair, a grab bag of great software programs. But still, a grab bag nonetheless.

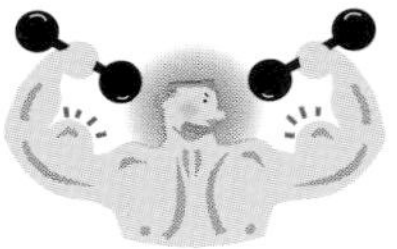

DEFINITION

Compound document: *A compound document uses objects—chunks of information—created by different applications.*

If you buy the "standard" version of Office, for example, you get the Word, Excel, PowerPoint, and Outlook programs. If you buy the "professional" version of Office, you get everything you get with the standard version plus you get the Access database program. Word, in case you don't already know, is Microsoft's word processing program, and it lets you create textual documents such as letters, reports, and memos. Excel is Microsoft's spreadsheet program, and it lets you perform numerical analysis such as for home budgets and business forecasts. PowerPoint is Microsoft's presentation program, and it lets you create online presentations and slide shows as well as web pages for the Internet or an intranet. Outlook is Microsoft's personal information manager (PIM), and it provides you with e-mail, a names-and-addresses manager, a to-do list manager, group scheduling, and some other minor bells and whistles. Finally, Access is Microsoft's database program, and it lets you create and manage computerized databases of information.

DEFINITIONS

Internet: *A global network of computers that share information.*

Intranet: *A company's internal network. An intranet often resembles the Internet and uses Internet technology—such as the World Wide Web.*

To summarize, Office isn't a single program (even though many users mistakenly think it is). And Office isn't really some radically new technique for integrating different types of information (even though some of the marketing types at Microsoft apparently seem to think it is). Office is really just a clever way for Microsoft Corporation to market and sell the Word, Excel, PowerPoint, Outlook, and Access programs—and a clever way for you to acquire great software at a bargain price.

Gaining this bit of knowledge is more important than you might first think. Once you understand that Office is really a family of products, how you should learn the individual Office programs becomes crystal clear. You need to learn the programs one by one—starting with the one you'll use most often (probably Word.) You'll want to ignore those programs you won't use. (Don't worry about this because you basically got them for free anyway.) And you'll want to close your ears and eyes to all of the marketing hyperbole and propaganda that pretends Office is something it's not. (That stuff will just confuse you.)

Does this approach seem as logical to you as it does to me? I hope so. I don't want to beat a dead horse here, but I worry (on your behalf) that the marketing fiction created by Microsoft will muddy the waters for you and complicate your learning. Make no mistake. You've made a great choice in picking Office. But we can't let a successful marketing strategy obfuscate your learning. That'd just be plain silly.

How this Book Is Organized

Now that you understand what Office really is, I can tell you how I've organized this book.

The *Office 97 for Busy People* book provides eleven chapters and three appendixes. You can take a look at the table of contents if you're curious about where I stuck stuff. But I do want to mention a handful of quick points about what the different chapters cover. For example, for starters, you should definitely read the first chapter. It explains how you can make your life (or at least your use of Office) easier.

Chapters 2, 3, and 4 describe the basics of working with Word, Excel, and PowerPoint. As incredulous as this may seem to the people who write (and read!)

those 1000-page books on Word, Excel, and PowerPoint, these manageable chapters will teach you what you need to know to create simple-but-useful Word, Excel, and PowerPoint documents.

Chapter 5 describes how you use Excel's Chart Wizard. If you want to add a chart to any Office document—a Word document, an Excel workbook, or a PowerPoint presentation—read Chapter 5. That's one of the great things about Office—it's easy to share chunks of information, such as an Excel chart, between programs.

The Office programs look the same and work the same in many ways.

The rest of the chapters cover a hodge-podge of topics. You can refer to the table of contents for specifics, but let me say that new users will probably benefit most from Chapters 6, 7, and 8. Chapter 6 describes those commands, features, and tools that are common to all or almost all of the Office programs. I suggest that everyone read Chapter 7 since it describes in detail how you save, open, and print Office documents. Oh, and then there's Chapter 8; it describes how you share *objects* (those "chunks of information" I mentioned earlier) between Office applications.

The last three chapters of the book cover more specialized topics. Anybody who's interested in the Internet—and more specifically in the World Wide Web—should consider reviewing Chapter 9 since it describes how Office's new Internet-ability works. If you want to use Outlook, the personal information manager, take a peek at Chapter 10. Finally, if you want to work with the Access database program that comes with the professional version of Office 97, read Chapter 11.

I also included some appendixes. Appendix A explains how you install Microsoft Office. Appendix B describes how you retrieve and use a handful of Excel templates that I created because those that come with Office are so limiting. (Curiously, Office 97 supplies a rich set of templates for Word and you really don't need templates for PowerPoint or Access.) Appendix C covers the basics of Windows 95 and Windows NT.

Conventions Used Here

Busy People books use several common conventions. So that you get maximum value from your reading, let me explain them quickly.

Blueprints

At the very beginning of the book, Busy People books provide Blueprints. In essence, Blueprints clue you into some of the neat things you can do with Office. They also often work as visual indexes in that they show you pictures of items or features you may have questions about and then point you to appropriate pages.

Fast Forwards

Each regular chapter begins with a "Fast Forward" section that summarizes the main points of the chapter. You can use a Fast Forward to preview the chapter's material. If you've already read the chapter or you know the material covered in the chapter, you can also use the Fast Forward to review the chapter's information. (For example, if you were back in college and you were studying for a test, you could probably use the Fast Forwards as a study review.)

STEP BY STEP

Step by Steps

To help clarify some of the more complicated procedures, or engrain some of the more *useful* procedures, these blue "Step by Step" boxes will walk you through the necessary steps, using illustrations from the program.

Expert Advice

You'll find "Expert Advice" boxes peppering the pages of this book. These are where I clue you in to some timesaving trick or technique that you may want to try or just be aware of.

Definitions

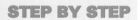

One of the challenges in reading a book about a technical subject is that you're bound to come across terms you don't understand. To minimize the head-scratching you'll have to do because I've used just bit of jargon or technobabble, I've included explanations of key terms in the "Definitions" boxes. (Perhaps you noticed the definitions I provided earlier in this Introduction.)

Notes

Every so often there's a miscellaneous bit of information that doesn't quite fit into the normal flow of the chapter—but that's still useful. I stuck these blurbs, along with cross references to other material in the book or chapter, into the margins as "Notes." (There was also one of these elements earlier in this Introduction.)

Caution

You can't get into too much trouble using Microsoft Office 97. Even so, there are a few places where you'll want to be careful and avoid making potentially time-consuming mistakes. To make these warnings stand out, they've been set off in separate "Caution" boxes. Keep an eye out for those black and yellow striped barricades.

Shortcuts

Oops. I almost forgot. The "Shortcut" boxes show you a way to accomplish something faster than by using the more full-featured method presented in the text.

On from Here

As I mentioned earlier, the place to start is Chapter 1. After that, you'll want to proceed to Chapter 2. And after that, well, pick your pleasure.

CHAPTER

1

Stuff to Do Once to Make Your Life Easier

INCLUDES

- Adjusting the Windows Desktop resolution
- Creating shortcut icons for applications and documents
- Turning on Word's spelling and grammar checking
- Telling applications where they should suggest saving documents

FAST FORWARD

Adjust the Windows Desktop Resolution ➤ *pp. 5-6*

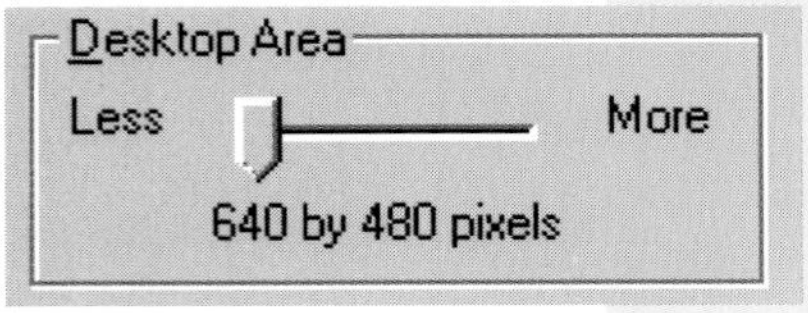

To boost your screen resolution, right-click the Windows desktop to display the shortcut menu, choose the Properties command, and then follow these steps:

1. Click the Settings tab.
2. Drag the Desktop Area slider button to increase the screen resolution.
3. Activate the Color Palette drop-down list and choose a color palette with more colors.

Create Shortcut Icons for Your Favorite Applications ➤ *p. 7*

To create an application shortcut icon, first close any open programs. Then follow these steps:

1. Start the Windows Explorer or Windows NT Explorer program.
2. Open the Microsoft Office folder. (It's probably named MSOffice.)
3. Hold down the CTRL key and then drag the application program shortcut from the MSOffice folder to the Windows desktop. (You may need to click the Restore tool first to expose the Desktop.)

Create Shortcut Icons for Oft-Used Documents ➤ *p. 8*

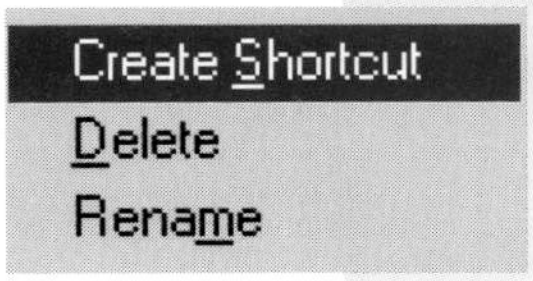

To create a document shortcut icon, again first close any open programs. Then follow these steps:

1. Start the Windows Explorer or Windows NT Explorer program.
2. Open the folder that holds the document.
3. Right-click the document and choose Create Shortcut from the Shortcuts menu. Explorer adds a shortcut to the folder for the document and then selects the shortcut.
4. Drag the document shortcut from its folder to the Windows desktop.

Turn On Word's Spelling and Grammar Checking ➤ pp. 8-9

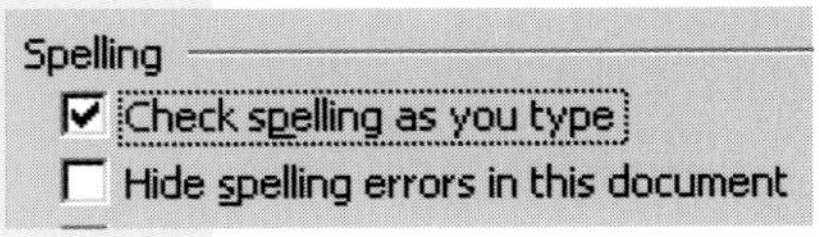

To turn on Word's spelling and grammar checking, start Word, choose the Tools | Options command, and click the Spelling & Grammar tab. Then follow these steps:

1. Mark the Check Spelling as You Type check box.
2. Mark the Check Grammar as You Type check box.
3. Activate the Writing Style drop-down list and select the description of the writing style you will most commonly use.
4. Click OK.

Tell Word Where It Should Save Documents ➤ p. 10

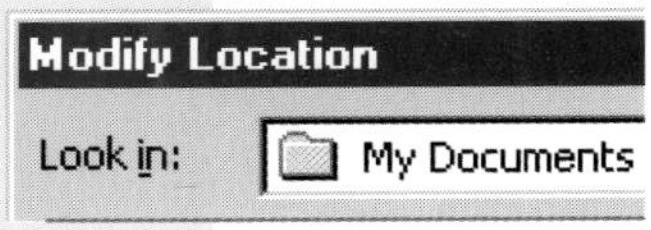

To tell Word where it should save documents and where it should assume documents are stored, choose the Tools | Options command, click the File Locations tab when Word displays the Options dialog box, and then follow these steps:

1. Double-click the Documents entry so that Word displays the Modify Location dialog box.
2. Use the Look In or Folder Name box to specify where Word should save your documents.
3. Click OK to close the Modify Location dialog box and click OK again to close the Options dialog box.

Tell Excel Where It Should Save Workbooks ➤ p. 11

To tell Excel where it should save workbooks, follow these steps:

1. Choose the Tools | Options command.
2. Click the General tab.
3. Provide the full path name of the folder where you want Excel to store documents and where you want it to assume you've saved documents.

Tell PowerPoint Where It Should Save Presentations ➤ p. 12

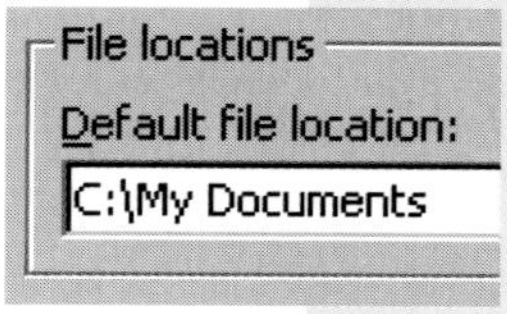

To tell PowerPoint where it should save presentations, follow these steps:

1. Choose the Tools | Options command.
2. Click the Advanced tab.
3. Provide the full path name of the folder where you want PowerPoint to store presentations and where you want it to assume you've saved presentations.

Busy People books, by convention, provide you with an early chapter that tells you how to customize the program so it works better or more smoothly, so that's what I'm going to do here. I'm going to tell you about half a dozen changes you can make to Windows and the individual Office applications. You'll have to do this stuff only once.

Adjust the Windows Desktop Resolution

The figures in this book use 640 x 480 resolution because, well, just because. You'll want to work at a higher screen resolution than this—800 x 600 resolution looks nice—because doing so allows you to see more of your work at one time, and because higher resolutions look better.

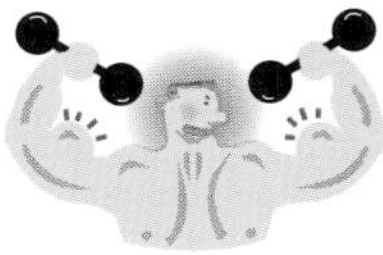

DEFINITIONS

Desktop: *What you see immediately after you start Windows. Icons, the Start button, and the task bar all appear on the desktop.*

Right-click: *Pressing the right-hand mouse button. This will cause a menu of options to appear onscreen.*

To boost your screen resolution, right-click the mouse on the Windows desktop. From the shortcut menu that appears, choose the Properties command to open the Display Properties dialog box, shown in Figure 1.1. Click the Settings tab.

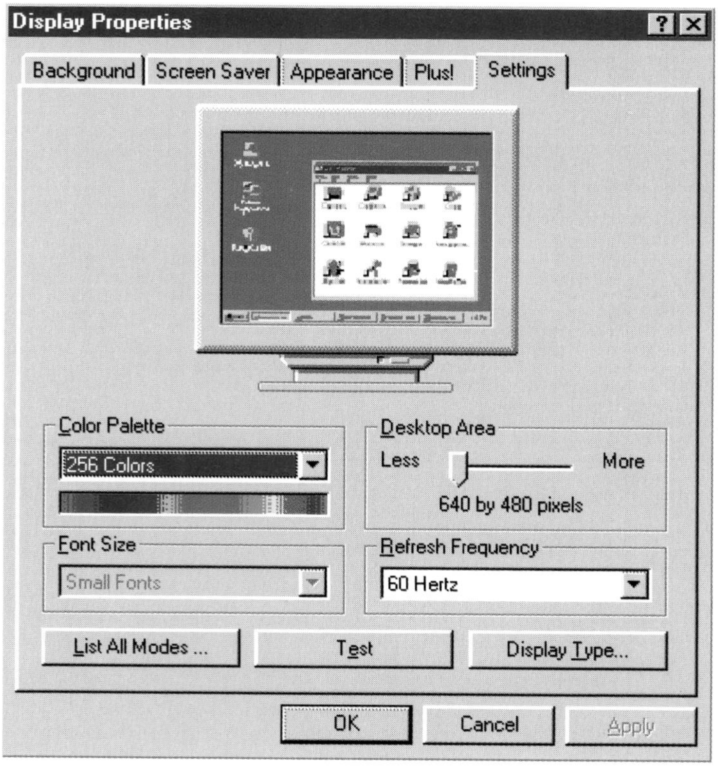

Figure 1.1 Use the Settings tab of the Display Properties dialog box to adjust your desktop resolution

For a quick course on the basics of Windows 95 and Windows NT, see Appendix C.

Next, drag the Desktop Area slider button to increase the screen resolution. You can also activate the Color Palette drop-down list and choose a richer color palette—a color palette with a greater number of colors.

Office lets you verify that your new display settings work by providing a Test button, also on the Settings panel of the Display Properties dialog box. You'll see on-screen instructions, contained in message boxes, for taking the test. Once you've performed this test and are happy with your changes, click OK to make your display property settings permanent (that is, of course, until the next time you go into the dialog box and change them).

Create Shortcut Icons for Your Favorite Applications

When you install Microsoft Office, Windows adds commands to the Programs menu for starting the individual Office programs. That's fine, I guess. But I think it's a lot slicker to place shortcut icons, like the one shown here, on your desktop.

In this way, you can start your favorite Office application—let's say it's Word—simply by double-clicking the shortcut icon.

To create a shortcut icon for an application, first close any open programs. Then follow the instructions I've laid out in the "Create a Shortcut Icon" Step by Step box.

STEP BY STEP Create a Shortcut Icon

1. **Start the Windows Explorer or Windows NT Explorer program. (Press the Start button, then choose Programs, then the appropriate Explorer option.)**

2. **Open the Microsoft Office folder. (It's probably named MSOffice.)**

3. **Hold down the CTRL key and then drag the application program shortcut from the MSOffice folder to the Windows desktop. (You may need to click the Restore tool first to expose the Desktop.)**

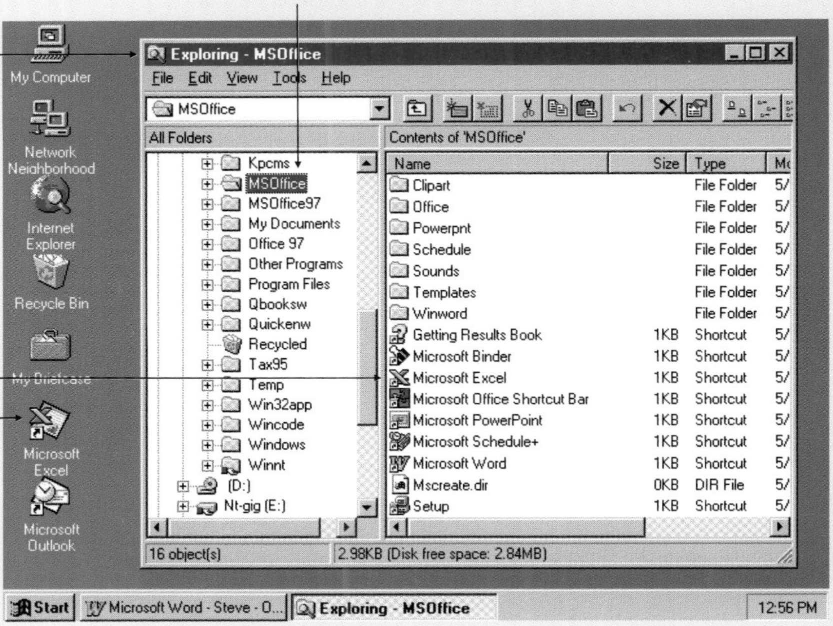

Create Shortcut Icons for Oft-Used Documents

It's not quite as common, but some people work with a particular document all the time. If this describes you, you'll also find it handy to place a shortcut icon for that document on your desktop. Almost every week, for example, I work with and update an Excel workbook that tracks my business revenues and costs. It's really handy to open the document with a double-click.

The process to create a document shortcut icon is similar to that for creating an application shortcut icon:

1. First, close any open programs.
2. After you start the Windows Explorer or Windows NT Explorer, open the folder that holds the document.
3. Right-click the document and choose Create Shortcut from the shortcut menu that appears. Explorer adds a shortcut to the folder for the document and then selects the shortcut.
4. Drag the document shortcut from its folder to the Windows desktop.

Turn On Word's Spelling and Grammar Checking

Microsoft Word checks the spelling and grammar of your documents automatically and will do it in the background (if you let it). Assuming you have a personal computer that isn't groaning under its workload, you definitely want to turn on both features. When you do so, Word underlines any misspelled words you enter with a red wavy line, and it underlines any poorly constructed sentences you enter with a green wavy line. (Note that for my example shown here, I colored the text blue so it would stand out on the page of this book. Usually, the text that makes up a Word document is black.)

Forescore and seven years ago,
our forefathers brought forth on
this continent a new nation,
conceives in liberty, and

EXPERT ADVICE

To fix or get more information on a spelling or grammar error, right-click the wavy green or wavy red line; then choose one of the commands from the shortcut menu that Word displays.

To turn on Word's spelling and grammar checking, start Word, choose the Tools | Options command, and then click the Spelling & Grammar tab. Then select the appropriate options, as shown in Figure 1.2. When you're done, click OK.

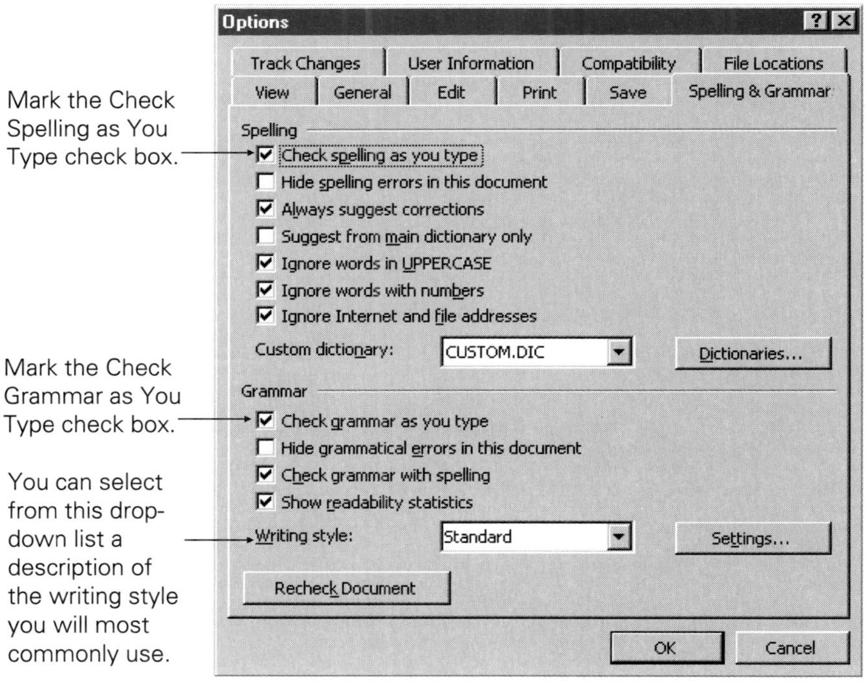

Figure 1.2 The Spelling & Grammar tab of the Options dialog box

Tell Word Where It Should Save Documents

Whenever you save or open a document, Word assumes you're using a particular folder. (I can't tell you which folder Word assumes because it all depends on whether you're running Word on top of Windows 95 or Windows NT and how you installed Word.) That Word assumes a particular folder is fine if it guesses right. But it's a waste of time—sometimes lots of time—if Word always guesses wrong.

If you find yourself in this circumstance, tell Word where it should save documents and where it should assume documents are stored. To do this:

1. Choose the Tools | Options command and click the File Locations tab when Word displays the Options dialog box.
2. Double-click the Documents entry in the unnamed list box so that Word displays the Modify Location dialog box, shown here:

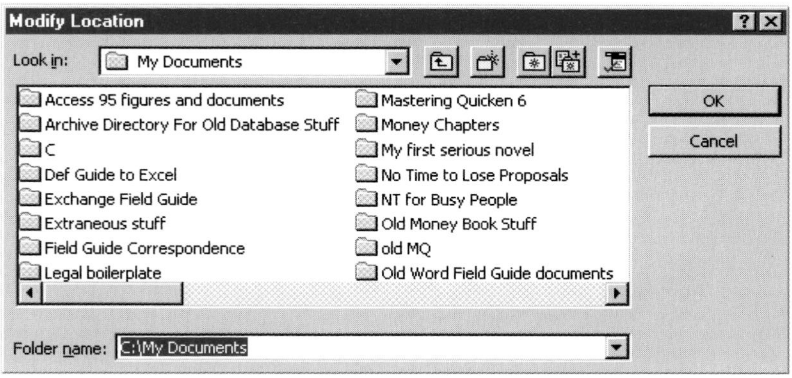

3. Use the Look In or Folder Name box to specify where Word should save your documents.
4. Click OK to close the Modify Location dialog box and click OK again to close the Options dialog box.

Tell Excel Where It Should Save Workbooks

If you use Excel, you'll want to specify where it should save workbooks and where it should assume you've saved workbooks. Then you won't have to spend a bunch of time hunting around your hard disk every time you choose the File | Open or File | Save As command.

Telling Excel where it should save workbooks is similar to the process just described earlier for Word and saving documents:

1. Choose the Tools | Options command.
2. Click the General tab on the Options dialog box, shown here:

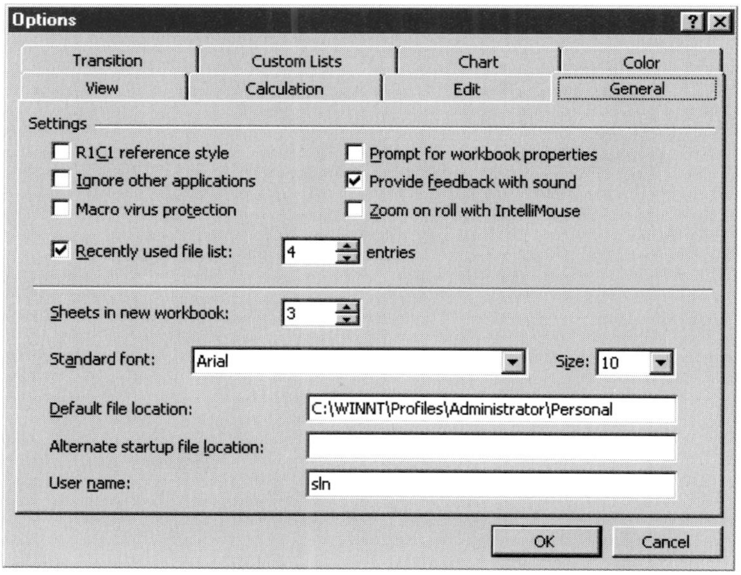

3. In the Default File Location text box, provide the full path name of the folder where you want Excel to store documents and where you want it to assume you've saved documents.

Tell PowerPoint Where It Should Save Presentations

As is the case with Word and Excel, if you use PowerPoint, you'll want to specify where it should save presentations and where it should assume you've saved presentations. Then you won't have to spend a bunch of time hunting around your hard disk every time you choose the File Open or the File Save As command. To tell PowerPoint where it should save presentations, follow these steps.

1. Choose the Tools | Options command.
2. Click the Advanced tab on the Options dialog box, shown here:

3. In the Default File Location text box, provide the full path name of the folder where you want PowerPoint to store presentations and where you want it to assume you've saved presentations.

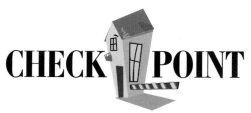

CHECKPOINT

This chapter describes a handful of up-front preparatory tasks you can complete to make working with Office more enjoyable or much simpler: how to adjust the Windows Desktop resolution, how to create shortcut icons, how to turn on Word's automatic spelling and grammar checking, and how to tell the individual Office applications where they should save your documents.

You're now ready to begin learning how to use Office. I suggest you start with the next chapter. It describes how you work with Word, the most popular and probably the most useful of the Office applications.

CHAPTER

2

Word Basics

INCLUDES

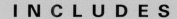

- Creating a document
- Checking spelling
- Using AutoText
- Copying and moving text
- Formatting a document
- Printing documents and envelopes
- Saving and opening documents
- Using the Office Assistant when you have questions

FAST FORWARD

Create a Document ➤ pp. 20-22

When you start Word, it creates a blank document, initially named Document1, which you can use. If you want to create another blank document, you can

- Click the New tool.
- Choose the File | New command to use one of Word's templates. Some templates also start wizards that help you begin the work of creating a document.

Enter and Edit Text ➤ pp. 22-23

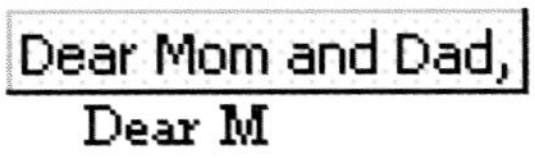

Enter and edit text as follows:

- To enter text into a Word document, just type.
- To end a paragraph, press ENTER.
- Use the BACKSPACE key to erase the character behind the insertion point.
- Use the DELETE key to erase the character ahead of the insertion point.
- To reposition the insertion point, just click the mouse where you want to start typing.
- To delete a chunk of text, select the text and press DELETE.
- To replace a chunk of text, select the text and then type the new text.

Check Your Spelling ➤ p. 23

If you misspell a word, Word (by default) alerts you to your error by underlining the word with a red, squiggly line. To correct the misspelling:

- Double-click the word (to select it) and then type the correct spelling.
- If you don't know the correct spelling and want Word to suggest a spelling, right-click the word to display the shortcuts menu and then choose the correctly spelled word from the menu.

Copy and Move Text ➤ pp. 24-26

To move text:

1. Select the text you want to move.
2. Drag the text to a new location.

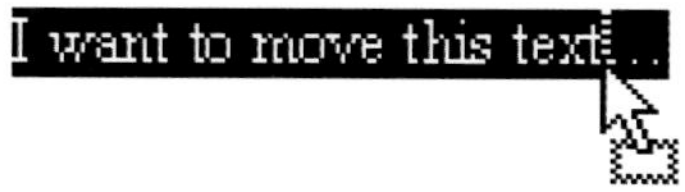

To copy text:

3. Select the text you want to copy.
4. Hold down the CTRL key and drag the text to a new location.

Format Text ➤ pp. 26-28

You can format characters and paragraphs by using the Formatting toolbar's buttons and list boxes. For example, if you want to make text bold:

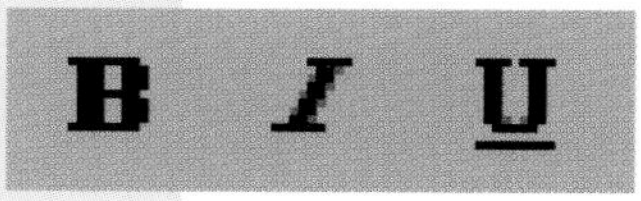

1. Select the text you want to be bold.
2. Click the Bold tool.

Print Documents ➤ p. 32

To print a single copy of a document:

1. Open the document you want to print.
2. Click the Print tool. This tells Word to print the active document in the usual way using the usual printer.

Save Documents ➤ p. 32

To save a document you've already named, click the Save tool.

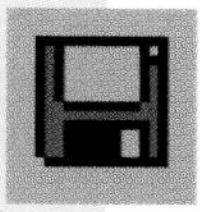

To save a document for the first time or under a different name:

1. Choose the File | Save As command.
2. Name the document by typing a name in the File Name box of the Save As dialog box.
3. Click Save.

Open Documents ➤ *pp. 32-33*

To open a document you've just created with Word, just select the document from the Start menu's Documents submenu. If the document you want doesn't appear there:

1. Start Word.
2. Activate the File menu.
3. Choose the Word document from the numbered list of documents there.
4. If the document you want doesn't appear here either, choose the File | Open command so that Word displays the Open dialog box.

Use the Office Assistant ➤ *pp. 33-35*

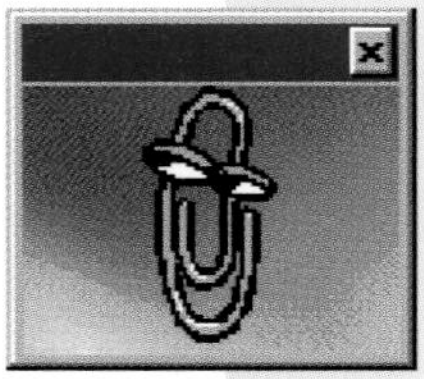

To use the Office Assistant:

1. Choose the Help | Microsoft Word Help command to display the Office Assistant.
2. Click the Office Assistant so that the yellow balloon appears if it isn't already there.
3. Type your question in the box provided.

The best part of Word is that it's so easy to use. If you know how to type and you know how to work with the Windows graphical user interface (choosing commands, fiddling with windows, and filling out dialog boxes), you know almost everything you need to write the next best-selling novel with Word.

In spite of Word's ease of use, however, you'll benefit tremendously if I give you some background information on the program, clue you in to a few of the booby traps you'll encounter, and point out some of the shortcuts you might otherwise miss.

What a Document Is

Let's start off by talking about what a document is. A document is the thing you create with Word: A one-page memo to a co-worker. A 300-page dissertation. A letter to a pen pal. You get the picture, right? A document is (usually) just a bunch of words.

In fact, the only thing that's different about a Word document as compared to those you create with a pen and paper is that Word doesn't create documents by putting ink on paper. It creates digital documents, and it stores them on your computer's hard disk or in your computer's memory. Don't worry—I'm not going to waste your time with some long-winded discussion about how Word stores a document as digital information on a disk. No way. I bring up the digital document business for a couple of important (and very simple) reasons. First, because Word's documents are digital, you can easily make changes to them and copy them. (You probably already know this—if only intuitively.) A second ramification of Word's digital documents isn't quite as obvious, however: because its documents are digital, Word happily lets you create documents that include things besides words and numbers. In fact, Word lets you include in its documents just about anything you can store as a file on your computer's hard disk. For example, you can stick pictures in your documents as shown here.

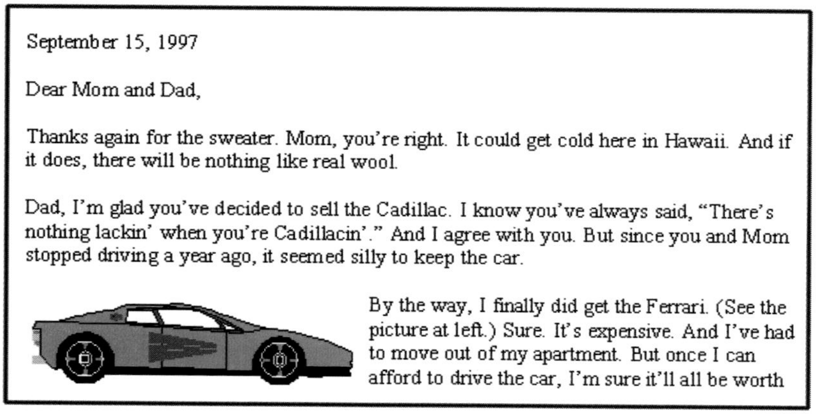

September 15, 1997

Dear Mom and Dad,

Thanks again for the sweater. Mom, you're right. It could get cold here in Hawaii. And if it does, there will be nothing like real wool.

Dad, I'm glad you've decided to sell the Cadillac. I know you've always said, "There's nothing lackin' when you're Cadillacin'." And I agree with you. But since you and Mom stopped driving a year ago, it seemed silly to keep the car.

By the way, I finally did get the Ferrari. (See the picture at left.) Sure. It's expensive. And I've had to move out of my apartment. But once I can afford to drive the car, I'm sure it'll all be worth

If you keep in mind what you've just read—that Word (with the help of your computer) lets you create and fiddle with digital documents and that you can include not only words and numbers in your documents but other stuff as well—everything else you need to learn about Word will fall into place.

Creating a Document

When you start Word, it creates a blank document, named Document1, which you can use (see Figure 2.1). If you want to create another blank document, you can click the New tool.

EXPERT ADVICE

If you don't know a Microsoft Office toolbar box or button name, point to the tool. The Office application displays the tool name in a pop-up box called a tooltip.

Or you can choose the File | New command so that Word displays the New dialog box, shown next. In essence, the New dialog box provides various tabs—General, Letters & Faxes, Memos, Reports, and so forth—that list Word templates you can use as starter documents for the new documents you want to create.

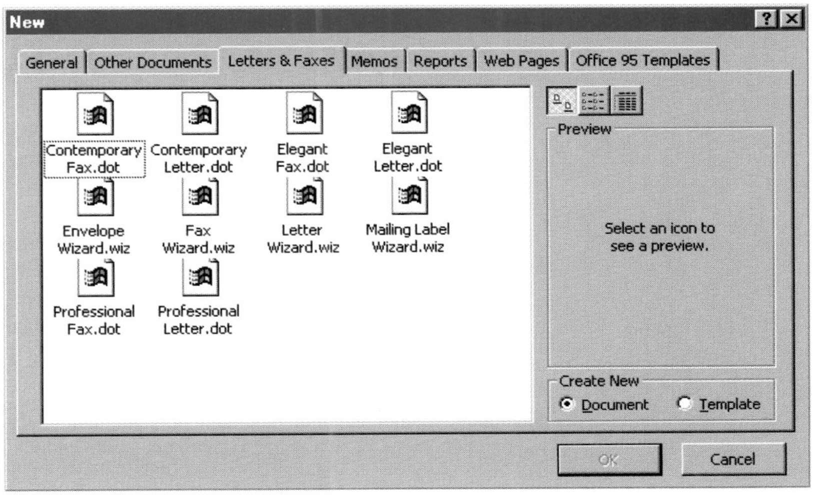

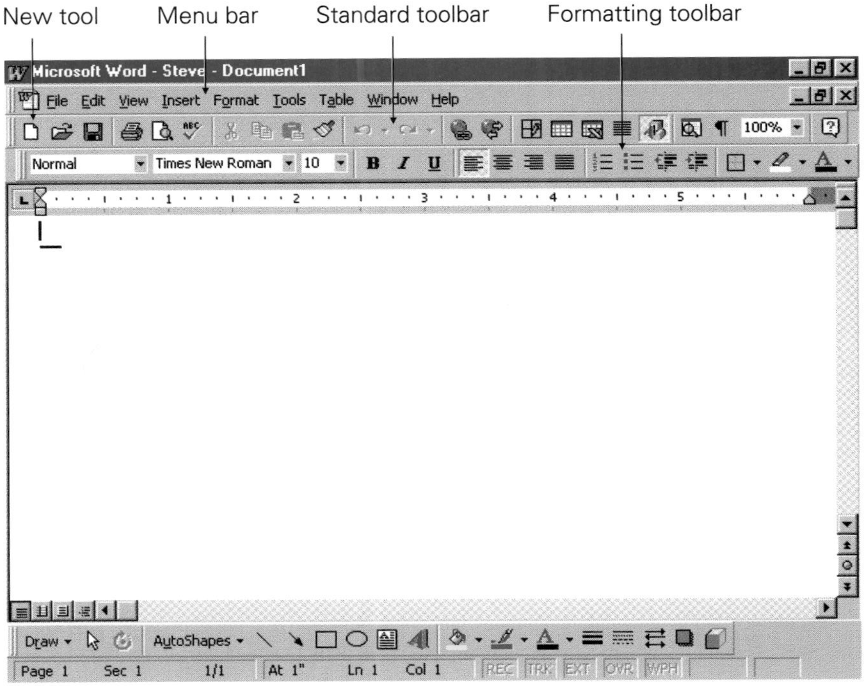

Figure 2.1 The Word program window

I'm not going to go into detail describing Word's templates. Instead, if you're interested, I recommend you open and experiment with them. Templates can save you much time if you're creating any standard document: a memo, letter, fax cover sheet, envelope, or mailing list.

DEFINITIONS

Template: *A prebuilt, preformatted document that Word provides and that you can use to save yourself some time. Some templates also start wizards that help you get started with the work of creating a document.*

Wizard: *A wizard leads you through the steps of some common but challenging task—such as printing envelopes.*

Entering and Editing Text

I'll talk more about the importance of pressing the ENTER key to signal the end of a paragraph. See the section "Paragraph Formatting" later in this chapter.

Most of what you put into a Word document—at least until you know Word better—will be text: words, sentences, and paragraphs. To do this, you just type. You don't even have to concern yourself with moving to the next line of the document when you get to the end of a line. Word automatically word-wraps your text. In other words, when you get to the end of one line, it automatically moves the insertion point to the next line. (The insertion point is the flashing vertical bar that moves ahead of the text as you type it.)

When you want to end a paragraph, press ENTER. Then begin the next paragraph by typing some more.

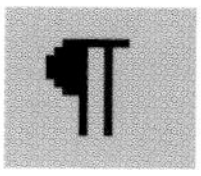

If you're sitting there in front of your computer, go ahead and bang out a couple of paragraphs of text. (Remember to press ENTER only when you want to end a paragraph!) You'll see how effortless word processing really is. If you want to view paragraph markers, spaces, and other nonprinting characters in your document, click the Show/Hide tool.

If you make a mistake, use the BACKSPACE key to erase the character behind the insertion point. To erase the character ahead of the insertion point, use the DELETE key. To reposition the insertion point, just click the mouse at the point to which you want to move the insertion point. (Go ahead and try these operations.)

If you want to delete a chunk of text, click the mouse button on the first character you want to delete and then, while keeping the button pressed, drag the cursor to the last character you want to delete. (This technique is called selecting.) When you select a chunk of text, Word highlights the text, as shown here:

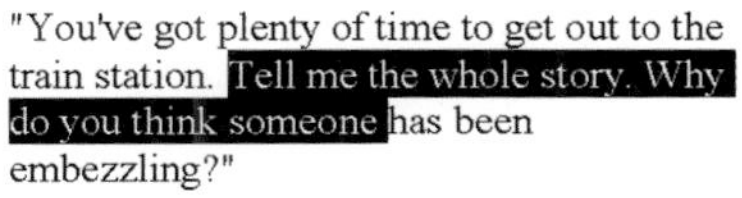

"You've got plenty of time to get out to the
train station. Tell me the whole story. Why
do you think someone has been
embezzling?"

To delete the selected chunk of text, press the DELETE key. To delete the selected chunk of text and replace it with some new chunk of text, just type the replacement text.

Checking Your Spelling

Word automatically spell-checks the words you enter. If you misspell a word, it underlines the word with a red, squiggly line:

To correct the misspelling, double-click the word (to select it) and then type the correct spelling. If you don't know the correct spelling and want Word to suggest a spelling, right-click the word to display the shortcut menu.

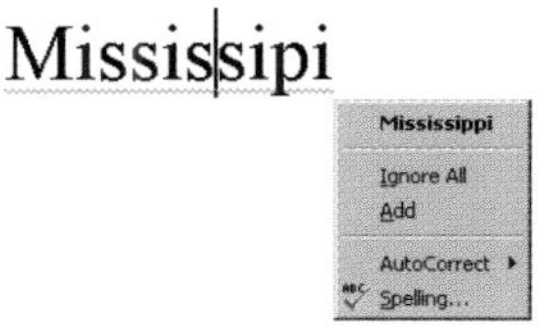

Then choose a suggestion from the menu. If Word can't make any sense of the misspelled word, there may not be any suggestions to choose from. If the word that Word thinks is misspelled is spelled correctly, right-click the word and then choose Ignore All from the shortcut menu.

The Weirdness of AutoText

While we're still sort of on the subject of entering text into your document, I want to mention one other, rather eerie feature of Word: AutoText. Here's the deal. Sometimes Word can guess what you're typing. For example, let's say you're just starting a letter to the folks back home. You begin typing the phrase, "Dear Mom and Dad." As soon as you've typed the first few letters of this greeting, "Dear M," Word figures out what you're typing and, as shown here, displays its guess about what you're typing in a pop-up yellow box called an AutoComplete tip.

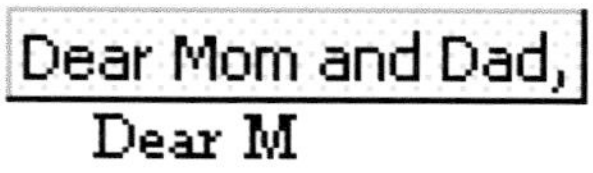

If Word guesses correctly, you can press ENTER to accept the suggestion and then go on with your typing. If Word doesn't guess correctly, you can just keep typing.

I'll tell you: AutoText is weird. There's no doubt about that. But it's really handy. Word can tell when you're starting to type a month name (such as September), a day name (such as Thursday), and any one of about four dozen common business words or phrases (such as Sincerely and Yours Truly).

By the way, although Word will automatically add things like your name and your business name to its list of AutoText entries, you also can expand the list of AutoText entries by choosing the Tools | AutoCorrect command and then following the instructions in the "Add an Entry to the AutoText List "Step by Step box shown opposite.

Copying and Moving Text

If you've been reading since the beginning of this short chapter, you now know most of what you need to know to work with Word. You know how to enter text. You know how to delete and replace text. And that's pretty much it.

STEP BY STEP Add an Entry to the AutoText List

1. Click the AutoText tab.

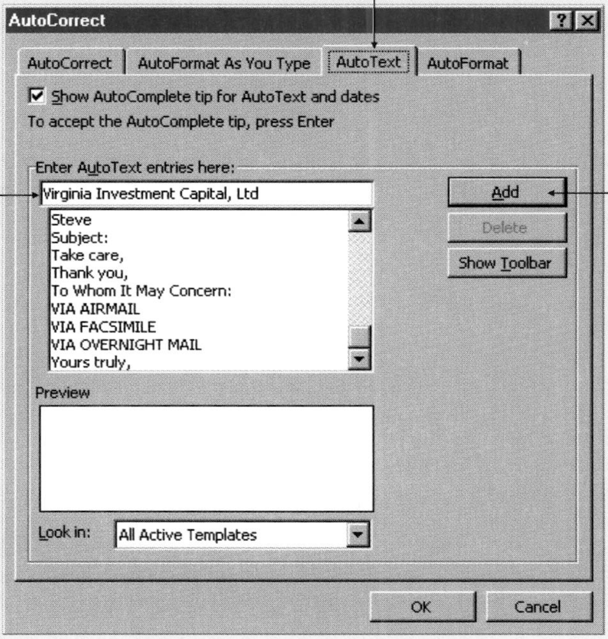

2. Enter the word or phrase you want Word to guess.

3. Click Add.

There are, however, a couple other editing tricks you'll want to know about. First, you can easily move and copy chunks of text. Using the mouse to move and copy text—the technique is called drag-and-drop—is really the slickest approach. To do this, select the chunk of text you want to fiddle with. (Remember that you do this by clicking the mouse button on the first character in the text chunk and, while keeping the button pressed, dragging the cursor to the last character in the text chunk.) To move the text selection, drag the highlighted text to a new location. To copy the text selection, hold down the CTRL key and drag the highlighted text to a new location. You'll need to try this a time or two before you really get the hang of it.

SHORTCUT

To select a single word, double-click it.
To select a single line, click to the left of the line.
To select a single paragraph, triple-click somewhere inside the paragraph.

If you don't like drag-and-drop, you can also use the Standard toolbar's Cut, Copy, and Paste tools. First you select the chunk of text you want to copy or move. Then you click the Cut tool if you want to move the text. Or you click the Copy tool if you want to copy, or duplicate, the text.

Next, you position the insertion point—remember that you do this by clicking the mouse—at the exact location you want the cut or copied text placed and then click the Paste tool.

Formatting Your Documents

In the old days, before toolbars and automatic formatting and other stuff like that, technical writers used to spend entire chapters discussing document formatting. We're (you and I, that is) not going to do that here. We're just going to cut to the chase and call it "good enough" at that. In this way, at the end of this chapter, you'll know everything you need to know to create 99 percent of the business and personal documents you need.

Character Formatting

Character formatting changes the way individual characters look: the typeface, or font, the color, the size (points), and so on. You can format characters by using the Formatting toolbar's boxes and buttons. For example, you can **boldface** selected text—notice you have to select it first—by clicking the Bold tool. You can *italicize* selected text by clicking the Italic tool. You can <u>underline</u> text...oh, you get it, I know. The only questions you'll have concern which tools perform which action. To get this information right now, take a look at Table 2.1.

Tool	Name	Description and Example of Formatting
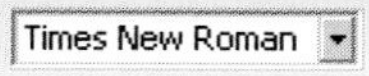	Font	Displays a drop-down list box from which you choose a font, or typeface.
	Font Size	Displays a drop-down list you use to specify the point size of the selected text. This text is 18 points.
	Bold	Alternately boldfaces and un-boldfaces the selected text. **This text is in boldface.**
	Italic	Alternately italicizes and un-italicizes the selected text. *This text is in italics.*
	Underline	Alternately underlines and un-underlines the selected text. This text is underlined.
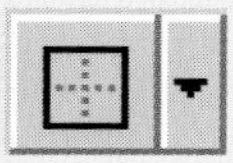	Outside Border	Draws a box around the selected text. (Click the down arrow at the end of the tool to display a list of other border choices.) This text has an outside border.
	Highlight	Changes the background color of the selected text. (Click the down arrow at the end of the tool to display a palette of color choices.) This text is highlighted
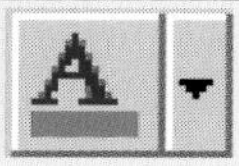	Font Color	Changes the foreground color of the selected text. (Click the down arrow at the end of the tool to display a list of color choices.) This text is colored red.

Table 2.1 Character Formatting Tools on Word's Formatting Toolbar

Word supplies a bunch of other character formatting options in addition to those on the Formatting toolbar, but most people won't need them. If you're curious, choose the Format | Font command or the Format | Borders and Shading command.

This text is highlighted

EXPERT ADVICE

One neat formatting trick that you can't create with the formatting toolbar is a drop-cap. To create a drop-cap, select the first character of a paragraph and then choose the Format | Drop Cap command. When Word displays the Drop Cap dialog box, click either the Dropped or In Margin button.

Paragraph Formatting

Most document formatting changes the way that individual characters or groups of characters appear. You can also change the way that paragraphs appear. A paragraph can be a word, several words, a number, or the traditional collection of sentences—anything—as long as it is ended by pressing the ENTER key. Several of the Formatting toolbar's tools change paragraph formatting, as detailed in Table 2.2.

I could describe how each of these tools works and when they come in handy, but why not try them out for yourself? Just type a few paragraphs (remember, a paragraph can be as short as one word as long as you've pressed ENTER afterwards). Then select a paragraph or two and click the various tools listed in the table. You'll see which tools perform which formatting.

As with character formatting, Word supplies a bunch of other not-so-common paragraph-type formatting options in addition to those found on the Formatting toolbar. To see these other options, choose the Format | Paragraph or the Format | Bullets and Numbering command. To learn how these other options work, just experiment.

Two Special Problems: Envelopes and Mass Mailings

Guess what? With what you now know about Word you can create almost any document. I need to tell you, however, about two problem documents—envelopes and mass mailings, or form letters—because as sure as the sun rises in the east, you're going to want to create both of these headaches sooner or later. If I give you just a bit of information here (and you remember it's here), you'll save hours of time.

Tool	Name	Description
	Align Left	Aligns the lines of the selected paragraph flush against the left margin of the document.
	Center	Centers the lines of the selected paragraph evenly between the left and right margins of the document.
	Align Right	Aligns the lines of the selected paragraph flush against the right margin of the document.
	Justify	Spaces the words of each of the lines of the selected paragraph so all lines are both flush against the left margin and flush against the right margin of the document.
	Numbering	Turns the selected paragraphs into a numbered list.
	Bullets	Turns the selected paragraphs into a bulleted list.
	Decrease Indent	Un-indents the selected paragraph.
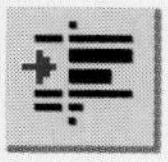	Increase Indent	Indents the selected paragraph.

Table 2.2 Paragraph Formatting Tools on Word's Formatting Toolbar

Envelopes

Envelopes present a series of problems—to the point, in fact, that in many offices you'll still see a typewriter in the corner that people use specifically and only for envelopes. (Envelopes cause problems, by the way, because in essence they look like these itty-bitty pieces of paper to Word, and because they often have to get stuffed through the printer in some kooky way.)

Fortunately, Word addresses the complexities of envelope printing. To print an envelope, choose the Tools | Envelopes and Labels command and then, when Word displays the Envelopes and Labels dialog box, follow the instructions in the next Step by Step box.

STEP BY STEP Print an Envelope

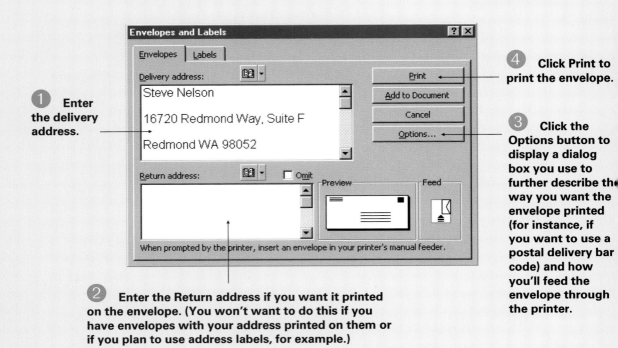

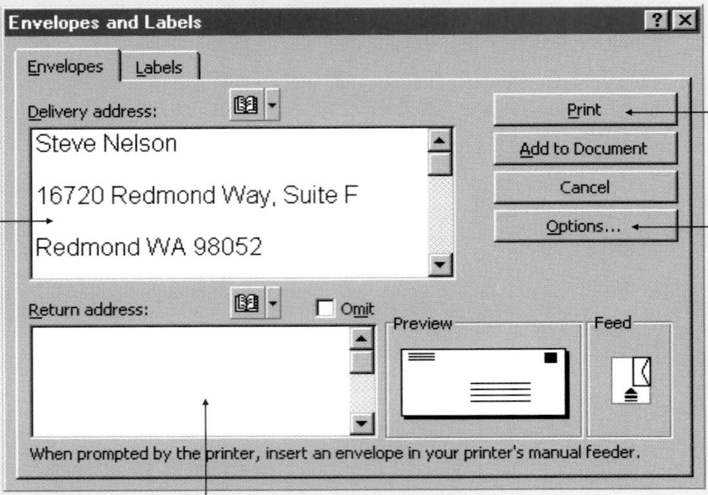

1 Enter the delivery address.

2 Enter the Return address if you want it printed on the envelope. (You won't want to do this if you have envelopes with your address printed on them or if you plan to use address labels, for example.)

3 Click the Options button to display a dialog box you use to further describe the way you want the envelope printed (for instance, if you want to use a postal delivery bar code) and how you'll feed the envelope through the printer.

4 Click Print to print the envelope.

Mass Mailings

If your mail is delivered by the U.S. Postal service, I can almost guarantee that you have been the recipient of a mass mailing. (Have you—and all of your neighbors, no doubt—returned your Super Prize winning numbers yet?) So, you know about mass mailings, I'm sure. And I bet most often you view them as an annoyance; however, consider the following. You have a letter—maybe it's just a simple note that says you've moved—that you want to send to fifty or five hundred different people and the only thing that's different about each letter is the mailing address and the salutation. Do you really want to spend time cranking out fifty or five hundred copies individually? I doubt it.

Word includes a special feature for situations just like this. You first create a names-and-addresses list, or database. Then you create a form letter with blanks that Word can fill in. Then, finally, you direct Word to use this names-and-addresses list and your boilerplate—your form letter—to produce all fifty or all five hundred letters.

I'm not going to give you a blow-by-blow account of how you do one of these mass mailings because Word comes with a wizard that does all the work for you. (Having me tell you how to use a wizard would be roughly akin to having me tell you how to watch a television show. Can you imagine—me, sitting there in your living room, saying things like, "Now pay attention here because something really crazy is going to happen next..."?)

To use the mass mailing wizard, choose the Tools | Mail Merge command. Then carefully follow the on-screen instructions. As Figure 2.2 shows, the first thing you do is click the Create button.

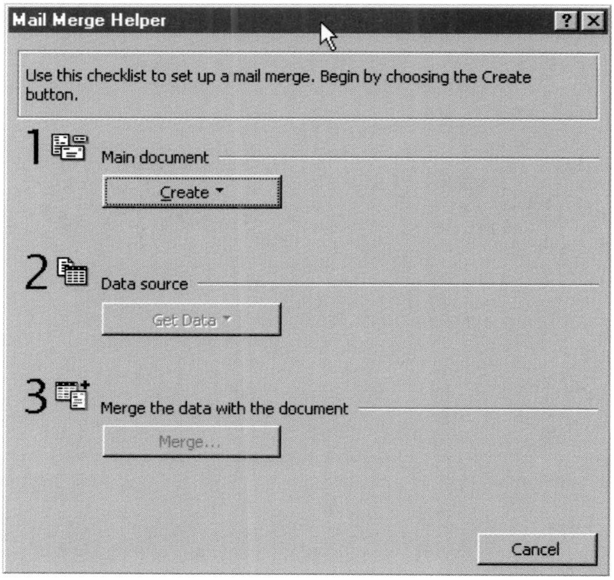

Figure 2.2 Beginning the Mail Merge wizard

Printing, Saving, and Opening Documents

I'm going to talk in detail about printing, saving, and opening office documents in Chapter 7. But just so I don't leave you hanging here, let me give you some quick instructions. If you want to print a single copy of a document, just click the Print tool.

In effect, clicking the Print tool tells Word to print the active document in the usual way using the usual printer. You don't get to control how Word prints when you use this tool, but it's easy.

If you want to save a document, click the Save tool or choose the File | Save As command. Then use the Save As dialog box (see Figure 2.3) to give the new document a name—by typing one in the File Name box—and click Save.

Chapter 7 offers a long, detailed, yet thoroughly captivating (of course) discussion of file opening and saving and document management in general.

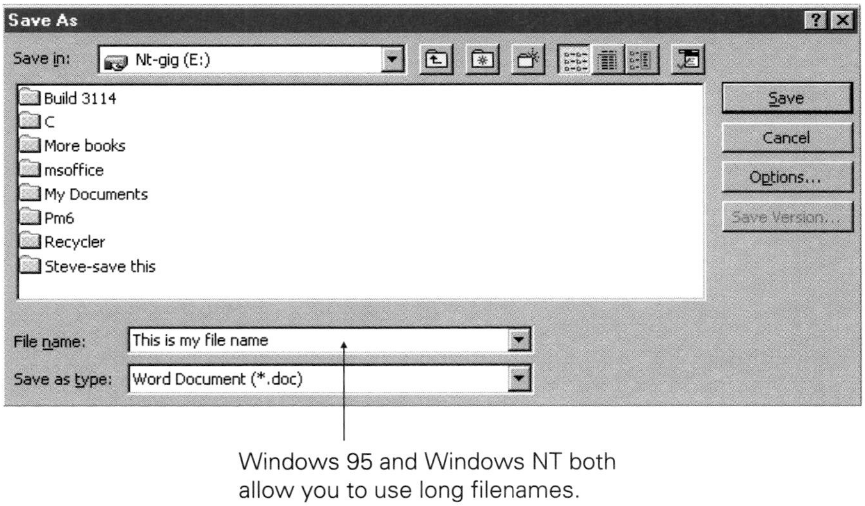

Figure 2.3 The Save As dialog box

To later use a document you've created with Word, your easiest tack is just to select the document from the Start menu's Documents submenu. (The Documents submenu lists the last 15 documents you've saved.) If the document you want doesn't appear there, start Word, activate the File menu, and choose the Word document from the numbered list of documents there. (The Word File menu lists the last 5 Word documents you've saved.) If the document you want doesn't appear here either, choose the File | Open command so that Word displays the Open dialog box (shown in Figure 2.4). When you see the document in the window beneath the Look In drop-down list, double-click it to open it.

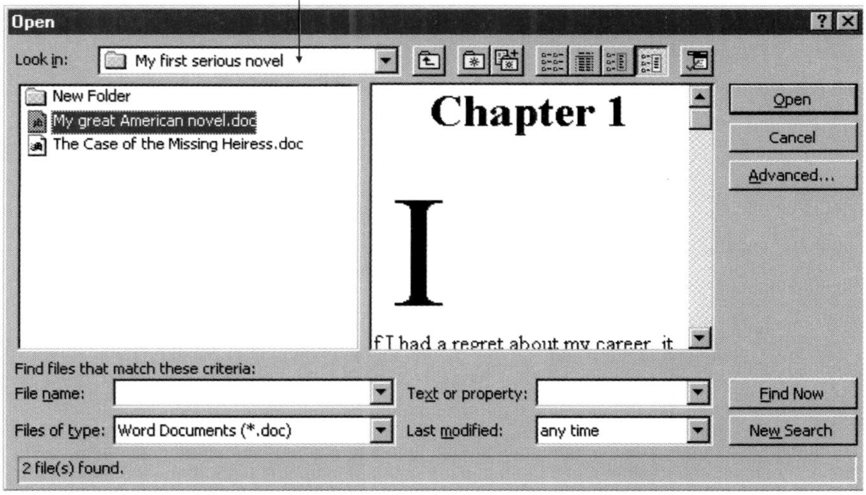

Figure 2.4 The Open dialog box

Using the Office Assistant

Believe it or not, you actually now know everything you need to productively and efficiently use Word. You know how to enter, edit, and format your text. You know how to spell-check your work. And you know (roughly speaking) how to print, save, and open documents. I dare say that you really can produce just about any document you want without knowing much more about Word.

If the Office Assistant doesn't appear, choose the Help | Microsoft Word Help command (or press F1).

Nevertheless, there is one other bit of knowledge you'll benefit from tremendously by knowing—one other bit of knowledge that may mean you don't have to read another word about Word: how the Office Assistant works. Have you met the Office Assistant yet? It's that animated and annoying paper clip character that appears over the Word program window.

The thing that makes the Office Assistant really neat is that it lets you ask questions about Word. To try this, click Office Assistant so that the yellow balloon appears, if it isn't already displayed. Then type your question in the box provided. For example, if you'd like to find out how to use the Format | Borders and Shading command to add shading to a paragraph, you might type, "How do I use shading?"

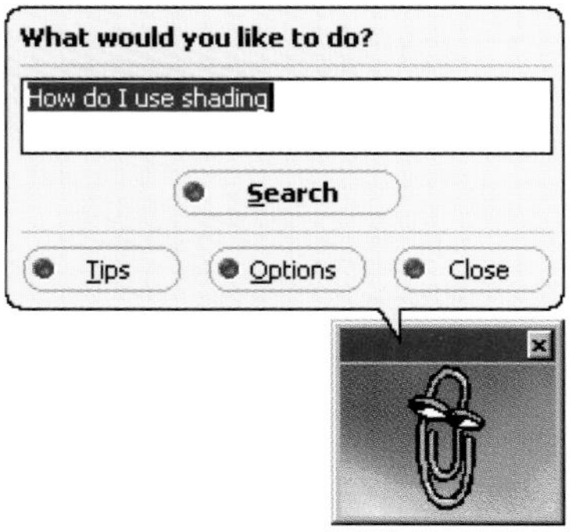

After you type your question, click Search or press ENTER. Office Assistant builds a list of online help topics that you can read to answer your question.

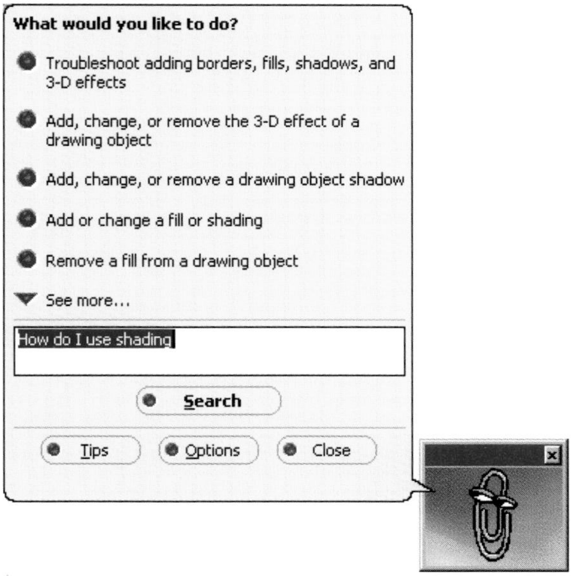

You review the list and then click the topic you want to read. I know this sounds corny—and I don't like Mr. Paperclip all that much—but Office Assistant is a wonderful tool that you can use to search through Word's online help.

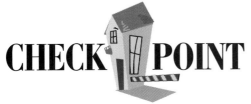

CHECKPOINT

You've actually learned quite a bit if you've been following along since the beginning of the chapter. You now know, for example, how to create a document— including how to spell-check the document, use the wackiness of AutoText, copy and move text, and format your document. You've learned how to print documents—including envelopes—and how to save and later open those documents. And, last but not least, you've learned where to get more information when you have questions I haven't answered here.

Note, though, that even if Word is the most important program inside the Microsoft Office box, it's not the only program. If you perform any numerical analysis—number crunching, in other words—take a few minutes and peruse Chapter 3. It explains what Microsoft Excel is and how you can use it to create spreadsheets, which you can use either as stand-alone documents or as components of Word documents.

THE INTERNET

CHAPTER

3 Excel Basics

INCLUDES

- Entering and editing worksheet data
- Understanding the types of data you can enter in cells
- Using functions
- Selecting cells and ranges
- Entering data into a range
- Formatting worksheets

FAST FORWARD

Enter Data into Worksheet Cells ➤ pp. 42-43

3	Rent	$500
4	Supplies	$500
5	Taxes	$250

To enter information into a cell:

1. Click the cell using the mouse.
2. Type what you want into the cell.

Whenever you press ENTER, click the Formula bar's Enter button, or click on another cell, Excel places into the cell whatever you've just typed.

Edit and Erase Data ➤ pp. 43-44

You can replace a cell's existing contents by typing over it. You can also edit a cell's contents. To do this, follow these steps:

1. Double-click the cell so that Excel turns the cell into an editable text box.
2. Make your changes.
3. To place the edited cell contents back into the cell, press ENTER or click the Formula bar's Enter button.

To erase the contents of some cells:

1. Right-click the cell.
2. When Excel displays its shortcut menu, choose the Clear Contents command.

Change Column Widths and Row Heights ➤ p. 45

	A	B
1	Sales	$10,000
2		
3	Rent	$500
4	Supplies	$500
5	Taxes	$250
6		
7	Profits	$8,750

To make a column wide enough to display its longest value or label:

1. Double-click the right border of the column letter box.
2. Drag the right border of the column using the mouse.

To make a row tall enough to display its characters:

1. Double-click the bottom border of the row number box.
2. Drag the bottom border of the row using the mouse.

Enter Formulas ➤ pp. 49-54

You enter a formula into a worksheet cell using the following steps:

1. Select the cell.
2. Type the equal sign.
3. Enter the formula using any input values and the appropriate mathematical operators that make up your formula; then press ENTER.

Use Functions ➤ pp. 54-60

You enter a function into a worksheet cell using the following steps:

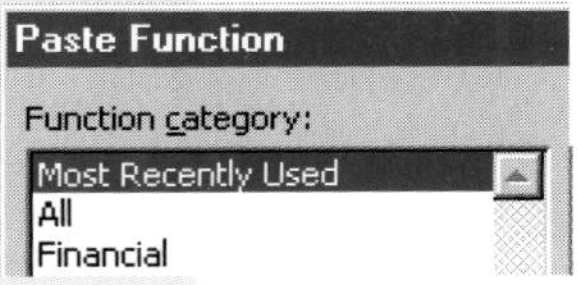

1. Select the cell.
2. Choose the Insert | Function command.
3. Select the function you want to use from the Paste Function dialog box.
4. Provide the arguments, or function inputs, necessary for the function's calculation; then press ENTER.

Select Ranges ➤ pp. 61-62

There are a number of techniques you can use to select ranges, depending on the size of the range:

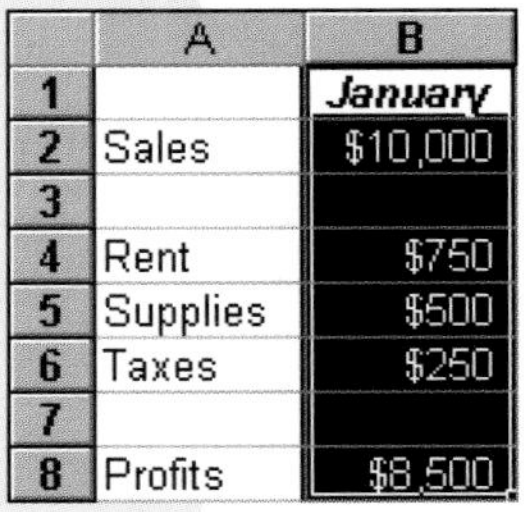

- To select a single-cell range, click the cell.
- To select a group, or multiple-cell range, click one corner of a rectangle of cells and then drag the mouse to the opposite corner.
- To select a three-dimensional range, first select the range on
- the first worksheet. Then press the CTRL key and click the sheet tabs of the other worksheets on which you want to select the same range of cells.
- To select a column or row with the mouse, simply click the column letter or row number.

Copy Ranges ➤ pp. 63-64

To copy a selected range's information using the mouse:

1. Hold down the CTRL key.
2. Drag the range to its new location by clicking the selection border.

Move Ranges ➤ p. 64

To move a selected range's information using the mouse, just click the border of the selected range and drag the range to its new location.

Insert Rows and Columns ➤ pp. 64-65

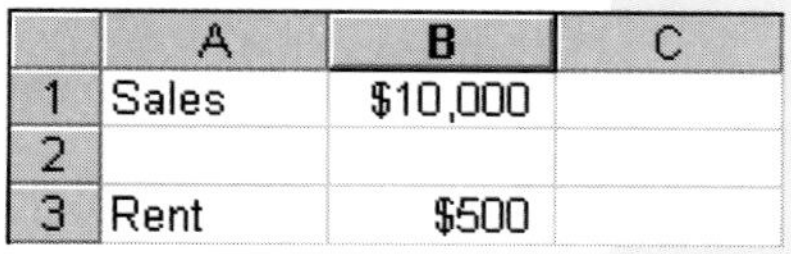

To insert a row:

1. Select the row above where you want to insert a new row.
2. Choose the Insert | Row command.

To insert a column:

1. Select the column to the left of where you want to insert a new column.
2. Choose the Insert | Column command.

To insert more than one row or more than one column, select more than one row or column before choosing the Insert | Row or Insert | Column command.

Format Worksheets ➤ pp. 65-66

To format a worksheet range:

1. Select the range.
2. Use the appropriate Formatting toolbar box or button.

Excel lets you easily perform numerical analysis. In other words, it's a tool for crunching numbers—for figuring out next year's budget or last year's profits or the price of tea in China.

Excel's basic building blocks—its worksheet pages—are simply tables, or grids, you use for storing information you want to analyze numerically. Figure 3.1 shows a sample worksheet page already filled in with a bit of data. Boiled down to its very essence, to use Excel all you have to do is learn to build worksheets like the one shown. That's what I'll explain how to do in the pages of this chapter.

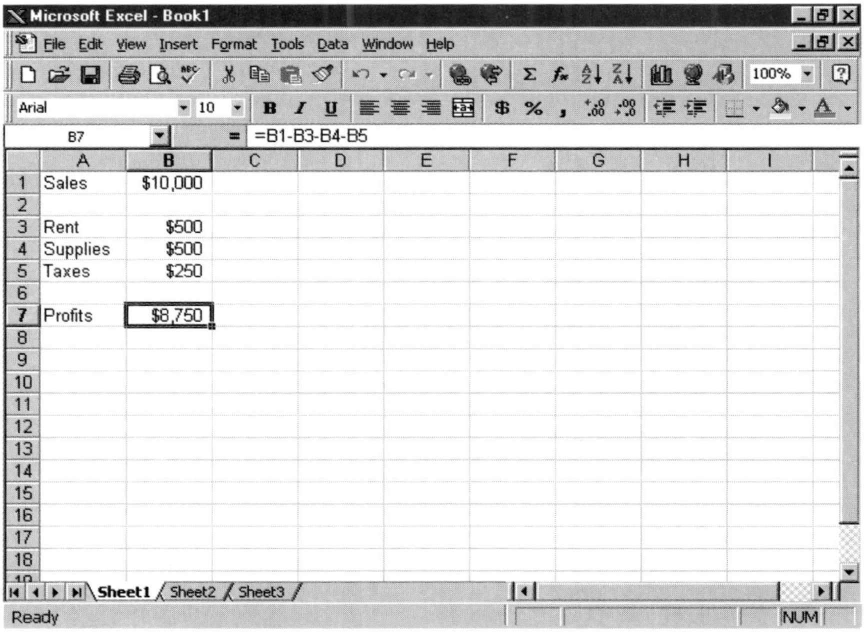

Figure 3.1 This simple Excel worksheet forecasts the profits of an imaginary business

Creating an Excel Document

I assume you already know how to start programs like Excel. If you don't, you might want to read Chapter 1. It explains how to add shortcut icons to your desktop that let you start Microsoft Office applications—like Excel—with a double-click of the mouse.

When you start the Excel program, it creates a blank Excel document for you to use. This document (it's okay to call it a document even though we aren't in Word) is more precisely described as a *workbook*. (You'll encounter this term if you read any of the Office printed or online documentation.)

A workbook is a notepad, or stack, of worksheets. The workbooks that Excel supplies initially provide only three pages (look at the bottom of Figure 3.1), but you can add more worksheets. You can also change the default number of pages for a workbook by choosing the Tools | Options command.

A worksheet is just a grid of rows and columns that you can use to organize information. Each row-column intersection creates a cell, which is simply a box you use to input information into the worksheet. Usually, the information includes numbers you want to manipulate mathematically as well as chunks of text that describe these numbers, as shown in Figure 3.1. But in real life, your own worksheets might easily be more complex or store more information. In any case, you get the idea. A workbook is like an electronic notepad, and each page of the notepad is a worksheet. (You can have pages in a workbook that aren't worksheets. I'll talk more about this in Chapter 5.)

Entering Data into Worksheet Cells

To enter some bit of information into a cell, you simply click the cell using the mouse and begin typing. When you press ENTER, click the Formula bar's Enter button, or click another cell, Excel places into the cell whatever you typed. If you begin typing some entry and then realize that you don't want your entry placed into a cell, press ESC or click the Formula bar's Cancel button.

The preceding paragraph describes the key to the most basic workings of Excel, so take a minute and test it yourself. Start Excel and enter some sample data into a few, randomly selected cells: Your birth date. The hourly pay rate you earned on your first job. The name of your first love. For fun, I created a simple spreadsheet, shown in Figure 3.2. You should be able to create a similar worksheet: Just click cells and type your entries.

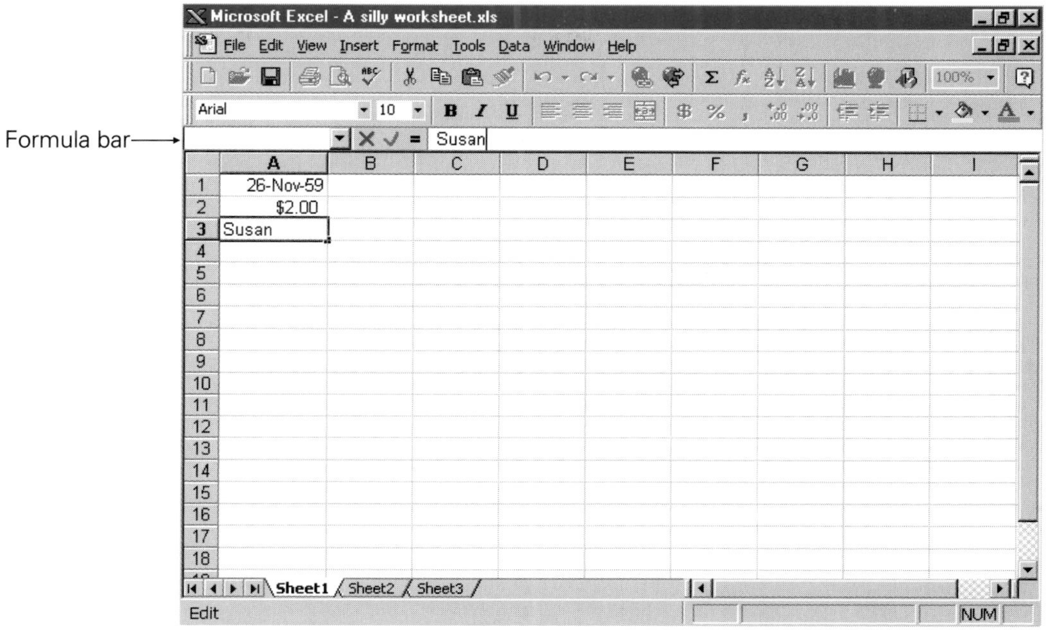

Figure 3.2 You enter data into a cell by clicking the cell, typing your entry, and pressing ENTER

Editing and Erasing Data

When you want to change a cell's information, you have two choices. You can

- Replace the cell's existing contents by typing over them. For example, you can click the cell, type your new entry, and press ENTER.
- Edit the existing entry. To edit a cell's contents:

    1. Double-click the cell so that Excel turns the cell into an editable text box.
    2. Make your changes.
    3. Press ENTER or click the Formula bar's Enter button to place the edited cell contents back into the cell.

When you make your changes, you can use the BACKSPACE key to erase the preceding character. You can click the mouse or use the LEFT or RIGHT ARROW key to move the insertion point and then press the DELETE key to erase the next character. Or you can insert new characters at the insertion point simply by typing.

To erase the contents of some cells:

1. Right-click the cell.
2. When Excel displays its shortcut menu, choose the Clear Contents command.

CAUTION

You can't erase the cell data by clicking a cell and pressing the spacebar. Although this technique appears to work, you really replace the cell's current contents with a space character.

Understanding the Types of Cell Data

You can enter three types of data into the cells of a worksheet: labels, values, and formulas. Labels are the simplest type of cell data, so I'll describe them first. Then after that, I'll describe values and formulas.

Labels

A label is usually a chunk of text or text and numbers that you don't want to use in a calculation. Your name or address. A telephone number. The name of the town you live in. Typically, you use labels to describe the values you want to use in calculations. Take another peek at Figure 3.1. All of the cell entries in column A are labels.

As a practical matter, you can enter labels as long as you need. (Okay—technically, there's a limit of 255 characters, but that is rarely really a limitation.) But if you type a label that's wider than the column you're placing it in, you'll often need to adjust the column width. Here's the reason: while Excel will let a long label spill over into the adjacent cell or cells if they are empty, if the adjacent cell or cells store data, Excel displays only the portion of the label that fits.

Take a look at the following worksheet fragment. Notice that the long label in cell A1—"Goethe took 50 years to write Faust"—spills over into cells B1, C1, and D1. This is because cells B1, C1, and D1 are empty. In comparison, only a portion of the label in cell A2 appears because cell B2 stores the number 50.

	A	B	C	D
1	Goethe took 50 years to write Faust			
2	Goethe toc	50		
3				
4				

I should point out that cell A2 stores the same label as cell A1. The two cells' contents are identical. It's only the display of the cells' contents that are different. This raises an important point which I'll talk about more in the coming discussion of values: what a cell stores and what Excel displays for a cell are often different. Stay tuned.

If a label's display does get cut off because it can't spill over into adjacent cells or you don't want a label spilling over into adjacent cells, you need to adjust the column width. There are a couple of quick ways to do this:

- To make a column as wide as the widest piece of data it holds—a label or a value—double-click the right border of the column letter box.
- Alternatively, drag the right border of the column using the mouse.

	A	B
1	Goethe took 50 years to write Faust	
2	Goethe took 50 years to write Faust	50
3		

Since we're on the subject of changing column widths, I'll also tell you that you can change the heights of rows using the same basic mechanics:

- Double-click the bottom border of the gray box that holds the row number label.
- Alternatively, drag the bottom border of the row using the mouse.

AutoComplete

Before we wrap up this discussion of labels, let me tell you about a special tool that Excel provides to make data entry of labels easier: AutoComplete. AutoComplete works like this. When you begin entering a label in a column, Excel looks at each of the other entries in the column to see if it looks like your entry might just match one of those. If Excel finds that the first few characters of your entry match the first few characters of another entry, it automatically completes, or AutoCompletes, your entry so it matches the earlier entry. This sounds kooky, perhaps, but let's take a quick look at a worksheet in which this AutoComplete tool would be really handy. Say you're building a list of employee names and addresses, as shown in the following example, and that you're using columns to store the individual fields of employee information.

	A	B	C	D	E
1	***Name***	***Street Address***	***City***	***State***	***Zip***
2	Peter	512 Wetmore	Redmond	WA	98053
3	Tom	5387 242nd PL	Redmond		
4					
5					

Take a close look at the entry I've started in row 3. When I began typing the first part of the city in which the employee lives, *Re,* Excel assumed there was a pretty good chance that I'd finish the entry is by typing *dmond.* (It's very likely that some of the employees live in the same town, right?) So Excel finished my city entry by typing *dmond* for me. If I do want to enter that employee's city as Redmond, I press ENTER or click the Formula bar's Enter button. If I want to enter something else, I just keep typing. Excel replaces *dmond* with whatever else I type. For example, if the employee described in row 3 really lives in Renton, when I type the last four letters of the city name, *nton,* Excel replaces the *dmond* with *nton.*

SHORTCUT

If you right-click a cell and choose the Pick from List command from the shortcut menu, Excel displays a list of all the labels you've already entered in that column of the worksheet. To enter one of the listed labels into the active cell, you just select it from the list.

Values

Values are numbers you want to use in calculations. If you were building a worksheet that tallied the cost of building a cabin—as Henry Thoreau did in his seminal work, *Walden*—you might build a worksheet like that shown in Figure 3.3. Notice that column A holds labels that describe the values, and that column B holds the values—the actual costs of Thoreau's cabin.

Figure 3.3 doesn't show any negative values, but worksheet cells accept negative values. To enter a negative value, just precede the number with a hyphen. If you wanted to enter "minus 42" into a cell, for example, you would press the hyphen key, then enter 42 (-42).

Using Special Values

Most users will enter values like those shown in Figure 3.3, but you should know that Excel will accept values that look or work differently. (Remember that a value is just a number you want to use later in a calculation.) For example, you can use scientific notation, date and time values, percentages, and fractions. I'm

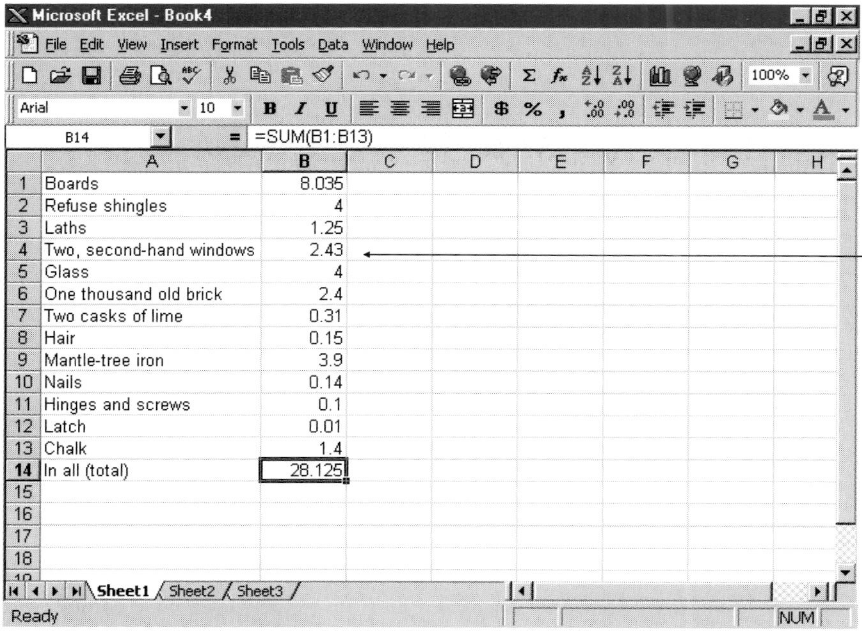

At this stage, you typically don't include any formatting: dollar signs, commas, etc. You do need to include a decimal point if a value includes decimal values.

Figure 3.3 Thoreau gave these numbers as the actual cost of building his cabin at Walden Pond

If you do enter a really large or really small value in a worksheet cell—one that uses more than about 20 digits—Excel will convert your value to scientific notation.

not going to talk about any of this scientific notation or date and time stuff here. Most people won't need this information. Nevertheless, if your job requires you to work with data in these formats, use the Office Assistant (described in Chapter 3) to ask Excel about how this stuff works. I will talk briefly about percentages and fractions.

You can enter percent values into worksheet cells by following the value with a percent symbol. Excel enters the decimal equivalent for the percent value into the cell, but displays the value as a percentage. Does that make sense? In other words, if you enter 75% into a cell, Excel stores the decimal value .75 in the cell, but displays it as 75%.

You can also enter fractional values into worksheet cells as long as Excel understands that what you're entering is a fraction. If you enter 1 2/5 into a cell, for example, Excel figures that you're probably trying to enter a fraction. So it plops the value 1.4 into the cell, formatting it to look like a fraction. Note that the way you enter this is by typing the integer first (1), then a space, then the numerator (2), then a slash (/), and then the denominator (5).

EXPERT ADVICE

Fractions illustrate an important point about Excel cells. What a cell holds isn't necessarily the same thing as what a cell displays. For example, if you enter 1 2/5 into a cell, the worksheet cell shows, or displays, this fraction, but the cell actually holds the value 1.4.

If you want to enter a fraction that doesn't contain a whole number and that could be misinterpreted by Excel as a date—for example, is the entry 2/5 a date value for February 5 or a fraction—just enter the fraction as 0 2/5.

Wide Values

If you enter a value with more digits than will fit into the width of a column, Excel does one of two things. If you haven't directly or indirectly told Excel to use special formatting for the cell (described later in the chapter in "Formatting Worksheets"), Excel displays the value using scientific notation, as shown here.

2.5E+22

If you have told Excel to use special formatting, Excel displays pound signs instead of the value. To make a column wide enough to display the value the way you want:

- Double-click the right border of the column letter box.
- Alternatively, drag the right border of the column using the mouse.

(These are the same techniques you use when a label is too big for a cell.)

Formulas

The final yet most important type of value is a formula. By entering a formula, you tell Excel to calculate some value using either values that the formula supplies or that the formula references. For example, if you entered the formula =2+2 into a cell, you would be telling Excel to add 2 and 2 together and display the result (which is 4, of course). If you entered the formula =A1+A2 into a cell, you would be telling Excel to add the value in cell A1 to the value in cell A2 and then to display the result. Formulas provide the very foundation of Excel, so I'm going to explain in detail how you use them.

Formula Basics

Entering a formula into a worksheet cell is easy. First, select the cell. Next, to tell Excel that you're about to enter a formula, type an equal sign. Finally, enter the formula using any input values and the appropriate mathematical operators that make up your formula. Table 3.1 describes the five basic operators and provides examples of simple formulas that show how the operators are used.

While the formulas in Table 3.1 can be useful to perform calculations, the neat part of Excel's formulas is that you don't have to include the actual values in a formula. You can instead reference other cells that hold the values. For example, let's say you want to calculate the monthly interest cost of a $50,000 loan when the interest rate is 9.5 percent annually. To make this calculation, you could construct a formula that looks like this:

=50000*9.5%/12

A better method (because it lets you quickly change formula values later) is to construct a simple worksheet that stores the loan values and then references

Operator	Description	Example	Result
+	Addition	=2+2	4
-	Subtraction	=4-3	1
*	Multiplication	=4*3	12
/	Division	=12/3	4
^	Exponentiation	=10^2	100

Table 3.1 The Basic Excel Operators

these values in the actual formula. Figure 3.4 shows just such a worksheet. To construct it, enter the labels and values shown in the range A1:B2, as well as the label shown in A3. Then enter the formula **=B1*B2/12** into cell B3.

DEFINITION

Range: A rectangular block of worksheet cells. You describe a range by entering the cell addresses (separated by a colon) of the range's opposite corners (for example, A1:B3).

The values 9.5% and 9.75%, by the way, are equivalent to the decimal values .095 and .0975.

When you do enter this formula into cell B3, what you're telling Excel to do is to multiply the value in cell B1 by the value in cell B2 and then to divide that result by 12. The neat thing about the formula in Figure 3.4 is that, by using cell references in the formula rather than actual values, you can easily recalculate the formula using different values. If interest rates pop up to, say, 9.75 percent, you can recalculate the monthly interest simply by replacing the existing value in cell B2, 9.5%, with the new value, 9.75%.

SHORTCUT

*Although you can type a formula, it's easier and more accurate to type the operators and then click the cells. For example, to create the formula =B1*B2/12, you could type =, click cell B1, type *, click cell B2, and then type /12.*

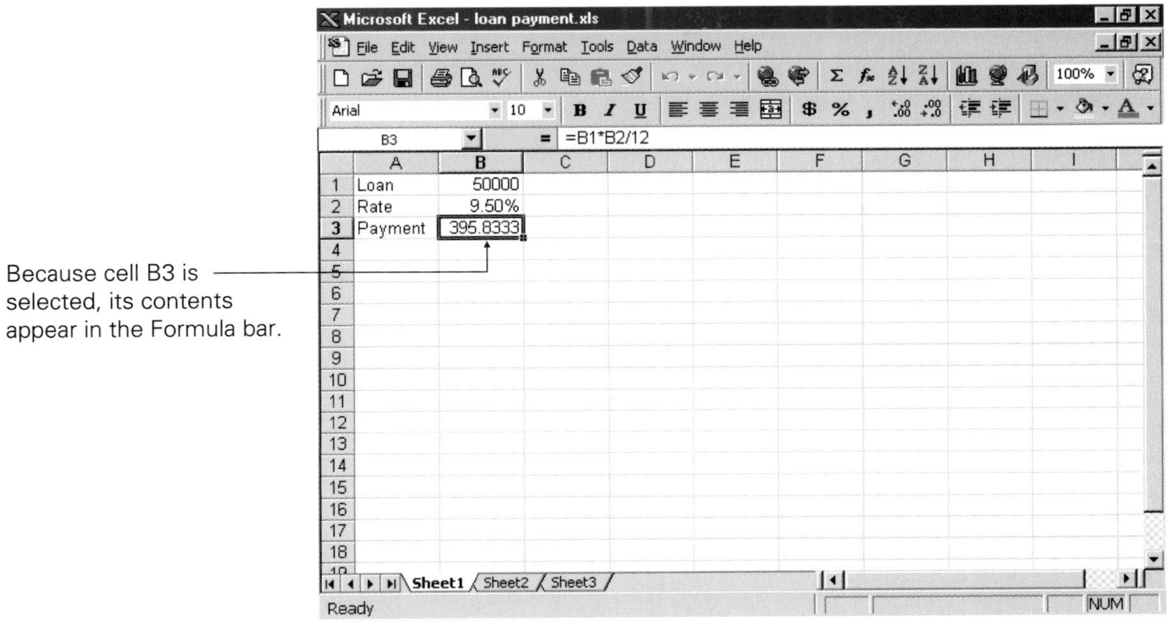

Figure 3.4 This simple worksheet calculates the monthly interest cost of a loan

As you write formulas for worksheet cells, you'll want to keep operator precedence in mind. Operator precedence determines the order in which a formula's calculations are made when a formula includes more than one operator. Take, for example, the case of the following formula:

=1+2-3*4/5^6

Do you know which calculations get performed first? (I might not if I didn't work with this stuff all the time.) The general rules are pretty easy:

- Exponential operations are performed first.
- Multiplication and division operations, which have equal precedence, are performed next.
- Finally, addition and subtraction operations, which also have equal precedence, are performed last.

If two operators in a formula have the same precedence—say there are two multiplication operations or a multiplication and a division operation—operators are used in left-to-right order. In the case of the formula given earlier, therefore, Excel first makes the exponential calculation, then does multiplication, then the division, then the addition, and finally the subtraction. (To verify that you understand how this works, try to calculate the preceding formula with a calculator and scratch pad and then test your result by entering the formula into an empty worksheet cell.)

To tell Excel that you want some part of the formula calculated first—in spite of the operator precedence rules—enclose the operator and its operands (the values the formula uses in its calculation) in parentheses. To tell Excel that you want some other part of the formula calculated second—in spite of the operator precedence rules—repeat the process: enclose the operator and its operands (which may actually be a calculation result) in parentheses.

Let's say, for example, that you did want to use the formula =1+2-3*4/5^6 in some worksheet cell, but that you wanted the operators used in exactly the opposite order that Excel would typically use them. In other words, rather than using the operators in the default order—exponentiation, multiplication, division, addition, and subtraction—you want them performed in this order: subtraction, addition, division, multiplication, and exponentiation. Here's how you would place your parentheses:

=((1+(2-3))*(4/5))^6

I describe functions later in the chapter in "Using Functions."

Excel uses different colors to help you identify different sets of parentheses to keep them straight. If you find this operator precedence business confusing—and it sometimes can be—your best bet is to keep your formulas simple. Don't construct long formulas that use a bunch of different operators. If you can, substitute a function. Alternatively, break a long formula into several shorter formulas and place these shorter formulas into separate cells.

Interpreting Error Values

You can create formulas that don't make sense because they aren't possible. For example, no one knows how to divide a value by zero—that operation is undefined. So if you enter a formula such as =1/0 into a cell, Excel can't calculate it. Instead, what Excel displays as the result of the formula calculation is an error value, #DIV/0!. This error value tells you, first, that Excel can't calculate the formula and, second, why Excel can't calculate it.

If you do create a formula that returns an error value, use the error value to identify the type of error. To figure out what an error message means, choose the Help | Contents and Index command. Click the Index tab and enter the error message into the text box provided.

Then, assuming the error isn't temporary—perhaps a result of the fact that your worksheet still isn't complete—correct the problem or problems that produced the error value.

How Excel Recalculates a Worksheet's Formulas

Excel calculates the formulas you enter in the order they need to be calculated. For example, it first calculates any formulas that are independent of any other formulas. (These might be formulas that use only values and not cell references, or they might be formulas that reference only cells that hold values and not other formulas.) After Excel has calculated these independent formulas, it begins calculating the dependent formulas, working its way from your least dependent formulas to your most dependent formulas. (By "dependent" here, I just mean formulas that need other formula's results in order to be calculated.)

Most of the time this all happens automatically. You don't need to think about it. You don't need to worry about it. However, you can create something called a *circular reference*, and that typically creates problems. A circular reference, quite simply, is a formula that either directly or indirectly depends on itself. So you can't calculate the formula because to calculate the formula you first need to calculate the formula. You see the circular nature of this.

If you build a worksheet that uses a circular reference, Excel may be able to iteratively solve the circular reference. It turns out that some circular references converge to a single solution. All Excel has to do is repeatedly recalculate the worksheet.

EXPERT ADVICE

If you create intentional circular references, you need to turn on iterative recalculation. To do so, choose the Tools | Options command, click the Calculation tab, and mark the Iteration check box.

Some circular references, however, can't be solved. In these cases, the formula that creates the circular reference doesn't converge to a single, correct solution. In that case, you've either made an error in entering the formula—perhaps you referenced an incorrect cell or the cell itself with the formula—or you've constructed a large, complex workbook, and your modeling logic has broken down someplace.

You'll always know when you create a circular reference. When you do, Excel displays a message box that says "Can't resolve circular reference" as you enter the formula that creates the circular reference. Then it displays the Circular Reference message box to identify the cells with the formulas that create the circular reference. Excel also draws an arrow or arrows to identify the circular reference. If the circular reference is intentional and the formula creating the circular reference converges on a single correct solution, you can leave the circular reference in the workbook. If the circular reference is unintentional or doesn't converge on a single correct solution, you should correct or replace the formula.

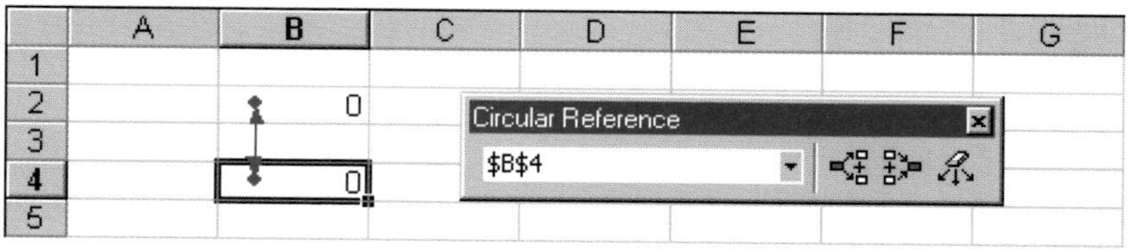

CAUTION

Excel doesn't alert you to circular references if you've already told it you want it to make iterative, or repeated, workbook recalculations. It figures that if you've told it to do this, you know you have circular references that you're trying to solve through convergence.

Using Functions

Using the formula operators described in the previous section of this chapter, you can actually create formulas that perform almost any calculation. But as a practical matter, some of your formulas—if you did do everything from scratch—would be very complicated. To make your formulas easier, Excel supplies what are called *functions*. In essence, a function is a prebuilt formula, so one advantage of functions is that they save you the time and trouble of building your own, complicated formulas. But there's another advantage of functions: they are usually very clever and efficient about the way they accept and handle any entries in the formula. If you're going to do any serious work with Excel, therefore, you'll want to know how to use Excel's functions. So that's what we'll discuss next.

Understanding How a Function Works

The best way to explain how a function works is to show you an example. Take a look at the worksheet shown here. It supplies the ages of an imaginary team of elementary school softball players.

	A	B
1	Sue	8
2	Beth	9
3	Carol	9
4	Britt	7
5	Marie	10
6	Lilly	9
7	Julie	8
8	Rachel	8
9	Claire	9

Let's suppose, for the sake of illustration, that you wanted to calculate the average age of team members and place this value in cell B10. To do this, you could construct a formula like the one shown here and then enter it in your worksheet:

=(B1+B2+B3+B4+B5+B6+B7+B8+B9)/9

But an easier approach would be to use a prebuilt function that calculates the average of a set of values stored in the range B1:B9. To do this, you would enter the following formula into your worksheet:

=AVERAGE(B1:B9)

Clearly, using the AVERAGE function is easier even in this simple example. You can imagine how much easier this function would make your work if you were calculating, say, the average age of all the players in a 100-person softball league.

You now understand what functions do, but let's talk for a minute about how you create function-based formulas. To create a function-based formula:

1. Type the equal sign (=).
2. Type the function name followed by a left, or opening, parenthesis [( ].
3. Enter the input values, or arguments, that the function needs or uses to make its calculation, followed by a right, or closing, parenthesis [ )].

In the case of the example AVERAGE calculation, I included only one argument, the range B1:B9. But many times functions accept or expect more than one argument, and in that case, you separate the arguments with commas. For example, it wouldn't make much sense—because all you would be doing is increasing your work—but you could rewrite the AVERAGE function shown earlier as follows:

=AVERAGE(B1,B2,B3,B4,B5,B6,B7,B8,B9)

Not all functions require arguments. For example, Excel supplies a function that returns the mathematical constant for pi, and it requires no arguments. In the case of functions that don't require arguments, you still follow the function name with parentheses, but you don't put anything between the parentheses. For example, the function-based formula to return the constant pi looks like this:

=PI( )

Although a function's arguments are often cell references, you can also use actual values, such as the players' ages, in a formula:

=AVERAGE(8,9,9,7,10,9,8,8,9)

You can also use as arguments the results of still other functions. For example, if you know that the SUM function sums the values included as its arguments, you might choose to enter the AVERAGE function's argument's like this:

=AVERAGE(SUM(B1),SUM(B2),SUM(B3),SUM(B4),SUM(B5),SUM(B6),SUM(B7),SUM(B8),SUM(B9))

The sum of a single value, of course, equals the value, so that last example doesn't really make sense. The argument SUM(B2) is the same as B2. But you get the basic idea: if a function wants a value as an argument, you can supply that value in several different ways.

Pasting Functions

While functions are terribly useful, they present a couple of problems to users. The first problem is that you may not know whether Excel supplies a function that provides a particular formula's calculations. I've said that Excel provides a lot of functions, but you don't really know whether Excel supplies functions to calculate loan payments or logarithms or whatever else you want to calculate. And even if I told you about each and every function, you wouldn't retain that knowledge for very long, especially if I provided you with a complete list of Excel's functions. (There are roughly 350 functions, if you include those supplied by the Analysis ToolPak add-in.)

The second practical problem with functions is you'll find it nearly impossible to remember which arguments a function needs and in which order you're supposed to supply them. For example, the function for calculating a loan payment needs at least three arguments: the loan balance, the interest rate, and the number of payments, and you have to enter these arguments in the right order, or the function can't perform its calculations.

Fortunately, Excel cleverly addresses and almost entirely solves these two problems. The Office Assistant first helps you find the function (if any) that performs a particular calculation. Then the Paste Function dialog box provides places for the arguments you need to supply and helps you to enter the arguments in the right order.

To see how all this works, suppose that you were considering the purchase of a new car and wanted to know what your monthly principal and interest payment would be. As a practical matter, it may be impossible for you to construct a formula, from scratch, that performs this calculation. So you might decide to use a function. Here's how the process would work:

1. Click the cell in which you want to enter the function.
2. Choose the Insert | Function command or click the Paste Function tool. Excel displays the Paste Function dialog box, shown next:

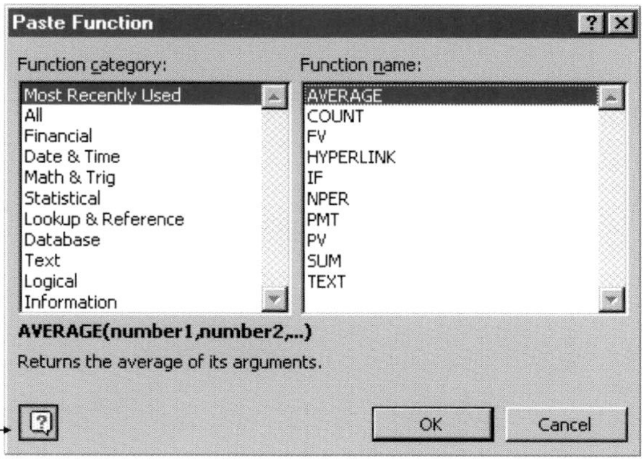

3. If the Office Assistant appears, click the Yes, Please Provide Help button. If it doesn't appear, click the Office Assistant button in the dialog box and then click the Help with This Feature button.
4. Describe what calculation you want to make by typing a description in the Office Assistant's text box. If you want to calculate a loan payment, for example, you might type **Calculate loan payment**.
5. Click Search. The Paste Function dialog box displays a list of recommended functions, as shown in Figure 3.5.
6. If you still can't figure out which function you want, pick the one that seems most likely and click the Office Assistant's Help On Selected Function button to have the Office Assistant display detailed help information, as shown here, about the selected function. You may need to repeat this process until you find the function you want.

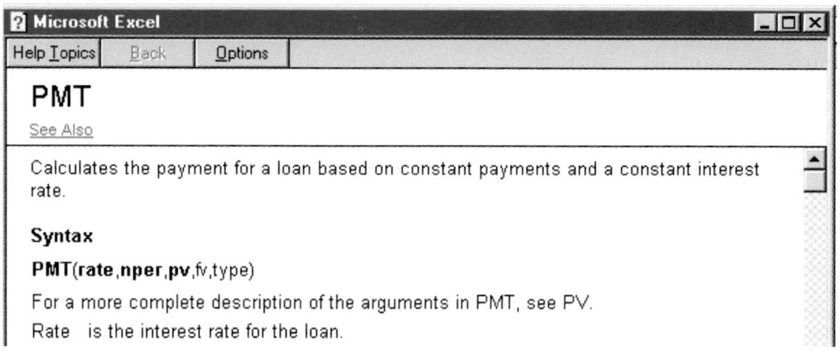

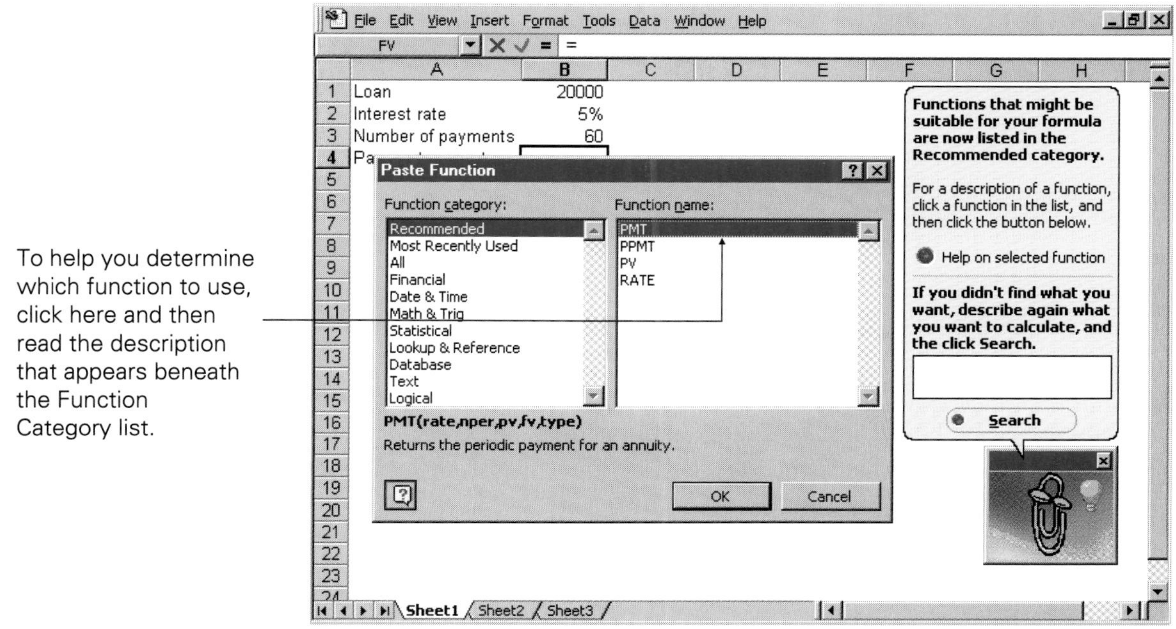

Figure 3.5 The Office Assistant after it's completed its job

7. After you identify the correct function, select it in the Paste Function dialog box and then click the Paste Function dialog box's OK button. Excel displays the second Paste Function dialog box, shown here:

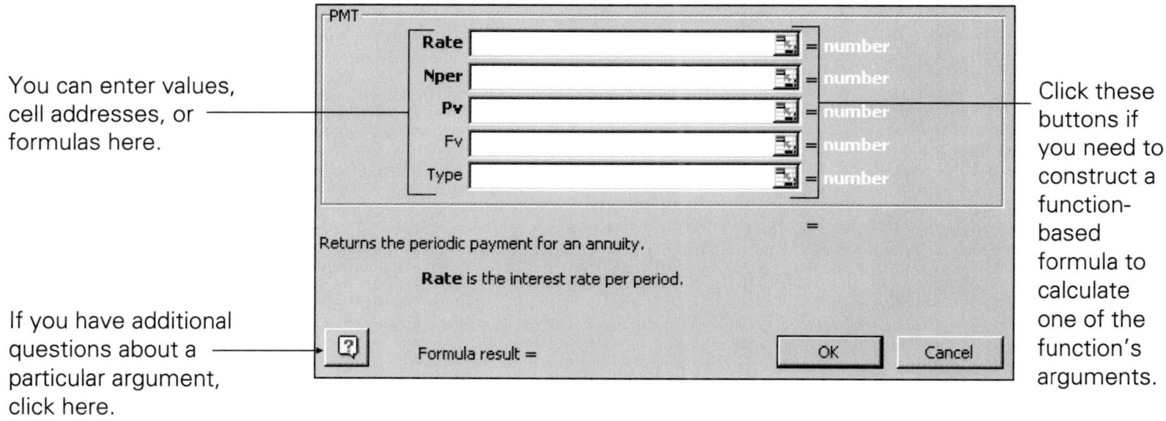

If you don't know a Microsoft Office toolbar box or button name, point to the tool. The Office application displays the tool name in a pop-up box called a tooltip.

8. Supply the arguments by filling in the text boxes. As you select an argument's text box, Excel describes what the argument should look like. As soon as you've supplied the last needed argument, Excel calculates the function result and displays this value at the bottom of the dialog box, on the left.
9. Click the OK button when you've finished supplying the arguments. Excel closes the Paste Function dialog box and places the function in the active cell (if you opened the Paste Function dialog box by clicking the Standard toolbar's Paste Function tool) or at the insertion point location (if you opened the Paste Function dialog box by clicking the Paste Function tool from either the Formula bar or one of the Paste Function dialog box's text boxes). Figure 3.6 shows a worksheet that calculates a car loan payment using a function.

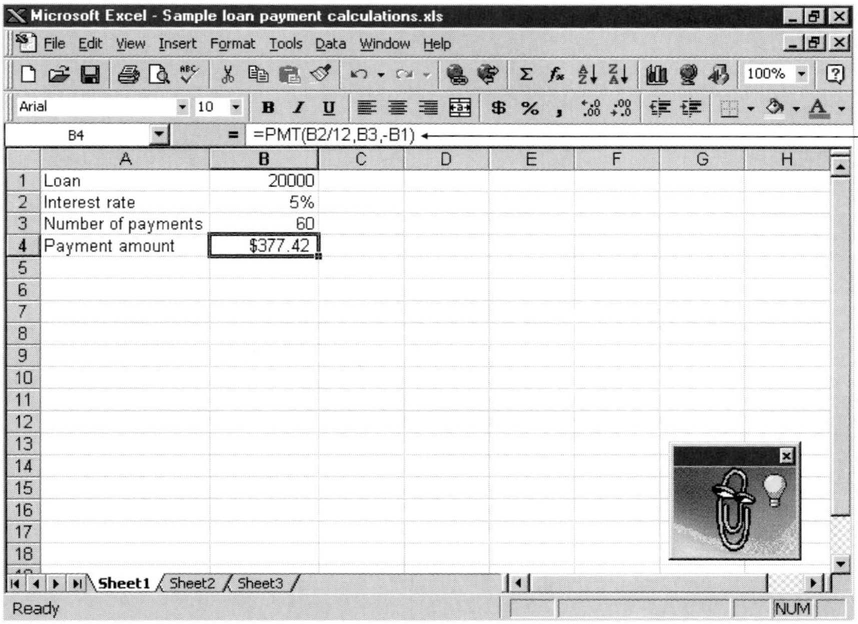

Figure 3.6 Using the Paste Function dialog box and some help from the Office Assistant, this worksheet was built to make a function-based calculation for the monthly loan payment on a new $20,000 car

Copying, Moving, and Filling Ranges

If you'll only ever build simple worksheets, you don't need to know how to copy, move, and fill ranges. In this case, skip ahead to the section "Printing, Saving, and Opening Workbooks."

In the preceding pages of this chapter, the assumption is that you enter data into a worksheet one cell at a time. Your simplest approach to do this is just to click the cell and then type your entry. You can, however, enter values, labels, and formulas into cells by copying and moving the contents of other cells. You can also enter values and labels into cells by using something called a Fill command.

As mentioned earlier, a range is just a rectangular chunk of a worksheet. So the smallest range is a single cell. But any rectangular worksheet chunk is also a range.

Selecting Ranges

To copy, move, or fill a range, you first select it. To select a single-cell range, you click the cell or move the cell selector to the cell using the arrow keys.

To select a group, or range, of cells, you click on one corner of a rectangle of cells and then drag the mouse to the opposite corner. The following illustration shows such a selection. (If you're following along in front of your computer, make sure that you can duplicate this selection using the mouse.)

Excel identifies your selection by placing a dark border around the cell(s).

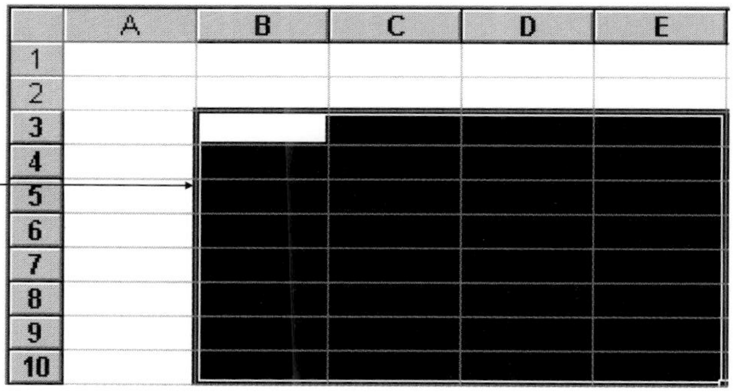

As mentioned earlier in the chapter, you describe a range selection by entering the cell address of the top-left corner of the range and the cell address of the bottom-right corner of the range, separating the two addresses with a colon.

For example, the range shown in the previous illustration is B3:E10. You'll often use range addresses in Excel dialog boxes and in constructing formulas.

You can also select more than one range of cells using the mouse, as shown here. To select multiple ranges, select the first range, hold down the CTRL key, and then select the second and any subsequent ranges.

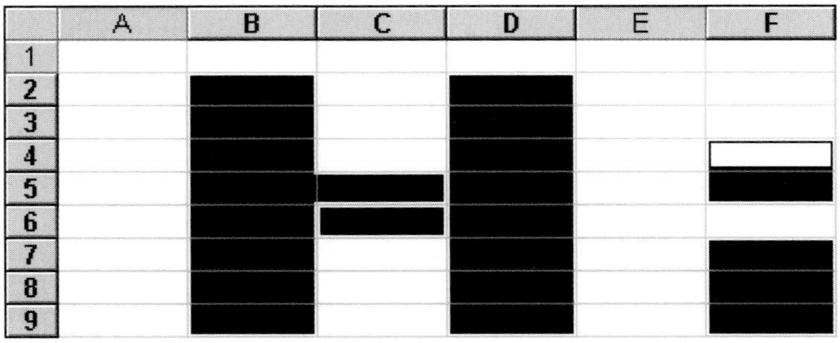

You can also use the keyboard to select a range of cells. First select one corner of the range using the arrow keys. Then, while holding down the SHIFT key, use the arrow keys to increase the size of the selection.

EXPERT ADVICE

To select a three-dimensional range—in other words, to select the same rectangle of cells on more than one page of a worksheet—first select the range on the first worksheet. Then hold down the CTRL key and click the sheet tabs of the other worksheets on which you want to select the same range of cells.

To select a column or row with the mouse, simply click the column letter or row number. Excel selects the entire column or row. (To select a column or row with the keyboard, use the arrow keys to select a cell in the row or column and then press CTRL-spacebar to select that cell's column or SHIFT-spacebar to select that cell's row.)

Copying Ranges

You can copy the contents of cells in one range to another range. For example, if you were building a budget worksheet as shown here, you might want to copy the contents of the range B1:B8 into the range C1:C8. To do this:

1. Select the range of cells that hold the labels, values, and formulas you want to copy (B1:B8 in this example).

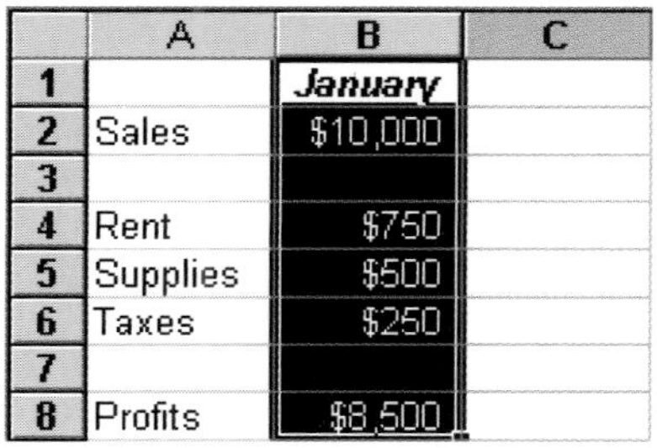

A
B
C
January
Sales
$10,000
Rent
$750
Supplies
$500
Taxes
$250
Profits
$8,500

2. Click the Standard toolbar's Copy button.
3. Click the top or top-left corner of the range into which you want to place the copied labels, values, and formulas (C1 in this example).
4. Click the Standard toolbar's Paste button. Excel pastes the copied cell contents into the new range.

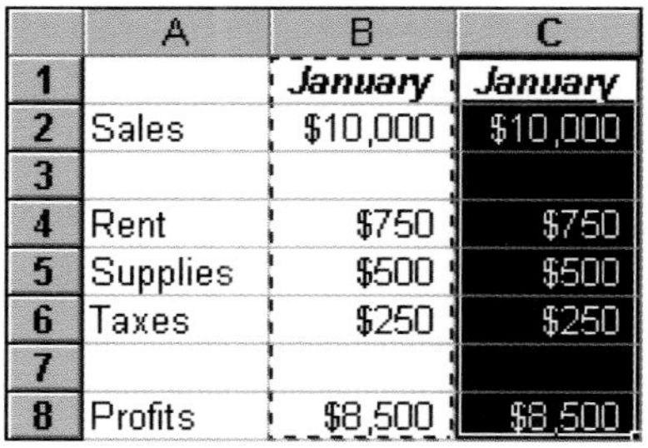

A
B
C
January
January
Sales
$10,000
$10,000
Rent
$750
$750
Supplies
$500
$500
Taxes
$250
$250
Profits
$8,500
$8,500

5. Edit cell labels and values as necessary. For example, you would replace the label January (in cell C1) with the label February.

Copying formulas works the same basic way—with one twist you might not expect. If you copy a formula, Excel adjusts the formula so it works in its new location. For example, if you want to copy the formula in cell B8 in the worksheet I just showed you—the formula is =B2-B4-B5-B6—the formula that is pasted into cell C8 is =C2-C4-C5-C6. Excel adjusts the cell addresses so the formula works in its new location. The big books on Excel spend several pages explaining how this works, but I won't do that here. As long as you know that Excel performs this adjustment—and that it usually adjusts correctly—you don't need to know more.

Moving Ranges

You can also move the contents of cells in one range to another range. To do this:

1. Select the range of cells that hold the labels, values, and formulas you want to move and click the Standard toolbar's Cut button.
2. Click the top or top-left corner of the range into which you want to place the copied labels, values, and formulas (C1 in this example) and then click the Standard toolbar's Paste button. Excel moves the cut cell contents to the new range.

EXPERT ADVICE

To move the selected range's information using the mouse, just drag the range to its new location. To instead copy a range, hold down the CTRL *key while you drag.*

Inserting Rows and Columns

You can easily insert rows and columns into a worksheet.

To insert a row:

1. Select the row above which you want to insert a new row.
2. Choose the Insert | Row command.

To insert a column:

1. Select the column to the left of which you want to insert a new column.
2. Choose the Insert | Column command.

If you want to insert more than one row or more than one column, no problem. Just select more than one row or column before choosing the Insert | Row or Insert | Column command.

Formatting Worksheets

Excel, like Word, provides a nifty Formatting toolbar that contains all sorts of neat buttons and boxes for formatting cell contents. Rather than reading some tedious explanation of how these tools work and what they do, take a peek at Table 3.2. Then create a sample worksheet and experiment as necessary.

Tool	Name	Description
	Font Size	Displays a drop-down list you use to specify the point size of the selected text.
	Bold	Alternately bolds and un-bolds the selected text.
	Italic	Alternately italicizes and un-italicizes the selected text.
	Underline	Alternately underlines and un-underlines the selected text.
	Align Left	Aligns the contents of a cell flush against the left side of the cell.
	Center	Centers the contents of a cell evenly between the left and right sides of the cell.

Table 3.2 Excel's Formatting Toolbar Tools

Tool	Name	Description
	Align Right	Aligns the contents of a cell flush against the right side of the cell.
	Merge and Center	Combines more than one cell into a single cell and centers text across the combined cell.
	Currency Style	Applies the currency style to the selected cells. (To change the type of currency, use the Numbers tab of the Format Cells dialog box.)
	Percent Style	Applies the percent style to the selected cells. (Note that Excel will change 10 to 1000% and 0.1 to 10%.)
	Comma Style	Applies the comma style to the selected cells. (This just means that Excel uses commas for numbers. The value 1000, for example, shows as 1,000.)
	Increase Decimal	Adds a digit to the right of the decimal point in the selected cells.
	Decrease Decimal	Removes a digit to the right of the decimal point in the selected cells.
	Decrease Indent	Un-indents the selected text.
	Increase Indent	Indents the selected text.
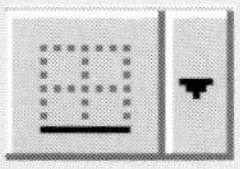	Borders	Displays the Borders toolbar so you can choose a border style for the selected cells.
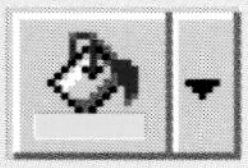	Fill Color	Lets you add, remove, or change the fill color of the selected object.
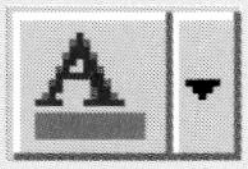	Font Color	Changes the foreground color of the selected text. (Click the down arrow at the end of the tool to display a list of color choices.)

Table 3.2 Excel's Formatting Toolbar Tools (*continued*)

Printing, Saving, and Opening Workbooks

In Chapter 2, I described how you can print, save, and open Word documents. These things work the same basic way in Excel as they do in Word. If you read Chapter 2, therefore, you already know how to print, save, and open Excel workbooks. If you didn't read Chapter 2, take the time to read, or at least skim, Chapter 7. It explains in detail how you manage (print, save, open, and so on) documents in Excel.

CHECK POINT

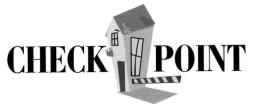

My editor was a bit frustrated with me about the length of this chapter. "Steve-buddy," she kept saying, "you're covering too much ground." Maybe she was right. But I'll tell you what. You, my friend, now know a lot of stuff about Excel. You not only know the easy stuff like how to enter and edit worksheet data, select cells and ranges, and format your data, but you also know other important and useful stuff including how to use functions and tricks for entering scads of data into ranges.

With the information provided in this chapter, you should find it pretty easy to build Excel worksheets. There's more to Excel than I've described here. (This bit of knowledge shouldn't surprise you: Excel does more complicated stuff than Word or PowerPoint.) But you should still have the requisite skills to build most worksheets.

Also, let me tell you (or remind you) that I've provided several handy business planning and financial planning templates at the Osborne/McGraw-Hill web site. If you're interested in learning more about these tools, refer to Appendix B.

FAX

CHAPTER

4

PowerPoint Basics

INCLUDES

- Creating a presentation
- Editing and formatting your presentation's slide text
- Creating new slides
- Customizing the slide show
- Viewing presentations

FAST FORWARD

Use the AutoContent Wizard ➤ pp. 73-77

To use the AutoContent Wizard, follow these steps:

1. Start PowerPoint in the usual way. When you do, PowerPoint displays its program window and dialog box.
2. Click the AutoContent Wizard to tell PowerPoint you want some help creating your presentation.
3. Click OK.

Edit Your Presentation's Slide Text ➤ pp. 77-79

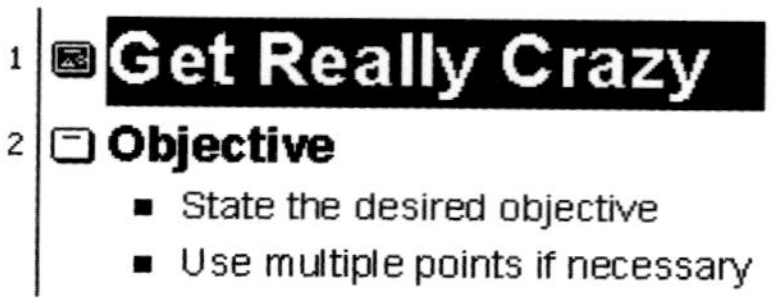

Editing a slide's text works the same way as editing the text in a Word document. To edit a slide's title:

1. Click at the point you want to place the insertion point. (You'll typically find this easiest to do using the Outline view, which you can always get to by choosing the View | Outline command or clicking the Outline View button.)
2. To add text, just type it.
3. To remove text, use the BACKSPACE or DELETE key.
4. To replace text, select the text you want to replace and then type the new text you want to substitute.

Format Slide Text ➤ pp. 79-81

To format slide text:

1. Select the text.
2. Use one of the Formatting toolbar's boxes or buttons.

Add a New, Blank Slide ➤ pp. 81-82

To add a new slide to the open presentation:

1. Display the presentation's Outline view and then position the insertion point (by clicking) at the point where you want to insert the new slide.
2. Choose the Insert | New Slide command.

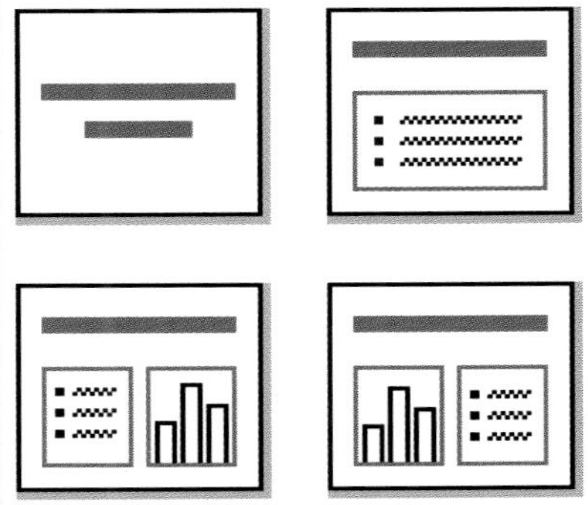

Fill a New Slide with Information ➤ pp. 82-84

To fill a slide with information:

1. Select the slide by, for example, clicking it in the outline.
2. Choose the View | Slide command.
3. When PowerPoint displays the slide in the Slide view, replace the placeholders with real text or objects.

Reorganize Slides ➤ p. 85

To rearrange the order of your slides:

1. Choose the View | Slide Sorter command.
2. When PowerPoint displays the Slide Sorter view of your presentation, rearrange the slides by dragging them to new locations.

Apply a Different Design Template ➤ pp. 85-86

To pick a different design template, choose the Apply Design command from the Common Tasks toolbar. (If the Common Tasks toolbar doesn't appear, choose the Format | Apply Design command.)

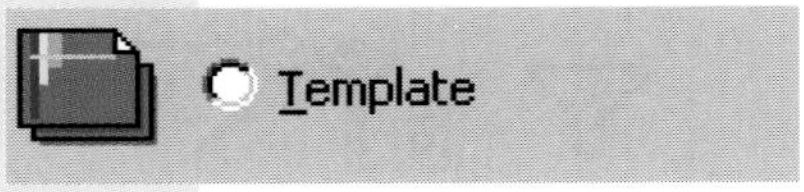

View a Presentation ➤ *pp. 89-91*

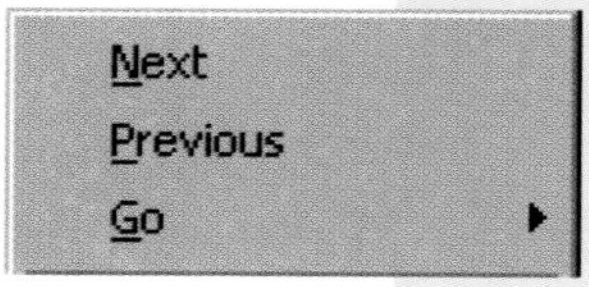

To view a presentation:

1. Choose the Slide Show | View Show command.
2. To move through the presentation's slides, use the PAGEDN and PAGEUP keys.

PowerPoint helps you create colorful, attractive, persuasive electronic slide shows you can use in presentations. You can display, or view, these electronic slide shows on a computer. And you can produce (by jumping through a variety of hoops) 35mm slides, overhead transparencies, printed-on-paper versions of the slides (in either color or black and white), and even World Wide Web documents.

Although all of this may sound complicated, it's really not. When you boil PowerPoint down to its very essence, it's pretty much just like Microsoft Word—except that the pages you create with PowerPoint (as compared to the pages you create with Word) are more colorful and show less text. You'll see exactly what I mean in a moment.

Creating a Presentation

Microsoft was pretty smart about the way it organized PowerPoint. The company figured—correctly, in my experience—that most PowerPoint users won't use PowerPoint all that frequently—maybe a few times a month, or even a few times a year. With this assumption in mind, Microsoft made PowerPoint really easy to use. PowerPoint does almost everything for you, thanks to such gizmos as the AutoContent Wizard, which I'll describe next.

Using the AutoContent Wizard

In Chapter 2, I introduced you to a couple of the wizards that Office supplies to make Word easier to use. While wizards are important in Word, they're even more important in PowerPoint because in PowerPoint you use wizards to do just about everything.

The most important wizard in PowerPoint is the AutoContent Wizard. It creates a rough-draft presentation for you based on your answers to a handful of questions. To use the AutoContent Wizard:

1. Start PowerPoint in the usual way. When you do, PowerPoint displays its program window and the dialog box shown here:

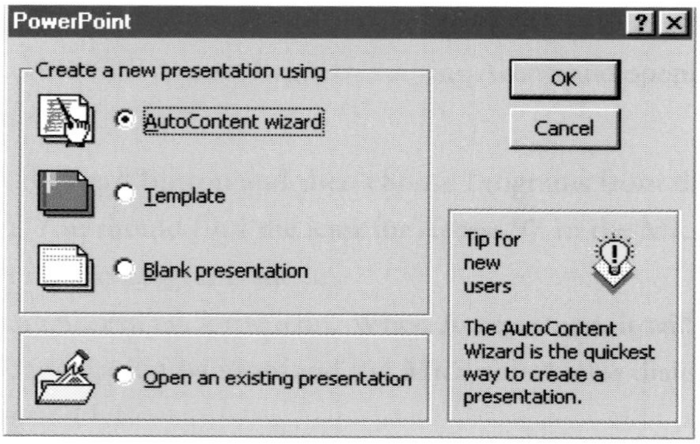

If you have questions about how to start PowerPoint, see Chapter 1. If you want to know more about opening an existing PowerPoint document (which PowerPoint calls a presentation), refer to Chapter 7.

2. Click the AutoContent Wizard to tell PowerPoint you want some help creating your presentation and then click OK.
3. When the AutoContent Wizard displays its first dialog box, click Next. The AutoContent Wizard then displays a dialog box, shown here, that asks what kind of presentation you want to create.

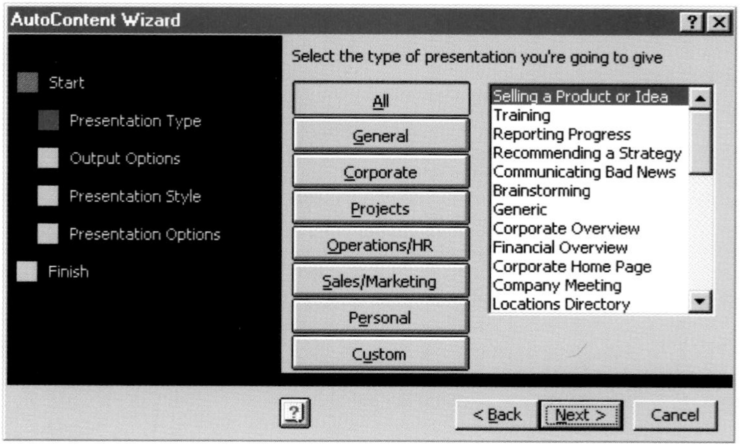

4. In the list at the right of the dialog box, select the description that most closely matches the presentation you're creating. (You select the presentation description by clicking.)
5. Click Next. The AutoContent Wizard next asks how your presentation will be used. Click the option button that most closely describes the way you will ultimately show your presentation.

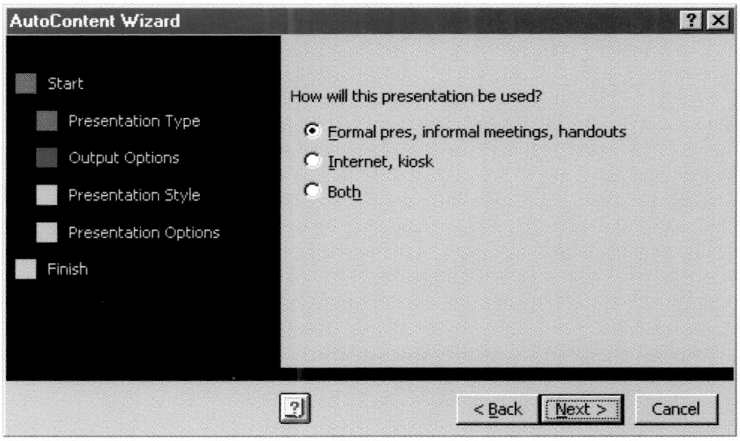

6. Click Next. The AutoContent Wizard asks how you'll share your presentation—as an on-screen presentation, as black and white handouts, as color overhead transparencies, or as 35mm slides—and whether you want to print handouts for the people who view your presentation. Click the option button that corresponds to the way you'll show your PowerPoint presentation.
7. Click Next. The AutoContent Wizard asks for some general information it will use for the opening slide, or page, of your presentation. Using the appropriate text boxes, give your presentation a title, provide your name, and supply any additional information you want on the first slide. (You might provide your company name, address, and telephone number here, for example.)

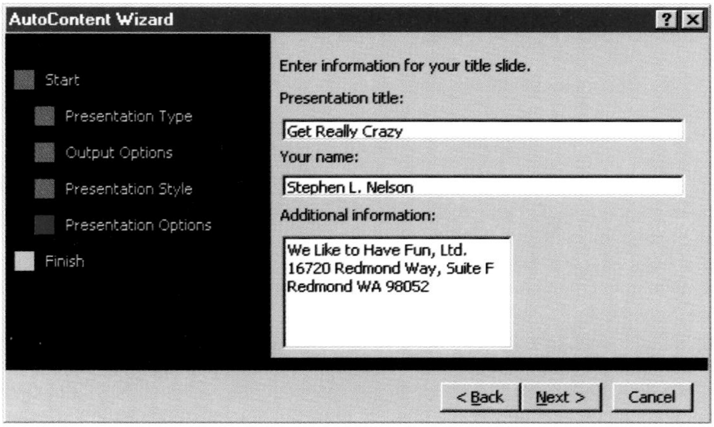

8. Click Next when you finish providing the information and then click Finish.

After you finish describing your presentation to the AutoContent Wizard, PowerPoint displays the presentation as an outline (see Figure 4.1). Each slide is

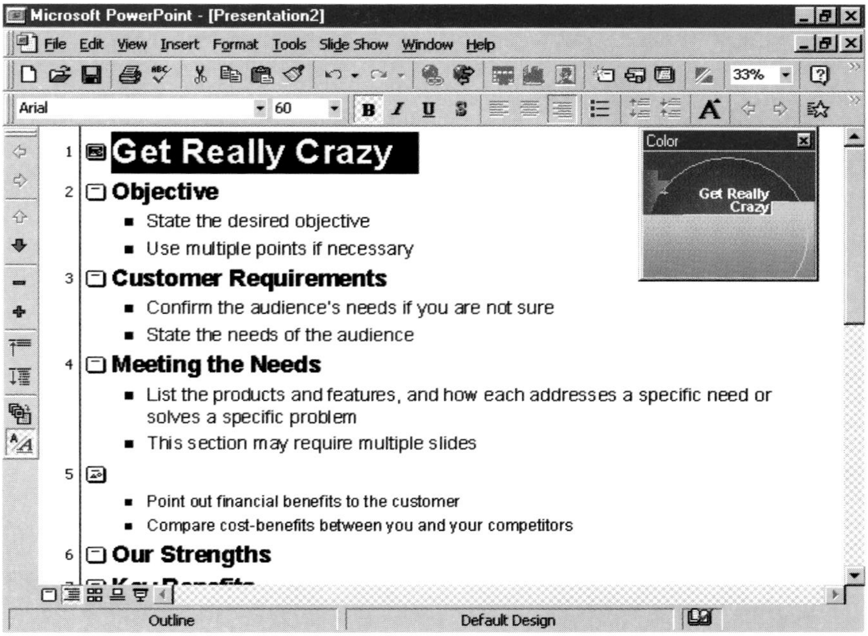

Figure 4.1 The Outline view of a PowerPoint presentation shows each slide's text

numbered, with its title text displayed in large, bold type. The first slide in Figure 4.1, for example, is titled, "Get Really Crazy." The second slide is titled "Objective" and includes as its other text two items in a bulleted list.

In the Color box, which appears in the upper-right corner of the presentation document window, you can see a small picture of the slide. If you instead want to see a full-screen view of the slide, double-click the title or the text of the slide you want to view and choose the View | Slide command. Figure 4.2 shows the Slide view of the second slide, the one named "Objective."

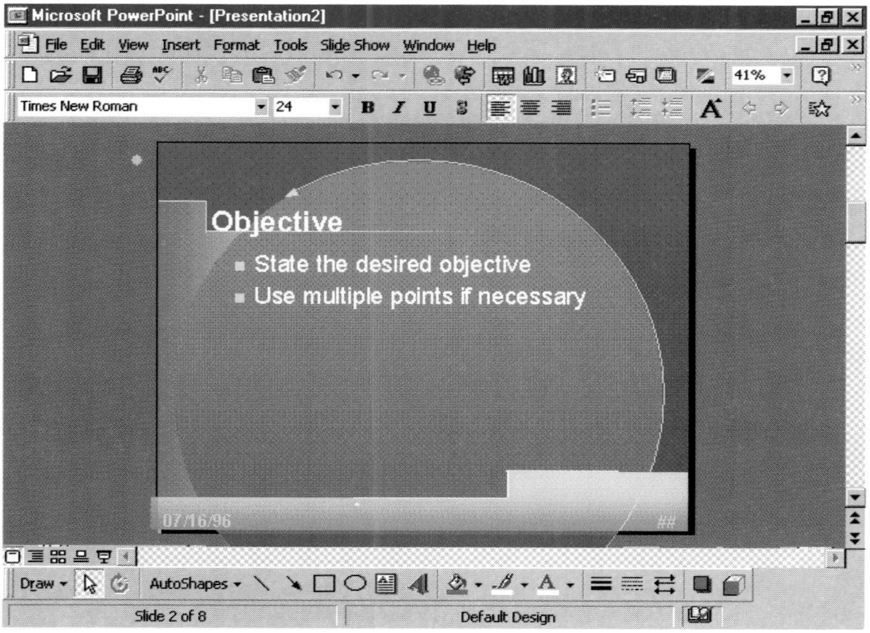

Figure 4.2 The Slide view of the second slide

Editing and Formatting Your Presentation's Slide Text

Editing and formatting a slide's text works the same way as editing the text in a Word document:

- To edit a slide's title, click at the point you want to place the insertion point. (You'll typically find this easiest to do using the Outline view, which you can always get by choosing the View | Outline command or clicking the Outline View button.)

- To add text, just type it.
- To remove text, use the BACKSPACE or DELETE key.
- To replace text, select the text you want to replace and then type the new text you want to substitute.

To change a bullet point's text, you use the same editing techniques as you do for a slide title (I just described these):

- To add a bullet point, click at the end of the line that you want the new bullet point to follow, press ENTER, and type the bullet point text.
- To remove a bullet point, select the bullet point text and press DELETE.

You can create bullet points within bullet points, as shown here, and you can promote bullets and subpoints to the next higher level:

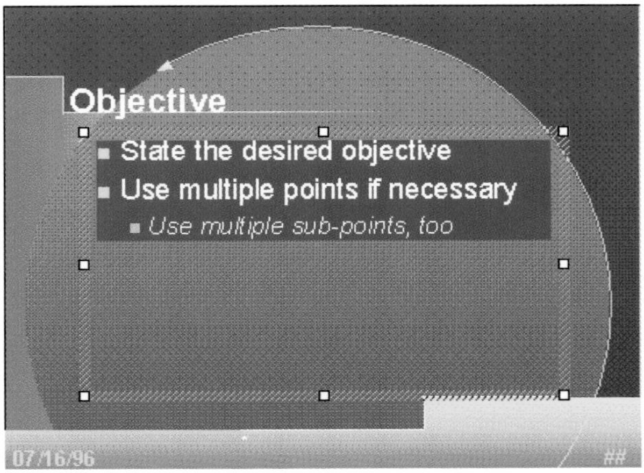

- To create a subpoint, first add the bullet point or points to the Outline view, as described earlier. Then click the bullet point you want to demote (to a subpoint) and press TAB.
- To promote a subpoint to a regular bullet point, click it and press SHIFT-TAB.

SHORTCUT

If you promote a bullet point, you turn it into a slide title and thereby create a new slide.

PowerPoint, like Word and Excel, provides a neat Formatting toolbar that contains all sorts of buttons and boxes for formatting slides. Take a peek at Table 4.1 and don't be afraid to experiment on your own with PowerPoint's formatting effects—you can always undo your formatting decisions if you decide you don't like them, or if you get a little carried away because you're having too much fun with them.

Tool	Name	Description
Times New Roman	Font	Displays a drop-down list from which you choose a font, or typeface.
10	Font Size	Displays a drop-down list you use to specify the point size of the selected text.
B	Bold	Alternately bolds and un-bolds the selected text.
I	Italic	Alternately italicizes and un-italicizes the selected text.
U	Underline	Alternately underlines and un-underlines the selected text.
S	Shadow	Alternately adds and removes shadow effects from the selected text.
	Align Left	Aligns the selected paragraph flush against the left margin of the text box.

Table 4.1 Formatting Tools on PowerPoint's Formatting Toolbar

Tool	Name	Description
	Center	Centers the lines of the selected paragraph evenly between the left and right margins of the text box.
	Align Right	Aligns the selected paragraph flush against the right margin of the text box.
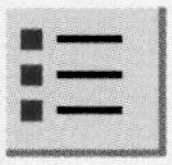	Bullets	Alternately adds and removes bullet points from the selected paragraphs.
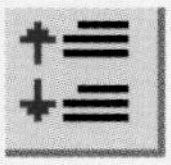	Increase Paragraph Spacing	Increases the space between paragraphs.
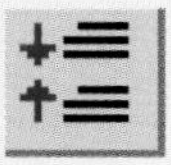	Decrease Paragraph Spacing	Decreases the space between paragraphs.
	Increase Font Size	Increases the font size of the selected text to the next larger font size.
	Promote	Promotes a bullet point to a slide or higher-level bullet point.
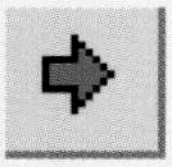	Demote	Demotes a slide to a bullet point or a bullet point to a lower-level bullet point.
	Animation Effects	Displays the Animation Effects toolbar, where you can decide how you want individual text or titles to arrive on the screen.

Table 4.1 Formatting Tools on PowerPoint's Formatting Toolbar (*continued*)

Chapter 9 talks in greater detail about how you create and use objects.

Okay. I know what you're thinking. "Geez, all he's doing is talking about slide text and formatting. When are we going to get to the real meat?" But let me clear up a possible misunderstanding. You probably now know everything you need to create presentation slides. Most of what you'll put on the slides that you show will be text—specifically, slide title text and bulleted lists. The only nontextual items you'll place on PowerPoint slides will be objects created by other Office programs (such as Excel) or objects created by other Office tools (such as

Organization Chart or WordArt). I'll talk a bit about these special cases in the next section, because you'll need to add new slides to a presentation if you want to use objects such as these.

DEFINITION

Object: *A document chunk you create with one program and then place in a document created or maintained by another program. Microsoft used to call these document chunks OLE objects. Now they are called ActiveX objects.*

Creating New Slides

When you use the AutoContent Wizard to create a starter presentation, PowerPoint creates a bunch of slides for you. But inevitably you'll need to add new slides. For example, you may want to add another slide that contains text or a bulleted list, or you may want to add a slide that contains an object created in some or with some other application.

To add a new slide to the open presentation, display the presentation's Outline view and then position the insertion point (by clicking) at the point where you want to insert the new slide. Then follow these steps:

1. Choose the Insert | New Slide command to display the New Slide dialog box.

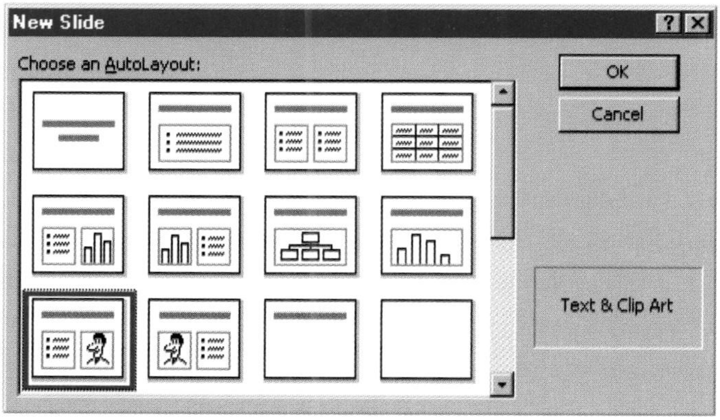

2. Select the type of slide you want to add to the presentation. You can select a slide with just text (in a variety of formats), or you can select a slide that contains placeholders for objects.
3. Once you identify the slide you want—say it's one with a clip art picture, for example—double-click the slide layout.

To fill the slide with information, select the slide by, for example, clicking it in the outline, and then choose the View | Slide command. PowerPoint displays the slide in Slide view showing object placeholders. I've detailed out the rest in the following "Filling a Slide with Information" Step by Step box.

When you double-click an object placeholder, PowerPoint starts the object's application program or its creation tool. For example, if you double-click a clip art object placeholder, PowerPoint displays the Microsoft Clip Gallery, as shown in Figure 4.3. You then scroll through the list of images until you find the one you want. Then you select the clip art image in the window on the right and click Insert.

Here is the new slide after I replaced the placeholders with a slide title, a little text blurb, and a goofy clip art image.

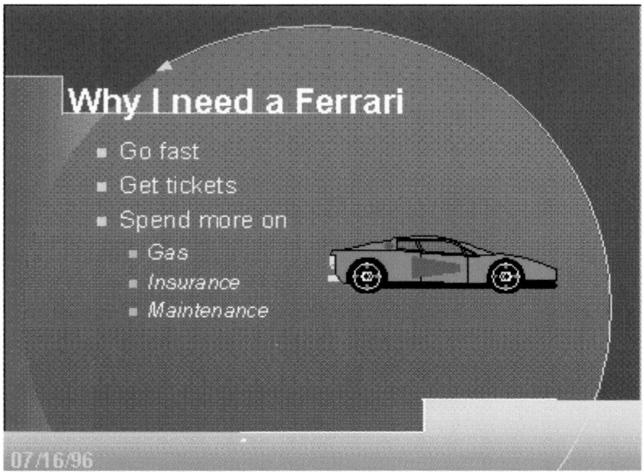

Chapter 5 describes how you create Excel charts, which you can place as objects in PowerPoint presentations or Word documents. Chapter 6 describes how to use several of the most popular Office tools and Office's Drawing tool.

By the way, if you insert another type of object—in other words, not a clip art image—PowerPoint displays the Insert Object dialog box (shown in Figure 4.4) when you double-click the object placeholder. If you want to create a

STEP BY STEP Filling a Slide with Information

1 To add a title to the slide, click the text "Click to add title" and then type the title.

2 To add a bulleted list or some other little snippet of text to the slide, click the text "Click to add text" and type the text.

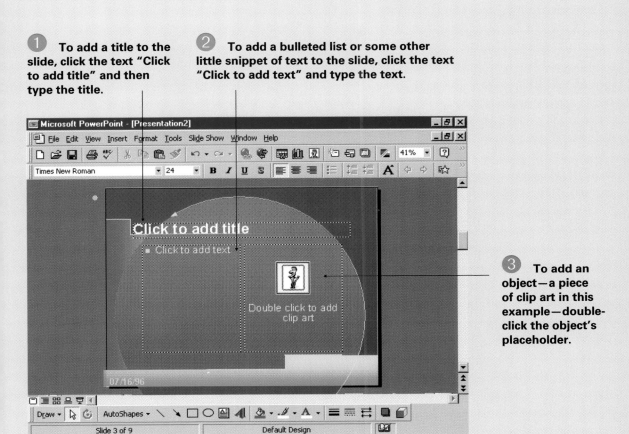

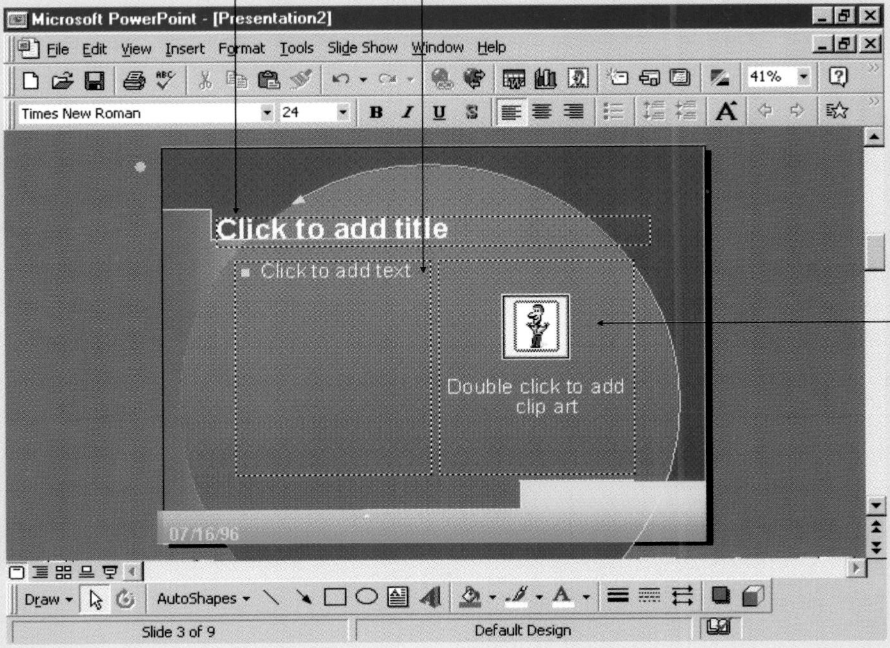

3 To add an object—a piece of clip art in this example—double-click the object's placeholder.

brand-new object, such as an Excel chart, select the Create New button. Then use the Object Type list to select the program you'll need to use to create the new object. Alternatively, if you want to insert as an object a document that already exists as a file somewhere on your hard disk, select the Create from File button. Then, when PowerPoint displays the File text box, use it to describe the file's location and give the file name.

To add an image, double-click it.

List of images

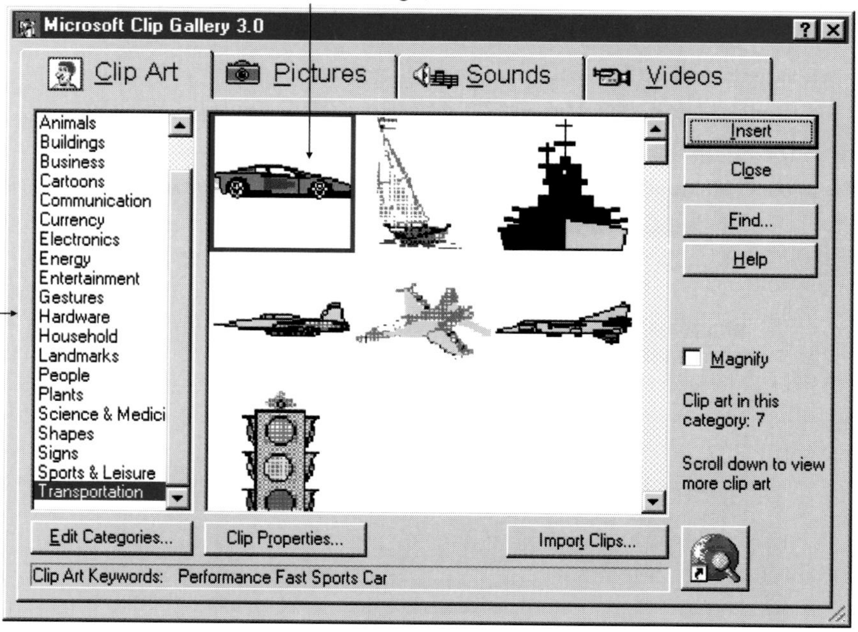

Figure 4.3 The Microsoft Clip Gallery tool lets you add clip art images to your PowerPoint slides

To select an object type from this list, just double-click it.

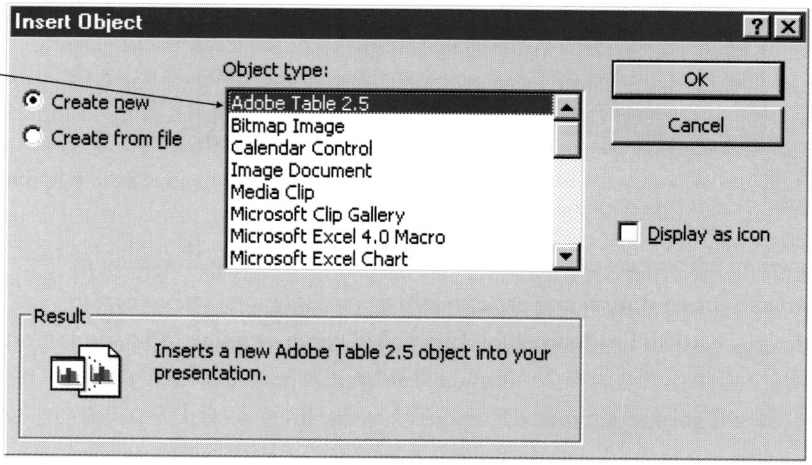

Figure 4.4 The Insert Object dialog box lets you place ActiveX objects in a slide

Reorganizing Slides

As you add slides to and remove slides from a presentation, you're bound to mix up their order. Fortunately, rearranging the order of your slides is easy to do. Choose the View | Slide Sorter command. When PowerPoint displays the Slide Sorter view of your presentation (see Figure 4.5), rearrange the slides by dragging them to new locations.

SHORTCUT

You can also easily delete slides using the Slider Sorter view. Just click a slide and press DELETE.

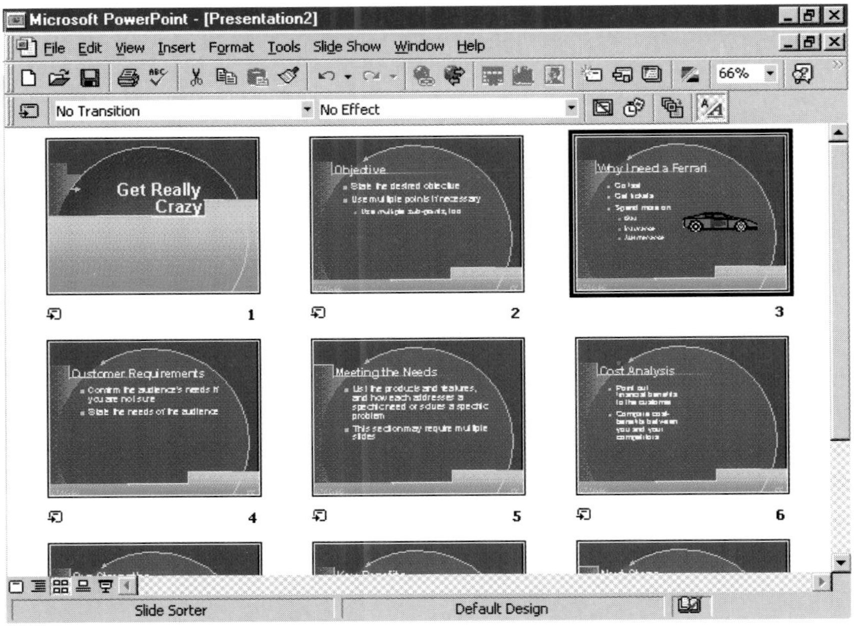

Figure 4.5 The Slide Sorter view lets you rearrange the order of your slides

Changing the Design Template

So far I haven't talked about the presentation's slide design—the way the slide background colors and shapes appear beneath the information you enter. So

PowerPoint's design templates were created by professional graphics designers.

let me take a quick minute and explain how this works. When you run the AutoContent Wizard, PowerPoint selects a design template based on the information you provide to the AutoContent Wizard. You aren't, fortunately, limited to the chosen design. You can pick a different design template. Select the Apply Design command from the Common Tasks toolbar (if the Common Tasks toolbar doesn't appear, choose the Format | Apply Design command) and then follow the instructions in the Step by Step box.

STEP BY STEP Changing the Design Template

1 In the Apply Design dialog box, verify that the Look In box specifies that the contents of the Presentation Designs folder be displayed. (If Presentation Designs does not appear in the Look In box, activate the Look In drop-down list and then select the Presentation Designs folder. It will be in the Templates folder, which will be in the Office folder.)

2 Verify that the Preview button is selected so that PowerPoint displays a thumbnail sketch of the design template.

3 Then view the various design templates by selecting them in the list beneath the Look In box.

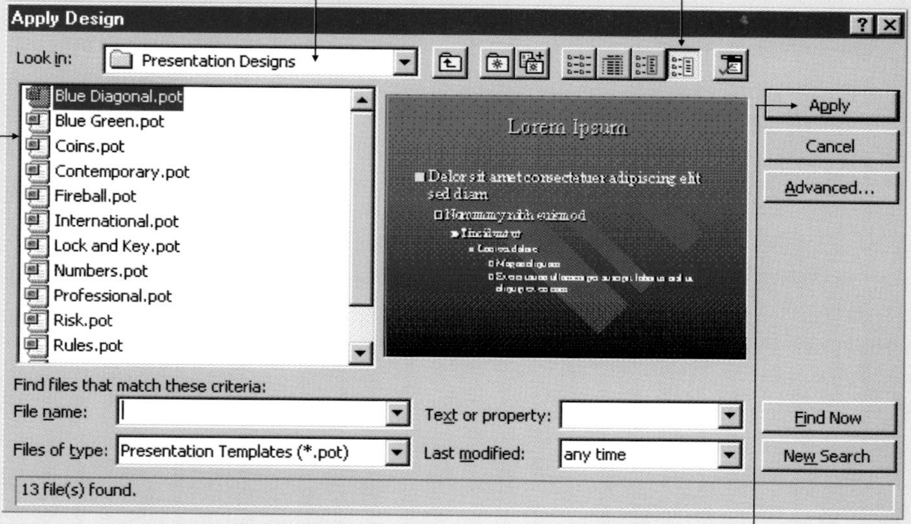

4 When you find the presentation you want, click the Apply button.

Customizing the Slide Show

PowerPoint has two fun and easy ways you can customize your slide show to fit the pace and style of your presentation: by changing the way slides come on the screen and by adding animation. Of course, customizing your slide show isn't necessary, but you actually might enjoy experimenting with these PowerPoint features.

When you create a presentation using the AutoContent Wizard, PowerPoint selects slide transitions for you, just as it chooses a design for your presentation. Luckily, you can easily change the transitions PowerPoint makes between the slides in your presentation. To change the way a slide comes onto your screen, select the slide and choose Slide Show | Slide Transition. And now, to the Step by Step box for the rest of the procedure.

STEP BY STEP Customizing Slide Transitions

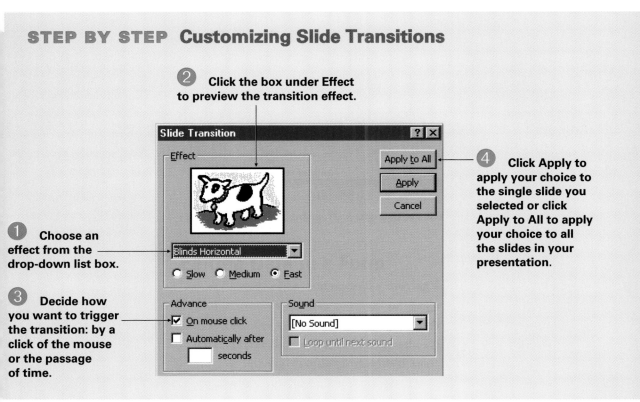

2 Click the box under Effect to preview the transition effect.

1 Choose an effect from the drop-down list box.

3 Decide how you want to trigger the transition: by a click of the mouse or the passage of time.

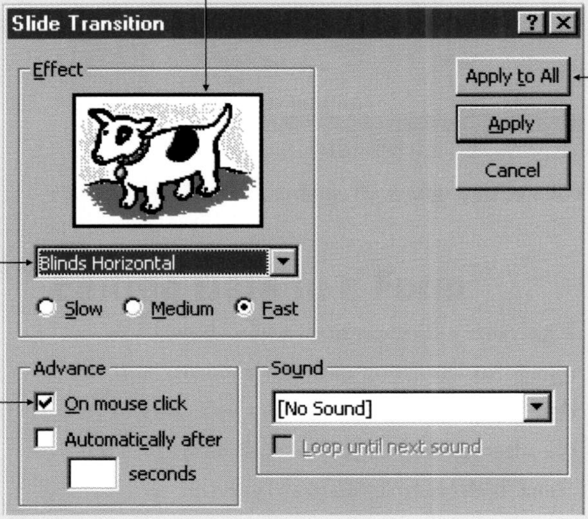

4 Click Apply to apply your choice to the single slide you selected or click Apply to All to apply your choice to all the slides in your presentation.

You can also customize your presentation using animation effects. To use animation effects:

1. Click the Animation Effects button on the Formatting toolbar.
2. On the Animation Effects toolbar, click either the Animate Title button to animate the slide title or the Animate Slide Text button to animate the paragraphs on a slide.

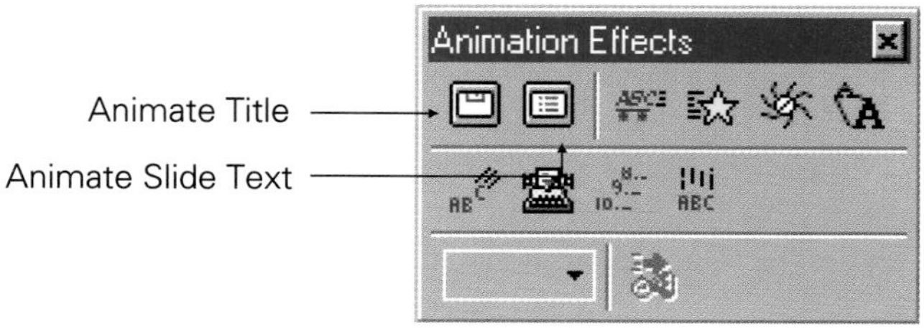

Animating the paragraphs on a slide allows you to display them point by point on a single slide. You'll probably want to use animation effects if you don't want your audience to see what you will talk about next, or if you want to draw attention to new points as you come to them. PowerPoint has several animation effects to choose from, complete with sound effects. You can have your paragraphs screech to a stop on the screen like a sports car, or you can have them open from the center like the shutter on a camera. You can even have the letters in your slide appear one by one as if you were typing them on a typewriter.

EXPERT ADVICE

To get an overview of the slide transitions and animation effects for the slides in your presentation, click the slides in the Slide Sorter view, and PowerPoint will identify on the Slide Sorter toolbar the effects for that slide.

Adding Speaker's Notes

I'd be willing to bet you're planning to use notes for your presentation. The easiest way of creating speaker's notes in PowerPoint is by using the Notes Page view. Click the Notes Page View button to view a slide in Notes Page view. To add notes to the slide, click the box below the slide and type.

What? You say you can't read what you're typing? The font size is probably too small for you to see it very well, so click the Zoom button on the Standard toolbar and choose a larger percentage size (somewhere between 66 and 100 percent should do).

Printing, Saving, and Opening Presentations

Chapter 7 describes in detail how you print, save, and open Office documents, including PowerPoint presentations.

You print, save, and open presentations in the same basic way you print, save, and open Word documents (described in Chapter 2) and Excel workbooks (very briefly described in Chapter 3). To print a presentation, for example, click the Print button. To save a presentation, click the Save button and then use the Save dialog box (which PowerPoint displays) to give your presentation a name and specify in which location you want it saved. To open a presentation, select it from the Start menu's Documents submenu (if it appears there) or from the PowerPoint File menu (if it appears there as a numbered command), or click the Open button and then use the Open dialog box to identify the presentation and specify where it was previously saved.

Viewing Presentations

If you want to view or show a presentation on the same computer you used to originally create the presentation, open the presentation (of course) and then choose the Slide Show | View Show command. PowerPoint displays the first slide. To display the next slide, press the SPACEBAR or click the mouse (depending on the option you chose in the Slide Transistion dialog box).

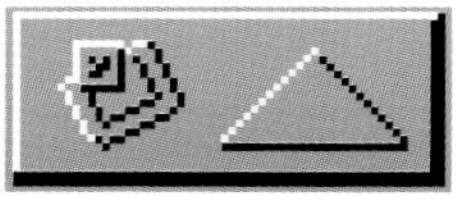

If you're viewing a PowerPoint presentation using the Slide Show | View Show command, you can also use commands from the slide show shortcut menu, which you display by clicking the triangle symbol you'll see in the bottom left corner of each slide.

When you click the triangle to display the slide show shortcuts menu, you see the menu shown here. Use the Next and Previous commands to move back and forth one slide at time.

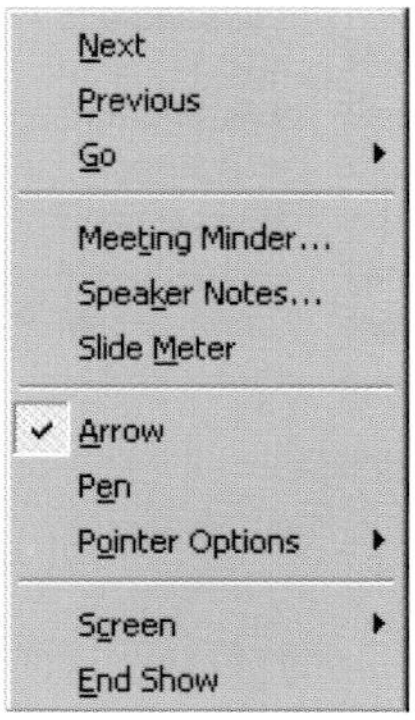

If you want to annotate a slide with meaningful scribbles (see Figure 4.6) as you're viewing your slide show, choose the Pen command. Then begin your

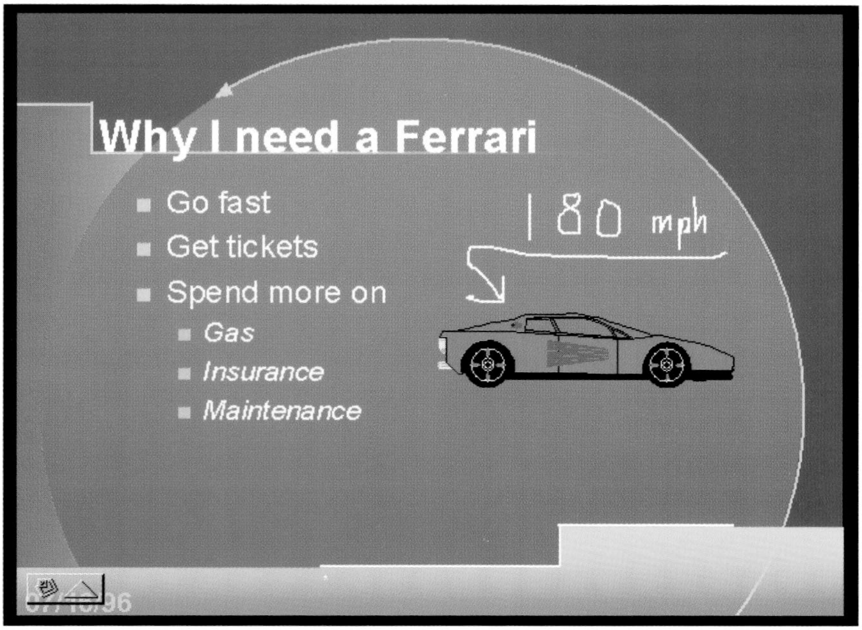

Figure 4.6 Use the Pen command to annotate your slides by hand

scribbling by dragging the mouse. This isn't hard, but you may want to practice a bit before you attempt this in front of a real, live audience.

If you want to show a PowerPoint presentation on a computer other than the one you used to create the presentation, open the presentation. Then choose the File | Pack and Go command. PowerPoint runs the Pack and Go Wizard, which copies to a floppy disk your presentation file and a special, stand-alone presentation-viewing program called Viewer.

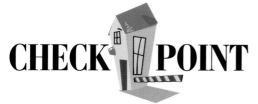

CHECK POINT

You've now learned the basics of creating and then showing PowerPoint presentations. You know, for example, how to start your work by using the AutoContent Wizard to create a rough draft of your presentation and how to finish your work by editing and formatting your presentation's slide text. You know how to customize your presentation by adding objects and using animation. And you know how to show your presentation.

However, while you now know enough to create an attractive, persuasive PowerPoint presentation, you'll still benefit (assuming you have time) from accumulating a bit more knowledge. Chapter 5, for example, describes how you use Excel's powerful-yet-easy-to-use Chart Wizard, which you can use to add chart objects not only to Excel workbooks but also to Word documents and PowerPoint presentations. Chapter 6 describes how to use many of Office's common tools. Chapter 7 describes in detail how you print, save, and open Office documents such as PowerPoint presentations.

CHAPTER

5

Creating Charts Using Excel

INCLUDES

- Understanding what data series and data categories are
- Collecting the data you want to plot
- Using the Chart Wizard
- Picking a chart type
- Formatting a chart
- Printing and saving charts
- Using a chart in another application

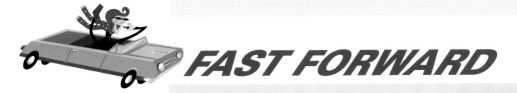

FAST FORWARD

Understand What Data Series and Data Categories Are ➤ pp. 96-98

A data series is a set of values you'll plot in a chart. Data categories, in effect, organize the data points—the individual values—within a data series.

Collect the Data You Want to Chart ➤ pp. 98-100

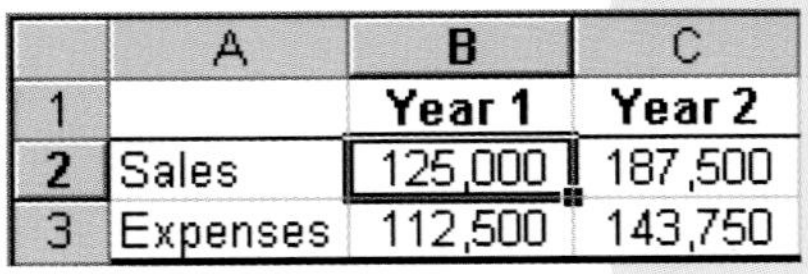

	A	B	C
1		Year 1	Year 2
2	Sales	125,000	187,500
3	Expenses	112,500	143,750

Enter the data series names and values into the Excel worksheet using a separate row or column for each data series. To enter a value or label into a cell:

1. Click the cell.
2. Type the value or label.
3. Press ENTER.

The actual data points must be values.

Use the Chart Wizard ➤ pp. 100-105

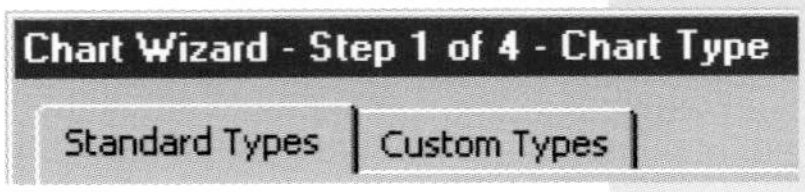

To use the Chart Wizard:

1. Select the range that holds the data series and the data categories information.
2. Choose the Insert | Chart command or click the Chart Wizard toolbar button.

Once you do this, Excel starts the Chart Wizard.

Pick a Chart Type and Subtype ➤ pp. 105-110

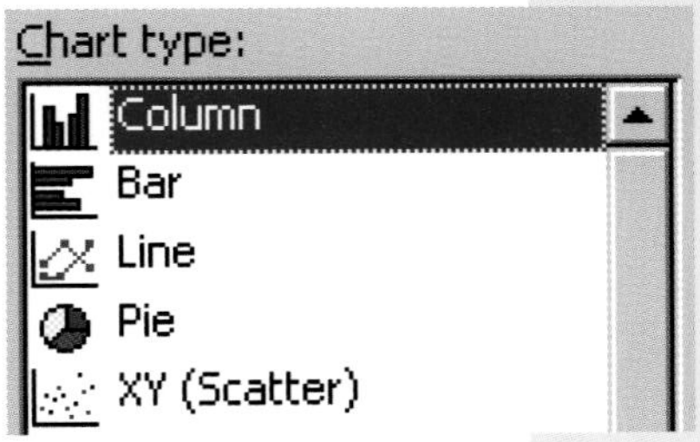

You can pick a particular chart type and subtype either as part of using the Chart Wizard or, later on, by using the Chart menu's Chart Type command after you've actually created the chart.

ormat Your Chart's Parts ➤ *pp. 110-111*

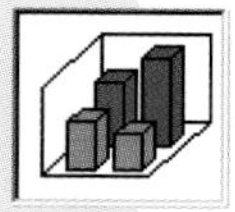

To format some element, or part, of a chart:

1. Right-click the chart part—this can be any element of the chart—and choose the Format command from the shortcut menu.
2. Use the Format dialog box that Excel displays to make your changes.

rint Charts ➤ *pp. 111-112*

- To print an embedded chart but not any of the worksheet page in which it's embedded, simply click to select the chart and then click the Print tool on the Standard toolbar.
- To print an embedded chart as part of the worksheet page in which it's embedded, print the worksheet page in the usual way (clicking the Print toolbar button or choosing the File | Print command).
- To print a chart that appears on its own chart sheet page, first display the chart sheet and then click the Print tool.

ave Charts ➤ *p. 112*

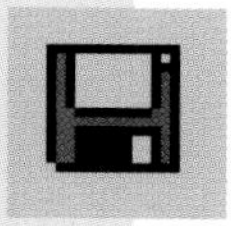

To save a chart, save the document in which the chart object is embedded—for example, by clicking the Save tool on the Standard toolbar.

se a Chart in Word, owerPoint, or Access ➤ *pp. 112-113*

To use an Excel chart in Word, PowerPoint, or Access:

1. Copy the chart object.
2. Paste the object into the other document.

You can include charts in Word documents, Excel workbooks, PowerPoint presentations—even in Access databases (although this last example might be sort of weird)—and it's very easy to do so. I'm going to surprise some readers here, however, by saying that you don't want to use the built-in Graph tool that comes with each of the Office programs. No way. What you want to do is create any chart in Excel and then copy that chart (if necessary) to the Office document you want to use.

The reason you want to create your charts using Excel—even if you don't know Excel and think it sounds terribly complicated—is that Excel's charting tool is vastly superior to the crummy, hard-to-use tools available in Word, PowerPoint, and Access.

Understanding What Data Series and Data Categories Are

Before you begin working with Excel's charting feature, however, you need to understand how Excel expects you to organize the to-be-charted data. Specifically, you need to understand what data series and data categories are—and how to arrange your worksheet data so that Excel easily identifies your data series and data categories. So let me explain.

A *data series* is a set of values you'll plot in a chart. If you plot mortgage interest rates over, say, the last five years, the set of mortgage interest rate values is a data series. If you plot credit card interest rates over, say, the same five-year time frame, the set of credit card interest rate values is another data series. The key thing to remember is that, fundamentally, data series are what you plot with charts.

Not surprisingly, a chart must have at least one data series. In fact, pie charts can depict only a single data series—but most charts can show numerous data series. Figure 5.1 shows two data series in a chart.

If you find yourself getting stuck on this data series business, here's another clue you can use. On a chart that already exists, you can identify data series by looking at the data markers, which are the graphical objects that the chart uses to show the plotted values. The data markers for a data series are usually visually connected in some way. In Figure 5.1, for example, Excel plots each data series using a separate line. The credit card interest rates show up as a red line. The mortgage interest rates show up as a blue line. In a bar chart—and we'll talk about these a little later—the bars for a particular data series are all the same color. The same thing is true for a column chart. You get the idea.

Data category is the other charting term you must understand. *Data categories*, in effect, organize the data points—the individual values—within a data

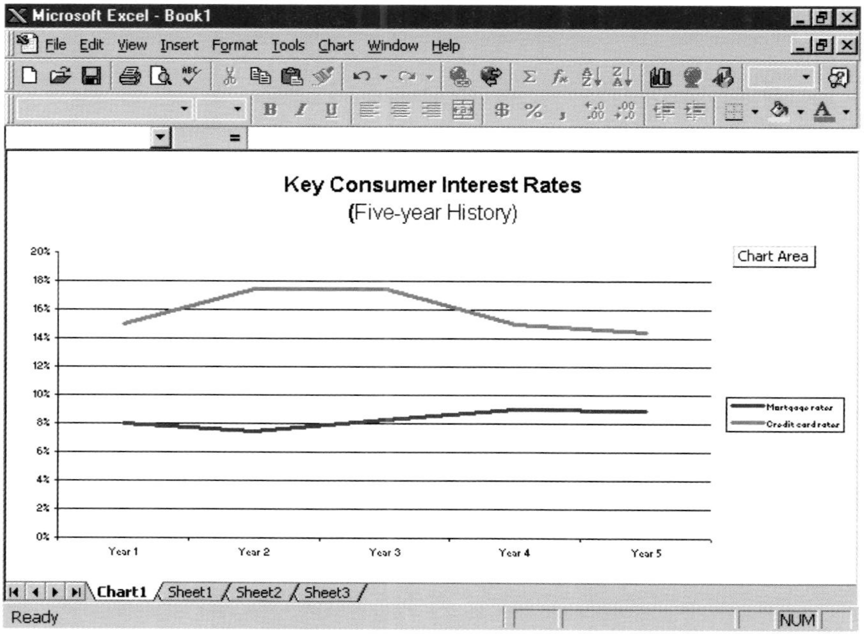

Figure 5.1 You plot data series—such as the fictional mortgage interest rates and credit card interest rates shown here—with a chart

series. For example, in any chart that shows how some value changes over time—what's called a time-series chart—time is the data category. In a chart like this, you use units of time—years, months, days, or whatever—to organize the individual data points within a data series. In Figure 5.1, for example, the data categories are years.

You can, however, use data categories other than time to organize the data points in a data series. Look again at Figure 5.1, for example. I could substitute the "Year 1, Year 2" etc. at the bottom of the chart with the names of fictional financial institutions. These fictional financial institutions would then become the data categories that organize the data points in the data series. The chart still plots interest rate information, and the two data series are still mortgage interest rates and credit card interest rates. The only other thing that needs to change is the title of the chart. This time, I'd call it "Key Consumer Interest Rates—(Five Largest Banks)."

Now that you know what data series and data categories are, you know how Excel organizes your to-be-charted data. With this information, you'll find it easy to first collect chart data using a worksheet and then later to plot the data using Excel's Chart Wizard.

EXPERT ADVICE

You can't plot more than 255 data series in a chart. You can't include more than 4,000 data points in a single data series, and you can't plot more than 32,000 data points in a chart.

Collecting the Data You Want to Chart

Once you know which data series you want to plot and what your categories are, you're ready to enter your data into an Excel worksheet. You can organize your data series into either rows or columns as long as your data series don't have more than 255 data points. If your data series do have more than 255 data points, you need to use separate worksheet columns for each data series—otherwise you won't have room in a row for all of a data series' data points. (A worksheet only has 256 columns, which means that if you used one column for the data series names you would have only 255 columns left for data points—assuming you've arranged data series by row.)

Your first data entry step, generally, is to enter the data series names and values into the worksheet using a separate row or column for each data series. To enter a value or label into a cell, click the cell, type the value or label, and then press ENTER. The actual data points must be values, of course. In the worksheet fragment shown here, for example, I used row 2 for the first data series, Sales, and row 3 for the second data series, Expenses.

	A	B	C	D	E	F	G
1		**Year 1**	**Year 2**	**Year 3**	**Year 4**	**Year 5**	
2	Sales	125,000	187,500	281,250	421,875	632,813	
3	Expenses	112,500	143,750	190,625	260,938	366,406	
4							

This worksheet organizes its data series by row.

I could just as well have organized the data categories by column, as shown here.

	A	B	C	D
1		Sales	Expenses	
2	**Year 1**	125,000	112,500	
3	**Year 2**	187,500	143,750	
4	**Year 3**	281,250	190,625	
5	**Year 4**	421,875	260,938	
6	**Year 5**	632,813	366,406	
7				

This worksheet organizes its data series by column.

Take a minute and look at both of these worksheets until you clearly see that they show the same information. The only difference is that the first organizes the data series by row while the second organizes the data series by column.

EXPERT ADVICE

You can provide the data points of a series by entering actual numeric values in the cells or by supplying formulas that calculate the values.

Once you've entered the data series, you can enter values or labels that identify the data categories. In the illustration earlier that shows the data series as rows, the data categories are described by the contents of the range B1:F1. In the example that shows the data series as columns, the data categories are described by the contents of the range A2:A6. Notice the placement of the data category information. In the example that organizes the data series by row, the data category information appears in the row above the rows with the data series. In the example that organizes the data series by column, the data category information appears in the column to the left of the columns with the data series.

Using the Chart Wizard

Once you've collected the data you want to plot, you're ready to use the Chart Wizard. To use the Chart Wizard, follow these steps:

1. Select the range that holds the data series and data categories information. If you were plotting the sales and profit information shown earlier, for example, you would select A1:F3. To select the worksheet range, click the top-left corner of the worksheet range and then drag the mouse to the lower-right corner of the worksheet range.
2. Choose the Insert | Chart command.

Once you do this, Excel starts the Chart Wizard. The Chart Wizard steps you through a series of four dialog boxes that ask, in essence, what you want your chart to look like.

Step 1: Chart Type

Later in the chapter, in "Using the Various Chart Types," I'll describe all of the Excel chart types and what they are typically used for.

The first Chart Wizard dialog box (see Figure 5.2) asks which type of chart you want. The most common type is the column chart, which plots data series as sets of vertical columns, or bars. You can choose any of Excel's 14 other chart types by selecting an entry in the Chart Type list. Select a chart subtype—in essence, a particular variant of the selected chart type—by clicking on the box in the Chart Sub-type area that shows a picture of the chart. After you pick the chart type and subtype, click Next to continue.

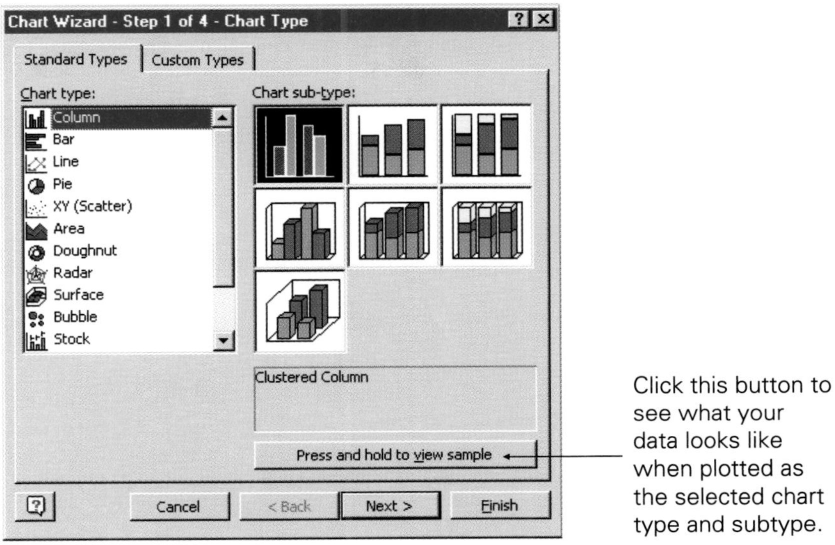

Figure 5.2 You use the first Chart Wizard dialog box to pick the type of chart you want

Step 2: Chart Source Data

The second Chart Wizard dialog box asks you to confirm the worksheet range with the to-be-plotted data and the way you've organized your worksheet data, as shown in Figure 5.3. If you've selected the correct range before choosing the Insert | Chart command, the Data Range text box will show it—so you shouldn't need to worry about this box. In a nutshell, the Data Range tab provides a box and buttons you use to fix misunderstandings (on the Chart Wizard's part) about how you've organized your data. The Series In option buttons, however, let you tell Excel how you've organized your worksheet data. Excel assumes that you'll have more data categories than you'll have data series, and it selects either the Rows or Columns button to show this assumption. If Excel's assumption is incorrect, you need to select the other button.

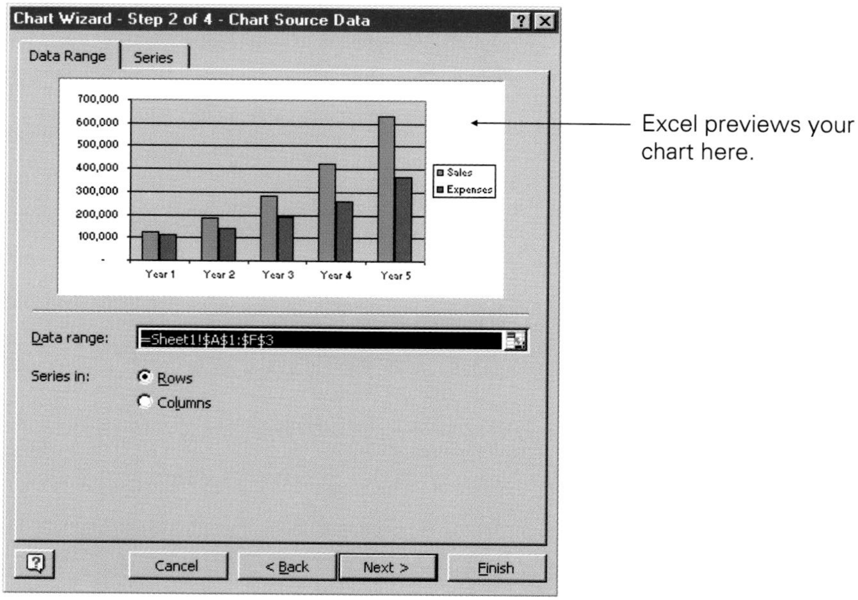

Figure 5.3 You use the second Chart Wizard dialog box to confirm that Excel has correctly identified your data range and data series

EXPERT ADVICE

As long as you organize your to-be-plotted data in the manner described and shown earlier in the chapter in "Collecting the Data You Want to Chart," you won't have to worry about (or use) the Series tab of the second Chart Wizard dialog box.

Step 3: Chart Options

After you complete the second Chart Wizard dialog box, click Next. Excel displays the third Chart Wizard dialog box, as shown in Figure 5.4.

To add a title to the chart, enter whatever you want to use for the title in the Chart Title text box. Typically, people use titles that are either the name of the organization ("Acme Trading Corporation") being described in the chart or a summary of the chart's message ("Acme's Sales and Profits Continue to Grow").

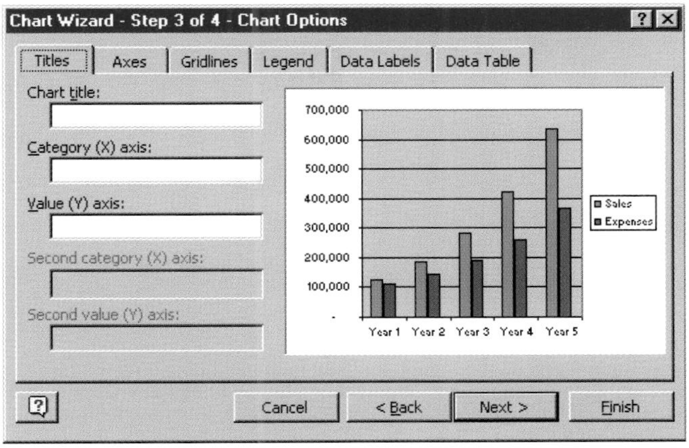

Figure 5.4 The third Chart Wizard dialog box lets you add, among other items, a title, axis, and a legend to your chart

The axis titles text boxes let you add titles to the Category (X) Axis, which indicates the categories (in Figure 5.4, the horizontal axis), and to the Value (Y) Axis, which calibrates the data series' data points (in Figure 5.4, the vertical axis). If what the categories show and how the data series' points are calibrated are obvious, you don't need to include these extra chunks of text. However, if the categories aren't clear or the data series values aren't adequately calibrated, you can often use the axis titles to mitigate confusion. For example, if the values plotted as data points are actually thousands—in other words, you've omitted the last three zeros (000) from the numbers—you could and probably should use an axis title to make this clear.

The Legend tab, which you view by clicking the third Chart Wizard dialog box's Legend tab, lets you add (or remove) a chart legend. To create the chart legend, Excel uses the data series names you supplied in your initial worksheet selection. (If you don't supply the data series names, by the way, Excel uses the rather meaningless names Series 1, Series 2, and so on.)

Step 4: Chart Location

After you finish adding any chart titles you want and specifying whether you want a legend, click Next. The fourth and final Chart Wizard dialog box, shown in Figure 5.5, asks whether you want your new chart to be created as an object plopped onto some existing worksheet page or to be created as an entirely new chart sheet. Select the option button that corresponds to the location you want for your chart and then click the Finish button.

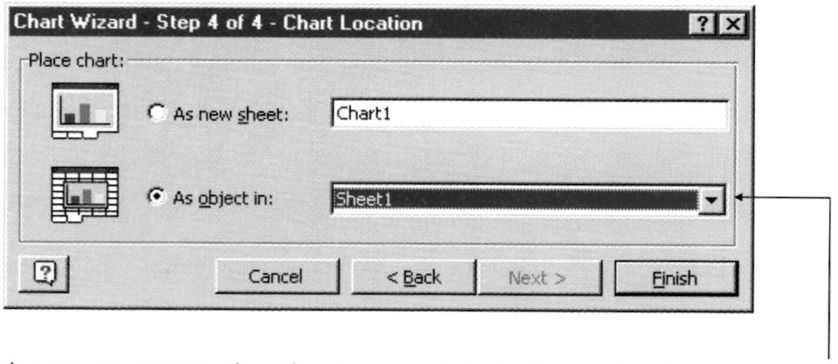

If you choose to create the chart as an object plopped onto some existing workbook page, you identify the worksheet by using this drop-down list box.

Figure 5.5 The final Chart Wizard dialog box lets you tell Excel whether you want the new chart to appear as an embedded object in some existing worksheet or on its own chart sheet

The Chart Wizard draws a chart like the one you've specified in the dialog boxes in the location you specified (see Figure 5.6). Notice that the chart in Figure 5.6 includes a chart title, a legend, and a value axis title.

As I noted earlier, charts can be embedded as objects that float on top of a regular worksheet page, or they can appear on their own chart sheet pages. Figure 5.6 is an example of an embedded chart. If you had chosen the Place Chart as New Sheet option in the fourth Chart Wizard dialog box (Figure 5.5) instead of the Place Chart As Object In option, the Chart Wizard would have added a separate page to the workbook, named Chart1 if it was the first chart sheet you'd added, and placed the chart there. Figure 5.7 shows the same chart as Figure 5.6 appearing on its own chart sheet page.

To resize the chart, drag these black squares, called selection handles.

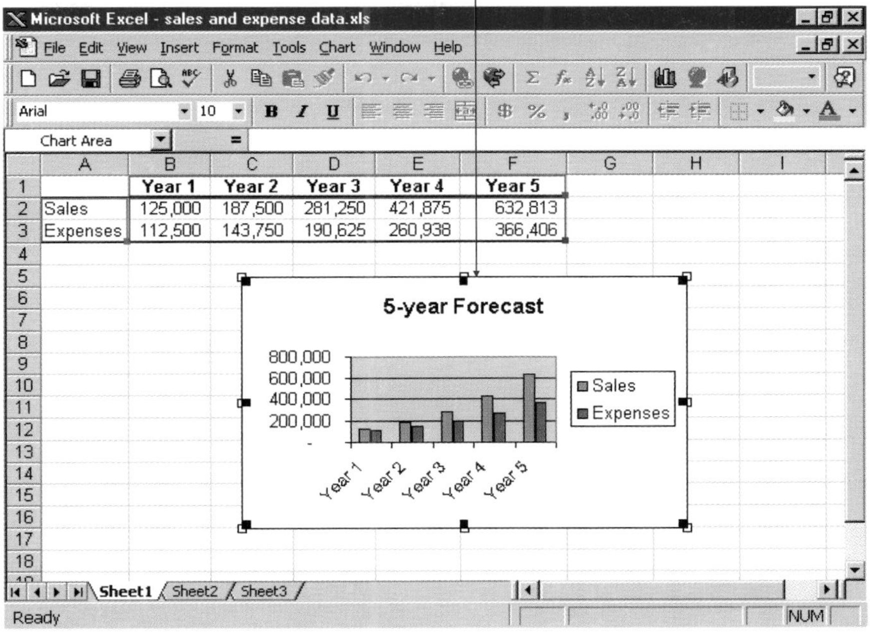

Figure 5.6 A worksheet with an embedded chart

Picking a Chart Type and Subtype

You can pick a particular chart type and subtype either as part of using the Chart Wizard or, later on, after you've actually created the chart. If you pick the chart type and subtype as you're creating the chart with the Chart Wizard, you simply select your chart type and subtype using the first dialog box that the Chart Wizard displays, as shown earlier in Figure 5.2.

To increase the size of this sheet's chart so it fills the window, choose the View | Sized with Window command.

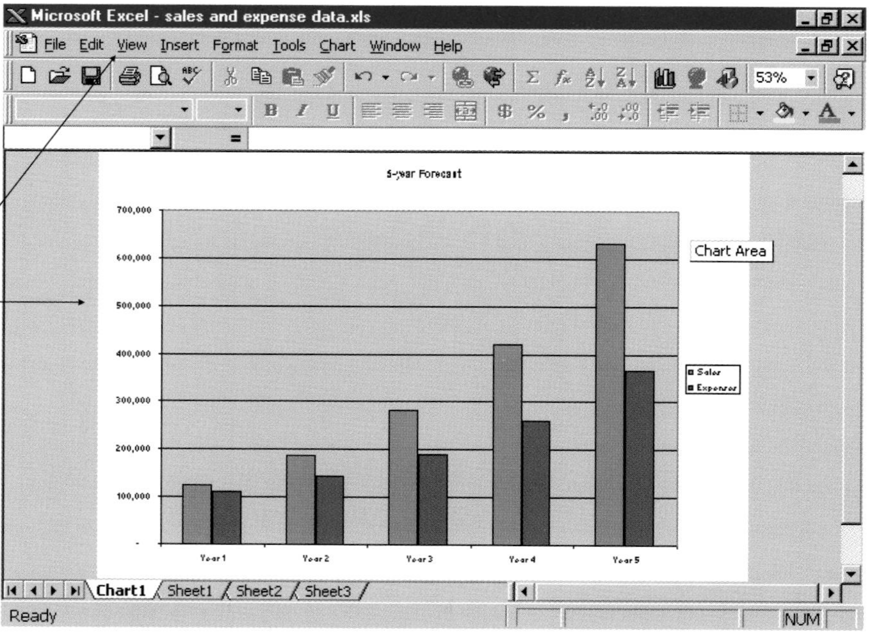

Figure 5.7 This chart appears on its own, separate, chart sheet page

Excel supplies a different menu bar for you to use when working with charts. To use any of the Chart menu bar commands, click the chart if it's an embedded object. If the chart appears on its own chart sheet page, display the chart sheet by clicking its tab.

If you change your mind about the chart type or subtype you want after creating the chart, Excel provides several ways to change your choice. The easiest way to change the chart type or subtype is to use the Chart menu's Chart Type command:

1. Choose the Chart | Chart Type command. Excel displays the Chart Type dialog box, which almost mirrors the first Chart Wizard dialog box (Figure 5.2) and lets you pick both a chart type and subtype.
2. To select another chart type or subtype, select the chart type from the Chart Type list and then click a Chart Subtype button.
3. After you choose the chart type and subtype, click OK. Excel redraws your chart so it reflects your changes.

It's that easy.

Using the Various Chart Types

So you can easily change the chart type and subtype you selected while using or after using the Chart Wizard. But knowing why you change or choose a chart type and subtype is probably more important that knowing how you change or choose a chart type and subtype. For this reason, take a couple of minutes to look over Table 5.1. It names each chart type, shows an example from the various subtypes available for that chart type, describes what the chart type does, and gives you hints about when you might want to use each one.

Chart Type & Example Subtype	Description	When to Use
Area 	Area charts plot your data series as colored areas, stacking these colored areas on top of each other.	Area charts do two things really well—they show how the data category totals of your plotted data change over time, and they show you how the proportion of an individual data series is relative to the total of all the data series' value changes over time.
Bar 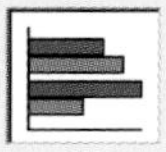	Bar charts plot your data points as individual horizontal bars.	Bar charts use individual data markers for each data point, thus they emphasize and let chart viewers compare the individual values. Because the bar chart category axis is vertical, not horizontal, the bar chart type often works well when your data category is something other than time (which many people equate with a horizontal axis).
Column 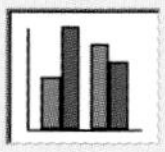	Column charts are very similar to bar charts, except they plot data points using vertical bars. Like bar charts, column charts use individual data markers for each data point.	As with bar charts, column charts emphasize and let chart viewers compare the individual values. Because, however, they use a horizontal category axis, column charts work particularly well for comparing individual values over time.

Table 5.1 Excel Chart Types: What They Are and When to Use Them

Chart Type & Example Subtype	Description	When to Use
Line 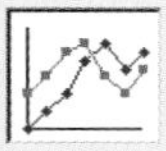	Line charts plot the data points of a data series in a line. Some of the line chart subtypes include additional data markers on the actual line to show the individual values being plotted.	Line charts tend to de-emphasize the individual data point values while showing how the plotted values change over time. One of the line chart subtypes uses a logarithmic value axis, which allows you to plot the *rate* of change in your data series' values. In this way, you can compare two data series' changing values and visually see which is growing or declining faster.
Pie 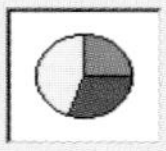	Pie charts plot only a single data series. In a pie chart, each data point is shown as a proportional slice of the pie (a segment of the circle).	Because they show only a single data series and because you typically can't plot more than a handful of data points in a pie chart before the slices of the pie become too small, pie charts should probably never be used, except, perhaps, as a way to explain what charts are to children. In almost all cases, if your data is so simple that it really fits in a pie chart, you should just put in a table instead. Sorry.
Doughnut 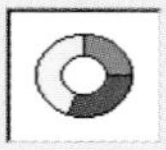	Doughnut charts resemble pie charts, but they allow you to show more than a single data series by plotting the multiple data series as concentric circles. Each data point is represented by a segment of the doughnut.	You know what I said earlier concerning when pie charts should be used? I'd say the same thing goes for doughnut charts.
Radar 	Radar charts plot data points as radial points from a central origin. Each data series' points are connected in a line, and the radar chart uses as many radial axes as there are data points in your series.	Although radar charts can be a little confusing at first, they can be very useful, as they allow you to more precisely calibrate each data series' points because each data point appears directly on an axis. The best time to use a radar chart may be when you want to easily compare the totals of all a data series' values.

Table 5.1 Excel Chart Types: What They Are and When to Use Them (*continued*)

Chart Type & Example Subtype	Description	When to Use
XY (Scatter) 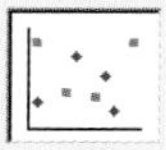	XY, or scatter, charts plot an independent data series (which replaces the data categories that other charts use) and one or more dependent data series. When you collect the worksheet data used to plot an XY chart, you should arrange the values of the independent data series in either ascending or descending order.	This is Excel's most useful chart type. Use XY charts when you want to explore or visually show the relationship between an independent variable and a dependent variable—for example, the effect of interest rates on new car sales.
Surface 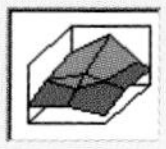	Surface charts are probably Excel's most interesting and perhaps most useful three-dimensional chart type. They plot a data set using a three-dimensional surface.	Use a surface chart when you want to explore relationships that exist both within a data series and within a data category. One indication of a data set that may be usefully plotted as a three-dimensional surface chart is when, even though you truly understand the difference between data categories and data series, you still have trouble defining which is which.
Bubble 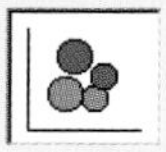	Bubble charts are a variation on the XY chart. Bubble charts also let you include a third data series in your XY chart that controls the size of the bubble marker.	Like an XY (scatter) chart, bubble charts visually explore the relationship of two or more data series. However, bubble charts are pretty hard to use unless you (and your chart viewers) are used to them. I'd say use this "maybe never."
Stock 	Stock charts, which are for technical analysis of security price and volume information, plot securities prices in a high-low-close chart.	If you believe in the religion of technical securities analysis, you already understand exactly how to use this chart type. If you don't believe, don't worry about this chart.

Table 5.1 Excel Chart Types: What They Are and When to Use Them (*continued*)

Chart Type & Example Subtype	Description	When to Use
Cylinder 	Cylinder charts work like column and bar charts with one minor twist: they use three-dimensional cylinders in place of bars.	You can use this chart type in the same situations as you use a column chart, although it probably doesn't make sense to do so. All you've done is unnecessarily complicate your chart.
Cone 	Cone charts also work like column and bar charts, but like cylinder charts, they come with a minor twist: they use three-dimensional cones in place of bars.	You can use this chart type in the same situations as you use a column chart. All you've done is add the illusion of depth without communicating any new information.
Pyramid 	Pyramid charts are almost exactly like cone charts except they have rectangular instead of round bases.	As with cylinder and cone charts, you can use this chart type in the same situations as you use a column chart. Why make your life more complicated?

Table 5.1 Excel Chart Types: What They Are and When to Use Them (*continued*)

Formatting Your Chart's Parts

I don't much like the default appearance and color of most parts of Excel's charts, and my guess is you won't like them much either. So let me quickly tell you how to change the appearance of just about any chart part. To start:

The precise name of the Format command and dialog box changes depending on what element of the chart you right-click.

1. Right-click the chart part—this can be any element of the chart—and choose the Format command from the shortcut menu. Excel will display a formatting dialog box with several tabs, similar to the one shown in Figure 5.8.
2. Click the Patterns tab (you can ignore the other tabs) and select from the options available:
   - Use the Line (sometimes called Border) boxes to describe how you want Excel to draw the chart part's border.
   - Use the Marker (sometimes called Area) boxes to describe how you want Excel to color the chart part.

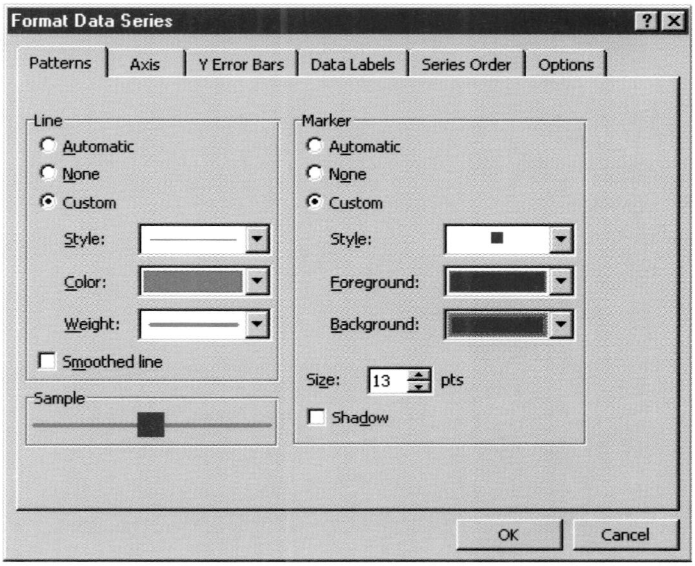

Figure 5.8 Options available for formatting a chart's elements

- For a column chart, use the Fill Effects button to describe how you want Excel to fill the columns. (The Fill Effects button only appears on the dialog box when you're formatting a column chart.)

If you want to format the text in your chart, you can do it the same way that you format text in a worksheet. For example, you select the text and then use a Formatting toolbar button or box.

Printing Charts

Printing charts is no more difficult than printing any other Office document. You just have to keep in mind a few options, depending on whether the chart is embedded or not. To print an embedded chart

- without the surrounding worksheet, simply click the chart and then click the Print tool on the Standard toolbar.
- with the worksheet page in which it's embedded, print the worksheet page by clicking the Print tool or by choosing the File | Print command.

To print a chart that appears on its own chart sheet page, first display the chart sheet and then click the Print tool.

Saving Charts

Because charts are always part and parcel of a workbook, you don't need to worry about separately saving a chart. When you save the workbook with the embedded chart object or with the chart sheet, you also save the chart. As discussed in Chapter 7, you can save a workbook in a variety of ways, but probably the easiest is just to click the Save tool on the Standard toolbar.

Using a Chart in Word, PowerPoint, or Access

Now that you've created your Excel chart, here's all you need to do to use it in Word, PowerPoint, or Access:

1. Save the Excel workbook.
2. Click the chart to select it and then click the Copy button.
3. Open the other Office document into which you want to place the chart (maybe this is a Word document, for example).
4. Position the insertion point at the exact location you want the chart placed and click the Paste button.

Figure 5.9 shows the mortgage rate chart—the same one constructed earlier in the chapter—after I've pasted it into a Word document.

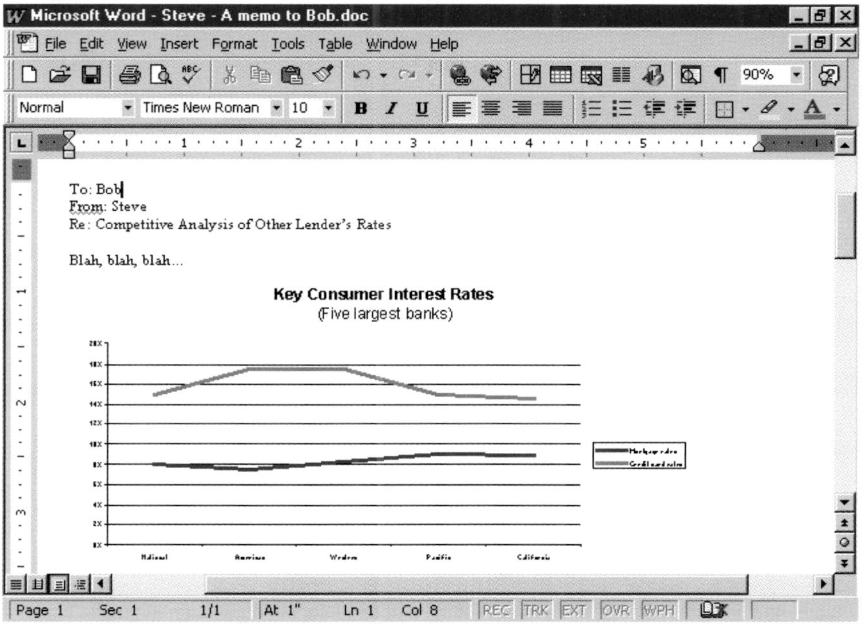

Figure 5.9 This Word document uses a chart created in Excel

CHECKPOINT

This chapter describes how you create, print and save Excel charts—as well as how you use Excel charts in other applications like Word or PowerPoint. Along the way, I've also thrown out some ideas as to when a particular chart type makes sense—and when it doesn't.

While you've now learned the basics of working with the major components of Microsoft Office—Word, Excel, and PowerPoint—there's still some additional knowledge you'll benefit by having. Specifically, you'll want to read (or at least review) Chapter 6's discussion of Office's common tools.

MAIL

CHAPTER

6

Common Tools in Office

INCLUDES

- Using the Format Painter
- Using the Undo and Redo commands
- Spell-checking
- Using AutoCorrect
- Drawing and working with drawn objects
- Working with WordArt
- Creating organization charts

FAST FORWARD

Use the Format Painter ➤ pp. 118-119

To copy some formatting from one object to another, use the Format Painter tool:

1. Select the object that already has the formatting you want.
2. Click the Format Painter tool on the Standard toolbar and the insertion point will change into a Paintbrush icon.
3. Select the object that you want to format, and the formatting is applied.

Use the Undo Command ➤ pp. 119-120

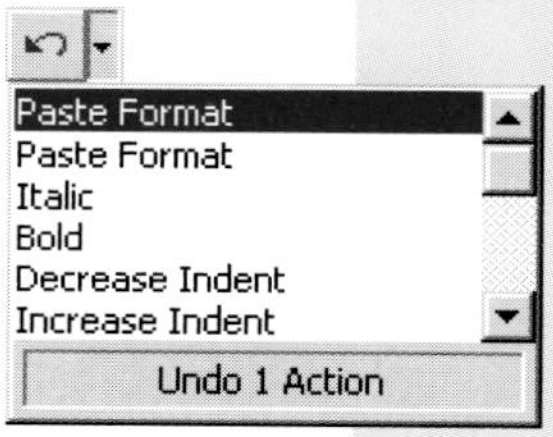

- To reverse the effect of your last action, click the Undo tool on the Standard toolbar.
- To reverse more than one action, click the down arrow that appears just right of the Undo tool. When you see the drop-down list of actions that Undo can undo, select (by clicking and dragging) as many as you want to undo.

Use the Redo Command ➤ pp. 119-120

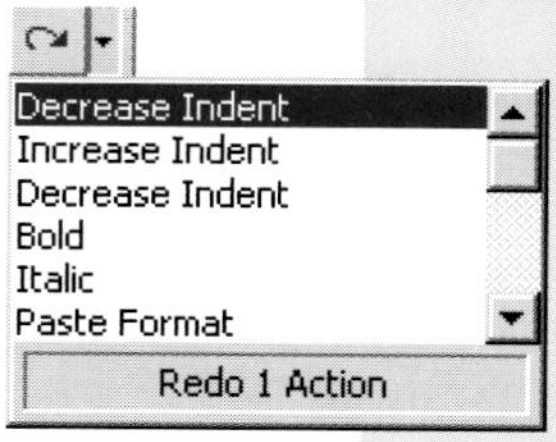

If you undo something by mistake, you can undo Undo:

- Click the Redo tool, which also appears on the Standard toolbar.
- To redo more than one Undo action, click the down arrow that appears just right of the Redo tool. When you see the drop-down list of actions that Redo can redo, select (by clicking and dragging) as many as you want to redo.

Check Spelling ➤ *pp. 120-122*

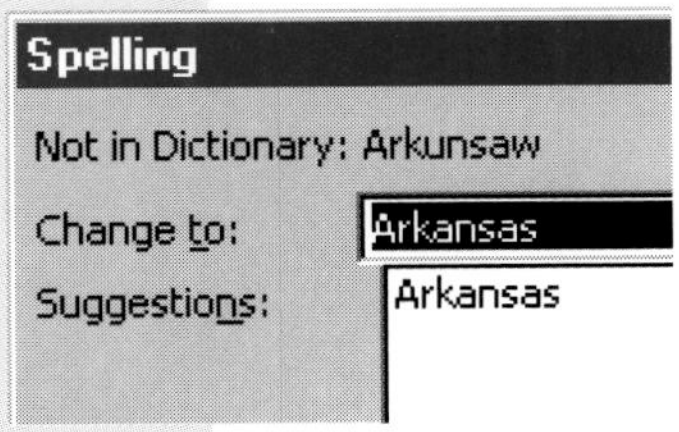

All Office applications include a Tools | Spelling command, which you use to check the spelling of text in a document: a Word document, Excel workbook, PowerPoint presentation, Outlook message, or Access database. To use the spell checker:

1. Open the Office document you want to spell-check.
2. Choose the Tools | Spelling command.

When the Office application finds what it thinks is a misspelled word, you can choose to ignore it, ignore all occurrences of it, or change it.

Use the Drawing Tools ➤ *pp. 124-131*

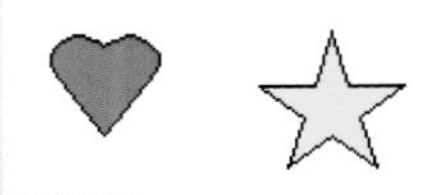

To use the Office drawing tools:

1. Display the Drawing toolbar by right-clicking one of the existing toolbars so the Toolbars shortcut menu appears. Then, click the Drawing command.
2. Use the Drawing toolbar's boxes and buttons to draw and color lines and shapes.

Use WordArt ➤ *pp. 131-135*

To add a WordArt object to a Word document, Excel workbook, or PowerPoint presentation, do either of the following:

- Choose the Insert | Picture | WordArt command.
- Click the WordArt tool on the Drawing toolbar.

Create Organization Charts ➤ *pp. 135-136*

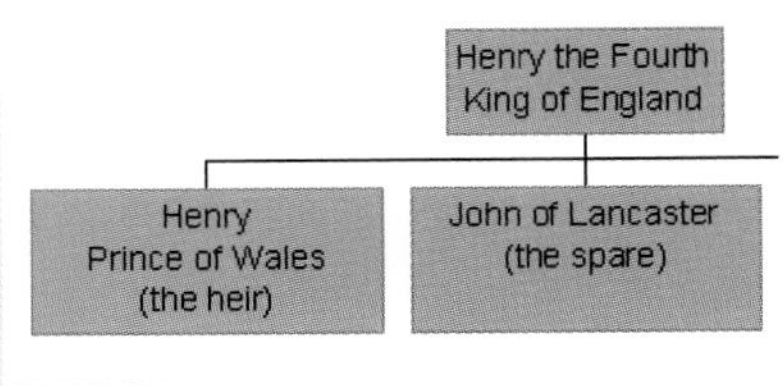

- To add an Organization Chart object to an Excel workbook or PowerPoint presentation, choose the Insert | Picture | Organization Chart command.
- To add an Organization Chart object to a Word document, choose Insert | Object and then select MS Organization Chart 2.0 from the Object Type list.

In the preceding chapters, I described in general terms how you create Word documents, Excel workbooks, and PowerPoint presentations. If you've read those chapters, you already have the skills to create very useful documents. Not surprisingly, however, you can do more than what Chapters 2, 3, 4, and 5 presented. In this chapter, I describe how you use and benefit from the common Office commands and tools available to you across all or most of the five Office programs: Word, Excel, PowerPoint, Outlook, and Access.

Using the Format Painter

Word, Excel, PowerPoint, and Access all provide a Format Painter tool on their Standard toolbars. The way the Format Painter tool works is pretty neat, and it isn't difficult to use. Usually, it's a matter of matter of click, click, and click:

You select the object in the usual way—such as by clicking or by clicking and dragging.

1. Select the object that already has the formatting you want: a blurb of text in a Word document, a spreadsheet range in an Excel workbook, a drawing in PowerPoint, or whatever.

> However, any one who eagerly seeks for celebrity and renown, might congratulate those select gods, call them *fortunate,* were it not that he saw that they have been selected more to their injury than to their honor.
>
> St. Augustine

2. Next, you click the Format Painter tool (to indicate you want to copy some formatting). After you've done this, the insertion point becomes a small paintbrush icon.
3. Then you select the object that you want to format. In other words, if you're copying formatting from one text blurb in Word to another text blurb, you select the second text blurb.

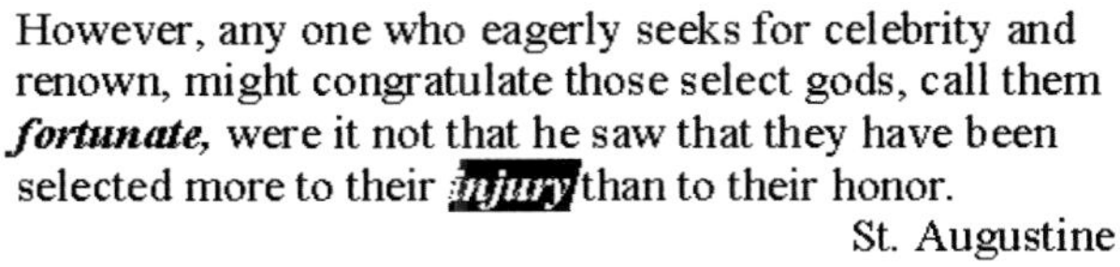

However, any one who eagerly seeks for celebrity and renown, might congratulate those select gods, call them ***fortunate,*** were it not that he saw that they have been selected more to their *injury* than to their honor.

St. Augustine

Using the Undo and Redo Commands

Ah, the wonderful world of Undo and Redo. Both commands are wonderfully useful—and have saved many careers.

Let me start with the Undo command. Undo undoes your last action. If you just deleted a sentence in a Word document, wiped out some critical formula in an Excel workbook, or added erroneous text to a PowerPoint slide, you can usually reverse the effect of your last action by clicking the Undo tool, which appears on the Standard toolbar.

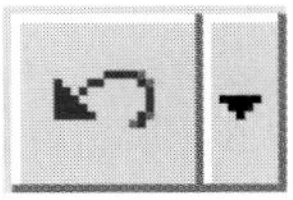

If you click the Undo tool, you reverse only your last action. But you can reverse more than one action if you wish. To do this, click the down arrow that appears just right of the Undo tool. When you see the drop-down list of actions that Undo can undo, select (by clicking and dragging) as many as you want to undo.

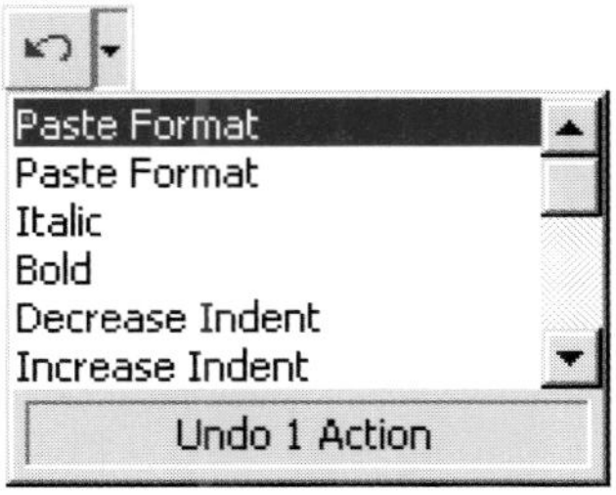

If you undo something by mistake, you can undo Undo by clicking the Redo tool, which also appears on the Standard toolbar.

As with the Undo tool, if you click the Redo tool, you redo only your last Undo action. You can also redo more than one Undo action, however. Click the down arrow that appears just right of the Redo tool. When you see the drop-down list of actions that Redo can redo, select (by clicking and dragging) as many as you want to redo.

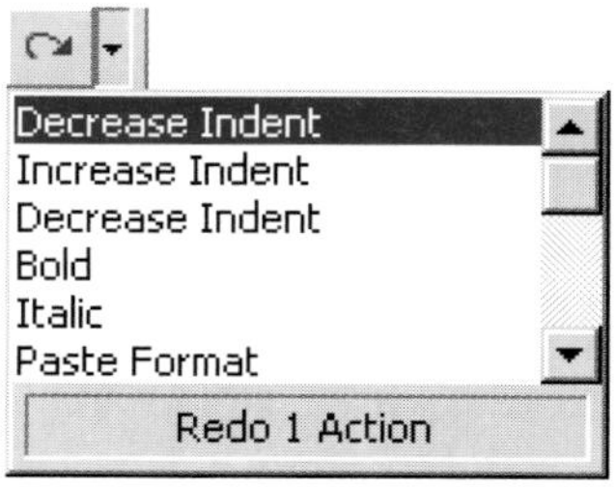

And by now, I'm sure you'll agree, we've made too much ado about Undo and Redo. So let's bid them adieu.

Spell-Checking

In Chapter 2, I discussed Word's spell-checking feature. Office also includes the Tools | Spelling command, which you use to check the spelling of words in a document: an Excel workbook, PowerPoint presentation, Outlook message, or Access database.

To use Office's spell-checking, first open the Office document you want to check. If you want, limit the portion of the document that's spell-checked by selecting it (you can do this by clicking and dragging the mouse). Then choose the Tools | Spelling command and the Spelling dialog box appears, as shown in Figure 6.1.

There are a few options that you can select in this dialog box that will affect how Office's spell-check works:

- If you don't want Office to automatically suggest replacements for your misspellings, unmark the Always Suggest check box.

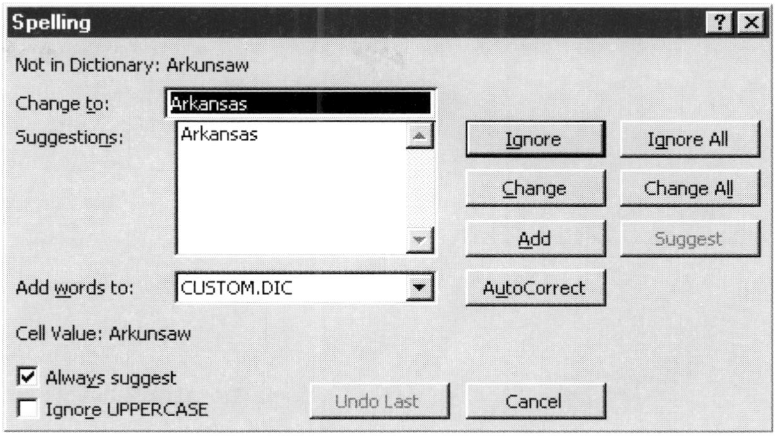

Figure 6.1 Check Spelling using Office's Tools | Spelling command

- If you want Office to ignore words that appear in all uppercase characters—such as ASAP, BTW, and FYI—mark the Ignore UPPERCASE check box.

Office will work through your document (or the area you selected in your document) and when it finds a suspect word, it will display in the Suggestions box the word (sometimes more than one) it thinks you were probably trying to spell. It also places in the Change To text box its best guess of the word you wanted to spell.

At this point, you have a few options:

- If you want to move one of the other suggested words to the Change To text box, click on that word in the Suggestions list.
- To ignore the misspelled word—maybe it's not really misspelled—click the Ignore button. To ignore every occurrence of the misspelled word in the document, click the Ignore All button.
- To replace the misspelled word with the word in the Change To text box, click the Change button. To replace every occurrence of the misspelled word with the word in the Change To text box, click the Change All button.
- To add the word to the dictionary that Office applications use for spell-checking, click the Add button.

EXPERT ADVICE

If you inadvertently ignore a misspelling or erroneously change a correctly spelled word, you may be able to undo the change using the Undo Last button.

Using AutoCorrect

AutoCorrect is an eerie little tool. In effect, it slyly observes what you enter into Word documents, Excel workbook cells, and PowerPoint outlines, correcting any obvious errors you make. For example, if you mistakenly type the word "occurrence" with only one "r" or only one "c," AutoCorrect fixes your mistake for you. (This is great for your document quality because it eliminates all of the most common spelling errors, but it isn't so good for any future spelling-bee competitions because you never even know you're misspelling certain words.)

AutoCorrect also substitutes dingbat or symbol characters when appropriate. For example, if you type a crude little smiley face using a colon and end parenthesis mark like this:

:)

AutoCorrect substitutes a slick smiley character like this:

Excel's AutoCorrect dialog box is shown in the Figure 6.2, but Word's and PowerPoint's look and work pretty much the same.

You can control the way AutoCorrect works by using the Tools | AutoCorrect command. When you choose this command while working with one of the Office applications, an AutoCorrect dialog box appears, much like the one shown in Figure 6.2.

The checkboxes specify which types of automatic correction the Office application should fix. Some of these are obvious, but let me give you the rundown on all of them just in case.

- The Correct TWo INitial CApitals check box fixes the kookiness that occurs when you leave your finger on the SHIFT key for just a bit longer than your should.
- The Capitalize First Letter of Sentence check box tells the Office application to capitalize the first letter following a period. (It assumes that this is the first letter in a new sentence.)
- The Capitalize Names of Days check box—well, you know, right? You have to spell Monday with a capital "M."
- The Correct Accidental Use of cAPS LOCK Key undoes the damage when the CAPS LOCK key is inadvertently pressed in.

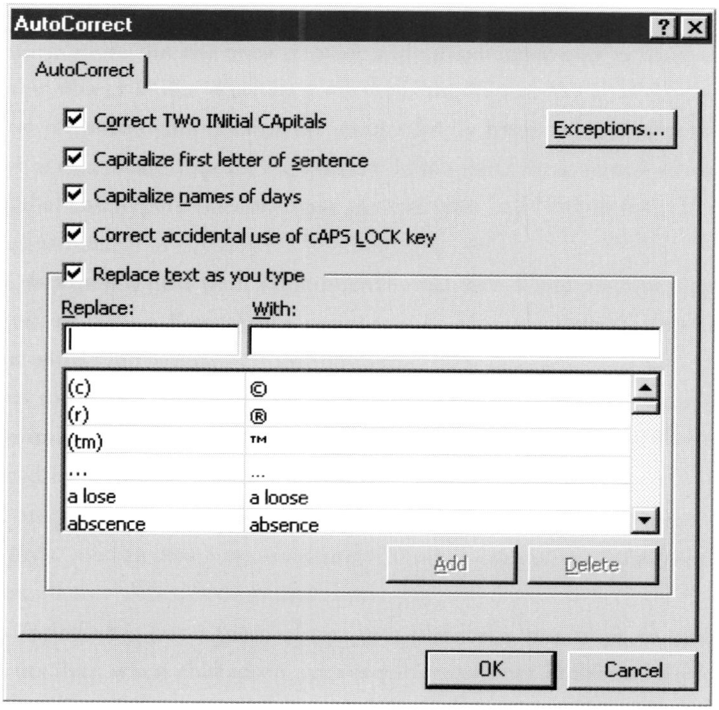

Figure 6.2 You can use the AutoCorrect dialog box to specify which errors AutoCorrect fixes

- The Replace Text as You Type check box controls the main functionality of AutoCorrect. When marked, this checkbox tells AutoCorrect to fix common misspellings and to replace typewriter art and bogus symbols with the real McCoy (where possible).

You can also add to the list of corrections that AutoCorrect makes so that Office can help you catch your own particular bugaboos:

1. In the Replace text box, enter a misspelling, typewriter art, or bogus symbol that you want AutoCorrect to fix.
2. Provide the replacement word or symbol in the With text box.
3. Click the Add button.

If you want to stay on your toes and police your errors yourself, you can prevent AutoCorrect from making certain corrections:

1. Scroll through the list of automatic corrections and click the ones you don't want AutoCorrect to make.
2. Click DELETE.

For more information about AutoText, refer to Chapter 2.

Let me mention one other tidbit regarding the AutoCorrect feature and Microsoft Word. In addition to AutoCorrect, Microsoft Word provides a related feature called AutoText. AutoText finishes the entry of certain commonly used words. If you type *Mon*, for example, Word displays the word "Monday" in a pop-up box.

Using the Drawing Tools

I'm going to talk about these drawing tools in the context of a PowerPoint presentation, but what I say here applies equally to Word, Excel, and PowerPoint.

Word, Excel, and PowerPoint—the three major Office applications—sport a powerful new set of drawing tools that you can use to add all sorts of drawing objects to your Word documents, Excel workbooks, and PowerPoint presentations: rectangles of any size and shape; circles, ovals, and arcs; lines and arrows, and freeform shapes limited only by your imagination. You can fill shapes with color and pattern, or leave them transparent, so your chart or worksheet shows through.

You can add text and format and spell-check it. And you can move, resize, group, and manipulate drawings in a multitude of ways. Figure 6.3 gives you a preview of some of the neat graphical effects you can achieve with Office's drawing tools.

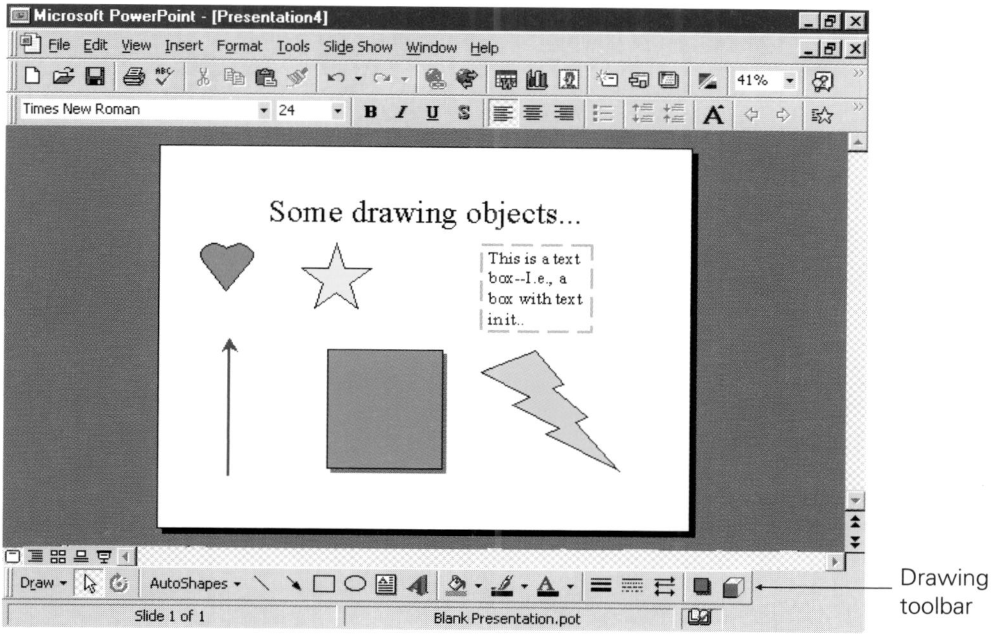

Figure 6.3 Here's a sampling of what you can do in Word, Excel, and PowerPoint with Office's drawing tools

Displaying the Drawing Toolbar

To use the Office drawing tools, you may need to display the Drawing toolbar (shown earlier in Figure 6.3):

1. Right-click one of the existing toolbars so the toolbar's shortcut menu appears.

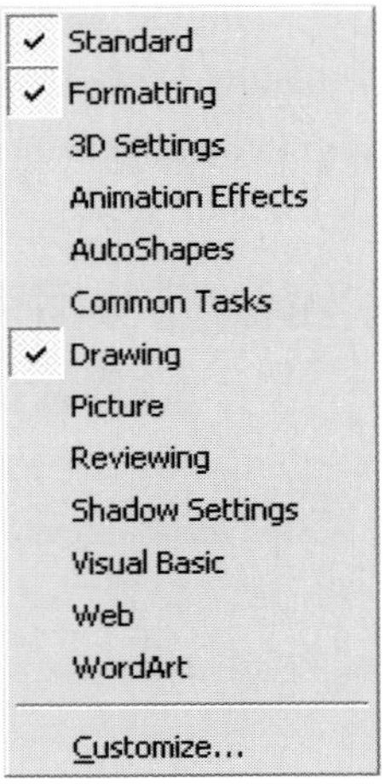

2. Choose the Drawing command from the shortcut menu.

The Office application adds the Drawing toolbar to the bottom of the application window.

Drawing Objects Using the Drawing Toolbar

You'll most often use the line, arrow, rectangle, and ellipse buttons to draw objects in a document.

Lines and Arrows

To draw a straight line:

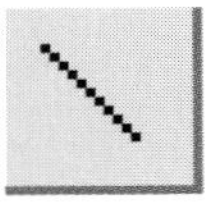

1. Click the Line button. When you move the mouse pointer into the document window, the cursor changes to a set of small cross-hairs.
2. Position the cross-hairs mouse pointer where you want one end of your line to begin and then click and drag. Release the mouse button where you want the line to end.

SHORTCUT

To draw more than one line at a time, double-click the Line button before you start. Then the cross-hairs pointer remains until you either click the Line button again or click another button.

If, after you click a button, you change your mind and decide you don't really want to draw a line after all, just click and release the mouse button anywhere in the worksheet (or click the button a second time).

The process is exactly the same when you use the Arrow tool:

1. Select the Arrow tool. (The cursor changes to a cross-hair.)
2. Click at the point where you want the arrow to begin and drag the mouse to the point where you want the arrow to end (and point). Then release the mouse button.

The Office application draws the arrow.

Rectangles and Ovals

You draw all the rectangles and ovals in the same way:

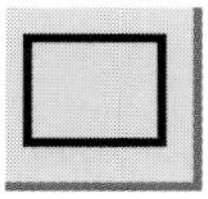

1. Click either the Rectangle tool or the Oval tool.
2. Position the cross-hairs where you want the upper-left corner of the rectangle or oval to be.
3. Drag down and to the right until you reach the spot where you want the lower-right corner of the rectangle or oval to be and then release the mouse button. (If you're drawing an oval, you size it as if it fit just inside an invisible rectangle.)

AutoShapes

The AutoShapes button displays a menu of line and shape commands. In effect, the menu's commands amount to predrawn shapes that you can plop right into your documents.

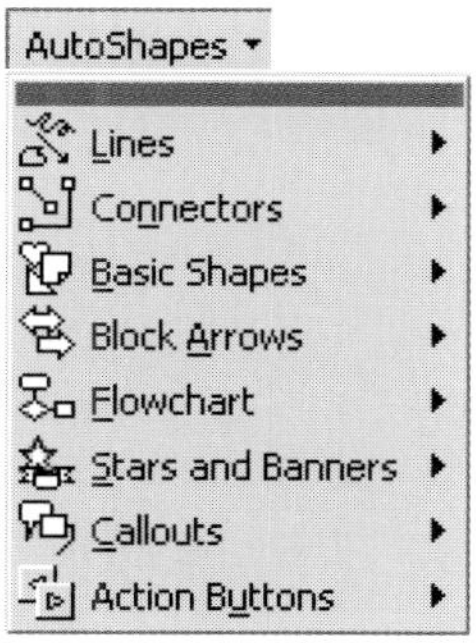

To draw an AutoShape line or shape:

1. Select an AutoShape menu command. Then select the line or shape you want from the submenu that the Office application displays.

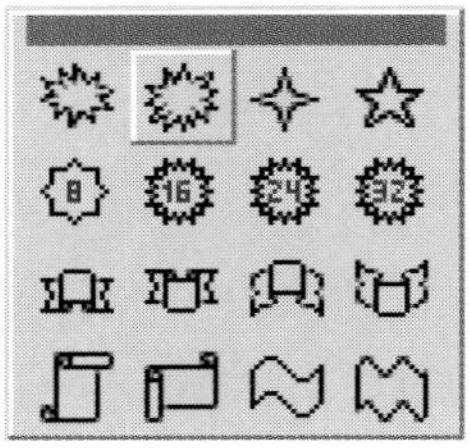

2. Position the cross-hairs where you want the upper-left corner of the shape.
3. Drag down and to the right until you reach the spot where you want the lower-right corner of the shape and then release the mouse button. Draw then sizes the shape to fit within the area you've defined.

Working with Drawn Objects

Now that you've learned how to draw objects in Office applications, you need to know how to work with them. Drawn objects can be moved, resized, reshaped, and formatted. So let me explain how you do all these things and more.

Moving Drawn Objects

You can move drawn objects around your worksheet:

- To move a line or unfilled shape, click on the line or shape to select it. Then drag it where you want it.
- To move a filled shape, click inside the shape to select it. Then drag it.

SHORTCUT

To copy drawn objects, hold down the CTRL key while you drag an object to a new location.

Changing the Size and Shape of Drawn Objects

You can also easily change the size or the shape of drawn objects. To resize or reorient a line or shape, first select it so that the Drawing tool adds handles (little white boxes) to its endpoints (if it's a line) or its edges (if it's a shape). Then drag the handles. When you click a handle, the pointer changes to a double-headed arrow:

- To resize an object in one dimension (for instance, to make a rectangle longer, but not higher), click and drag an endpoint handle (if a line) or a side handle (if a shape).
- To change both dimensions at the same time, click and drag a corner handle (if a shape).
- To resize an object proportionally (that is, without changing its shape), hold down the SHIFT key while you click and drag a corner handle.

Using the Free Rotate Tool

The Free Rotate tool rotates an object. This sounds complicated, but a quick example will quickly show you how it works:

1. Select the object you want to rotate. Then click the Free Rotate tool.
2. When round, green handles appear at every corner of the object, click on one of the handles and drag it in either a clockwise or counterclockwise direction to rotate the object.

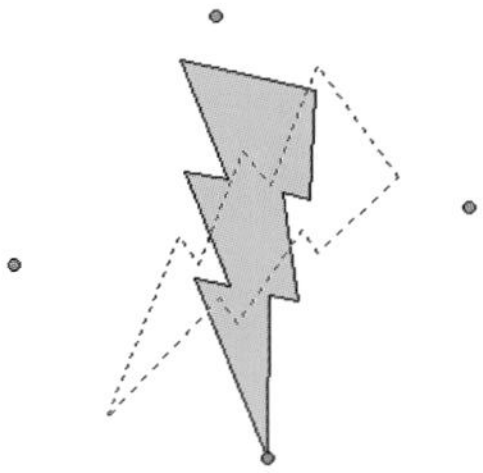

Text Boxes

Text boxes are just boxes that include text. (I often use them to add impossible-to-miss comments to a Word document, an Excel workbook, or a PowerPoint presentation.) To add a text box to a document:

1. Click the Text Box tool.
2. Draw a rectangle by dragging the mouse pointer between the rectangle's opposite corners.
3. Type your text in the box.

EXPERT ADVICE

You can format the text in a text box the same way you format other text. The easiest method is usually to use the tools on the Formatting toolbar.

Formatting Drawn Objects

Having created lines and shapes, you're only half done. You can, if you like, format them in a variety of ways to produce striking results. Formatting an object allows you to change its color and line weight and to add patterns and shading. The simplest way to reformat an object is to select it (by clicking it) and then to use the appropriate Drawing tool. Table 6.1 describes the tools on the Drawing toolbar that let you format existing drawing objects.

SHORTCUT

If you want to select more than one object, hold down the SHIFT key and then click each of the objects.

Tool	Name	Description
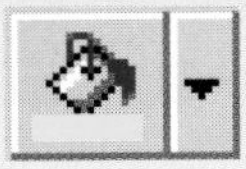	Fill Color	Fills a shape with the selected color. (To select the color, activate the Fill Color drop-down list and select the square with the color.)
	Line Color	Colors a line using the selected color. (To select the color, activate the Line Color drop-down list and select the square with the color.)
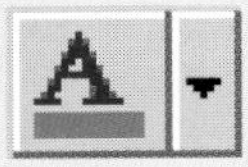	Font Color	Colors the text in a text box using the selected color. (To select the color, activate the Font Color drop-down list and select the square with the color.)
	Line Style	Displays a list from which you can choose a line thickness and style.
	Dash Style	Displays a list from which you can choose a dashed-line style.
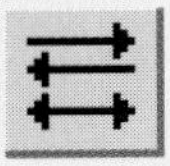	Arrow Style	Displays a list from which you can choose an arrow style.
	Shadow	Displays a list from which you can choose a shadow style.
	3-D	Displays a list from which you can choose a three-dimensional perspective.

Table 6.1 The Drawing Toolbar's Formatting Tools

Working with WordArt

Office comes with a clever little program called WordArt. WordArt lets you take little chunks of text and manipulate them in all sorts of interesting and sometimes goofy ways.

To add a WordArt object to a Word document, Excel workbook, or PowerPoint presentation, follow these steps:

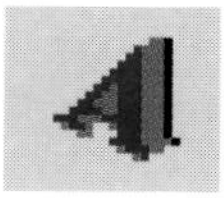

1. Choose the Insert | Picture | WordArt command. Alternatively, if the Drawing toolbar is on the screen, click the WordArt tool. The Office application opens the WordArt Gallery, shown in Figure 6.4.
2. WordArt next displays the Edit WordArt Text dialog box, shown next. Enter the text you want to display as a WordArt object here. Then click OK. WordArt adds the WordArt object to the open Office document.

Use the Font and Size drop-down list boxes and the Bold and Italic tools to change the appearance of your WordArt object.

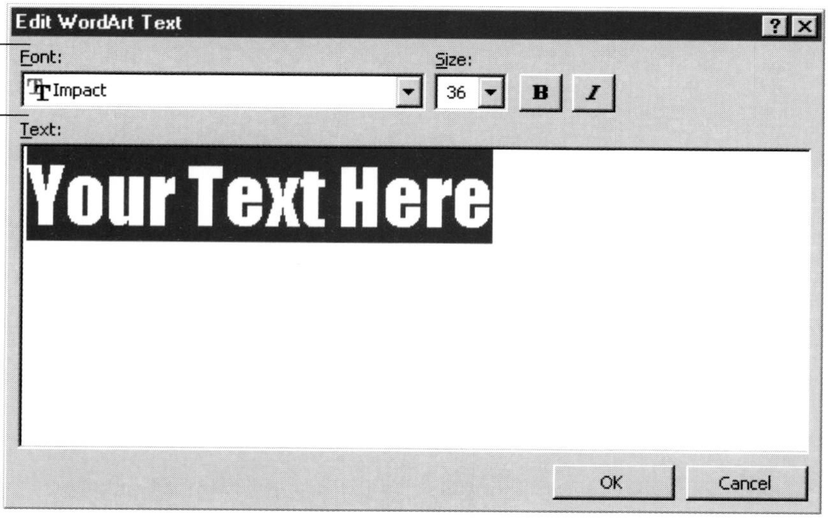

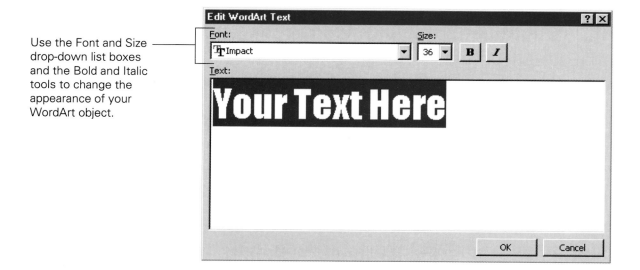

Figure 6.5 shows a PowerPoint presentation with a WordArt object.

The WordArt toolbar, shown in Figure 6.5, appears whenever you select (by clicking) a WordArt object. This toolbar provides many different tools, as described in Table 6.2, that you can use to further manipulate and format your WordArt object.

Select a WordArt style by double-clicking the appropriate button here. Then click OK.

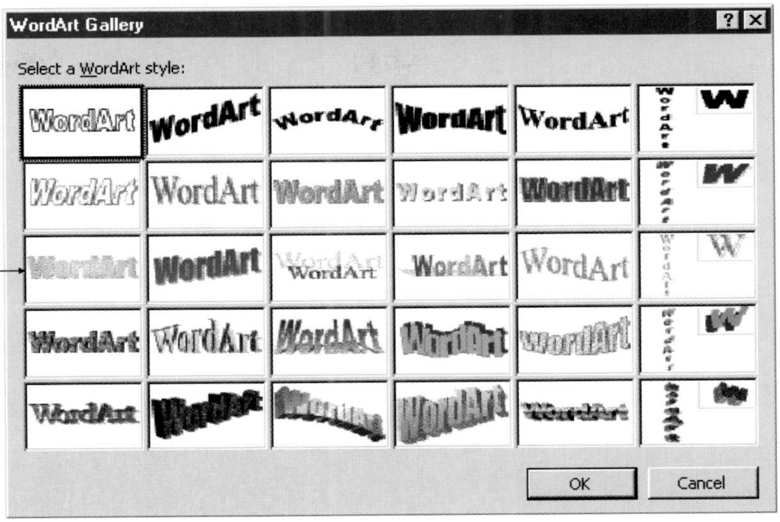

Figure 6.4 You use this dialog box to pick a style for your WordArt object

WordArt toolbar

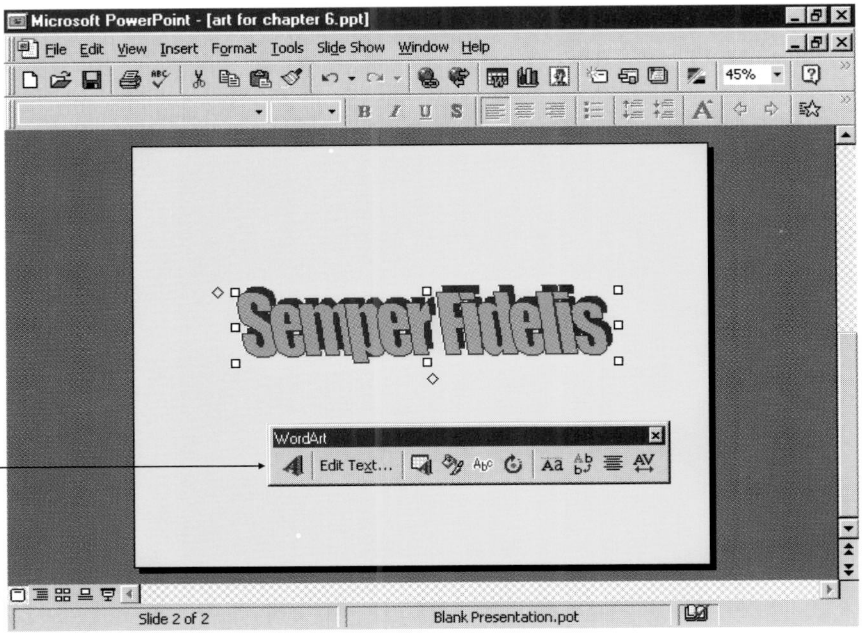

Figure 6.5 A PowerPoint presentation with a WordArt object

Tool	Name	Description
	WordArt	Lets you add a new WordArt object to the open Office document.
Edit Text...	Edit Text	Displays the Edit WordArt Text dialog box so you can change the WordArt object's text.
	WordArt Gallery	Lets you pick a new style for the WordArt object.
	Format WordArt	Displays a dialog box with a bunch of tabs that let you change things like the WordArt object's color and size.
	WordArt Shape	Displays a menu of kooky shapes you can use for your WordArt object.
	Free Rotate	Adds round, green handles to the WordArt object, which you can use to rotate the WordArt object by dragging.
	WordArt Same Letter Heights	Tells WordArt to make all the letters in your WordArt the same height.
	WordArt Vertical Text	Rearranges the WordArt object's text so it's vertical rather than horizontal.
	WordArt Alignment	Displays a menu of alignment options for your WordArt object's text.
	WordArt Character Spacing	Displays a menu of character spacing options for your WordArt object's text.

Table 6.2 The WordArt Toolbar's Formatting Tools

EXPERT ADVICE

If you have questions about what a particular tool on the WordArt toolbar does, go ahead and create a WordArt object, experiment a bit, and then delete the object when you finish. To delete a WordArt object, click it and press DELETE.

Creating Organization Charts

Before I close this chapter, I want to quickly tell you about another clever little program that comes with Office: Organization Chart. Organization Chart, as its name suggests, lets you create organizational charts and then plop these items into Office documents as objects.

To add an Organization Chart object to a Word document, Excel workbook, or PowerPoint presentation, choose the Insert | Picture | Organization Chart command. The Office application opens the Microsoft Organization Chart window, shown in Figure 6.6.

To show who's king of the mountain, for example, you click the top box. Then replace the filler text with a name and title.

Here are a few of the ways you can tailor the organization chart to your needs:

- To add boxes to the chart, use the Subordinate, Co-worker, Manager, or Assistant command button. Select an existing organization chart box, click the appropriate command button, and then fill in the new box with the right name and title information.

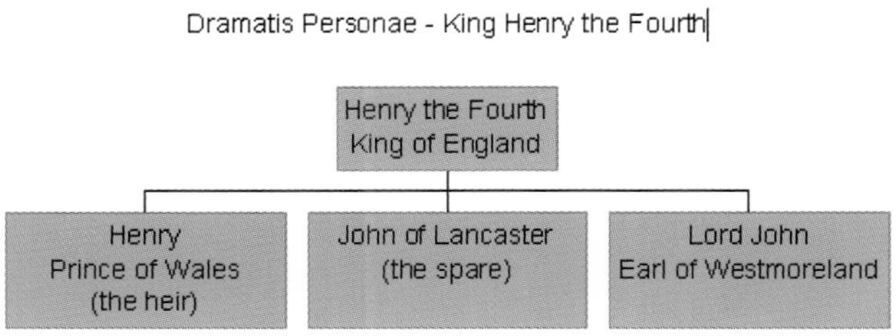

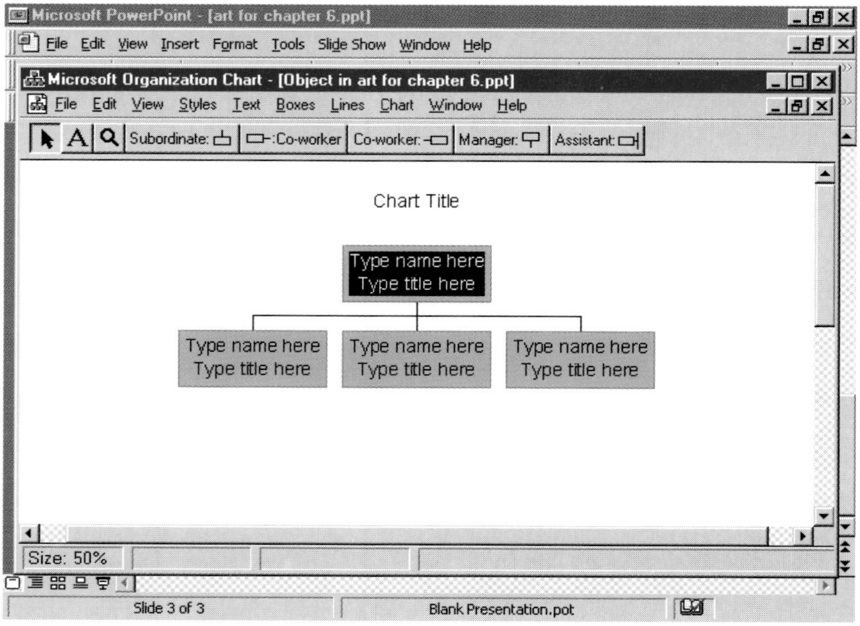

Figure 6.6 To create an Organization Chart, you simply fill in the boxes

- To remove a box from the organization chart, click the box and then press DELETE.
- To change the appearance of the Organization Chart object, use the commands on the Style, Text, Boxes, Lines, and Chart menus. I'm not going to describe here how these menu's commands work. Doing so would waste your time. When you create your first organization chart, just experiment with these commands to get the look you want.

When you finish creating your Organization Chart object, choose the File | Exit and Return To command. The Office document now includes your new Organization Chart object.

SHORTCUT

To delete an Organization Chart object from an Office document, click anywhere on it and press DELETE.

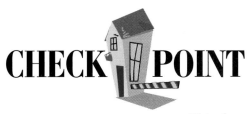

CHECK POINT

This chapter describes most of the common Office tools you'll use across the Office applications: the Format Painter toolbar button, the Undo and Redo commands, Office's spell-checking feature, AutoCorrect, the Drawing tool, Words Art, and Organization Chart. As silly as it might sound, you really will want to learn how to work with all of these tools because they're so useful in so many different places within the Office suite of applications.

With the material covered in this chapter and the previous chapters, you're well on your way to proficiency with the core Office applications: Word, Excel, and PowerPoint. There are still a couple of areas you'll benefit from by learning more about. Chapter 7 covers the topic of document management (saving, opening, and printing documents), so you'll probably want to read it if you have questions about any of these activities. Chapter 8 explains how you share objects created in one Office application with other Office applications—for example, how you take a chart you've created in Excel and place it into a Word document or PowerPoint presentation.

PRIORITY!
MEMO:
FIRST CLASS
RUSH!

CHAPTER

7

Managing Your Office Documents

INCLUDES

- Printing documents
- Saving documents
- Opening documents
- Creating new documents
- Searching for lost documents
- Sharing files electronically

FAST FORWARD

Print a Document ➤ pp. 142-144

To print a Word document, Excel workbook, or PowerPoint presentation, use either of the following methods:

- Use the Print tool, which appears on the Standard toolbar.
- Use the File | Print command.

Save a Document ➤ pp. 144-145

To save a Word document, Excel workbook, or PowerPoint presentation, use either of the following methods:

- Use the Save tool, which appears on the Standard toolbar.
- Use the File | Save As or File | Save command.

Resave an Office Document ➤ p. 144

To save a document a second and subsequent times, you have two options:

- Choose the File | Save command.
- Click the Save button on the Standard toolbar.

Protect Your Documents with Passwords ➤ pp. 146-149

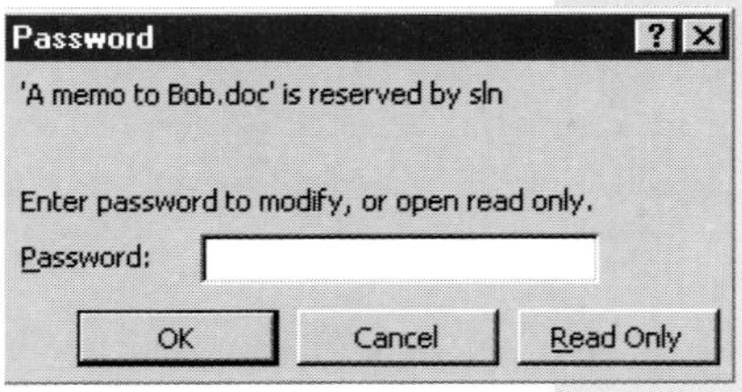

You can prevent your files from being read or changed without your approval by doing the following :

1. Choose the File | Save As Command.
2. Click the Options command button.
3. Enter a password and select the options you want to use.

Open Documents ➤ pp. 149, 150

Use any of these methods to open an Office document:

- Choose the document from the Start menu's Documents submenu. This is the easiest approach.
- Use the File menu to reopen any of the four files you used most recently. They are listed at the bottom of the file menu. Just click a file to open it.
- Click the Open tool on the Standard toolbar and choose the document in the dialog box that appears.

Create a New Document ➤ pp. 152-153

The easiest way to open a new document—a Word document, Excel workbook, or PowerPoint presentation—is to use the New tool on the Standard toolbar.

Search for Lost Documents ➤ pp. 153-157

To find lost documents, use the boxes that appear at the bottom of the Open dialog box, under the heading "Find files that match these criteria," to describe the file you want to find.

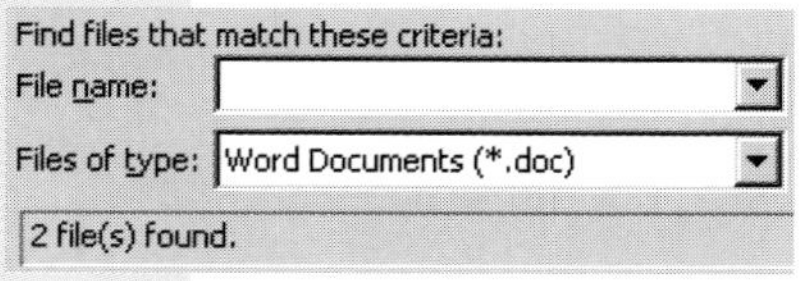

Share Files Electronically ➤ pp. 157-159

Use the commands that appear on the File | Send To submenu to share files in e-mail messages, routing lists, and Exchange folders and to fax documents.

In earlier chapters, I briefly described how you save and open Office documents and how you print them. But I didn't really give you all the information you'll need if you're going to be working with Office on a daily or regular basis. This chapter addresses this embarrassing deficiency by telling you everything you need to know about Office document management in Word, Excel, and PowerPoint: how to print documents, how to save documents (so you can use them again), how to open previously saved documents, and how to find documents you misplace.

Printing Documents

As I've mentioned maybe three or four times earlier in the book, you can easily print a Word document, an Excel workbook, or a PowerPoint presentation by clicking the Print tool. (The Print tool appears on the Standard toolbar of each of the Microsoft Office applications: Word, Excel, PowerPoint and so on.)

The one problem with the Print tool is that it doesn't give you any control over how an application—say it's Word—prints your document. So you should know how to use—and definitely want to know about—the other way you print documents, workbooks, and presentions: by using the File | Print command. Fortunately, this command is really easy to use. All you do is open the document, workbook or presentation you want to print, choose the command, and then select the various options in the Print dialog box, as described in the following Step by Step box, to specify how you want the document to print.

STEP BY STEP Print a Document

③ Specify how many copies of the document you want to print using the Number of Copies box.

① If you have more than one printer connected to your computer, select the printer from the Name drop-down list.

② Use the Print buttons and box to specify what pages of the document you want to print: all of the pages, only the current page, or some range of pages.

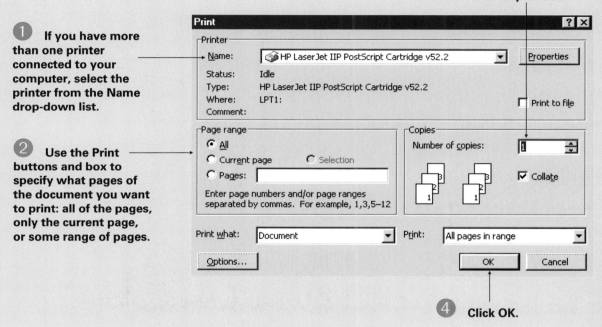

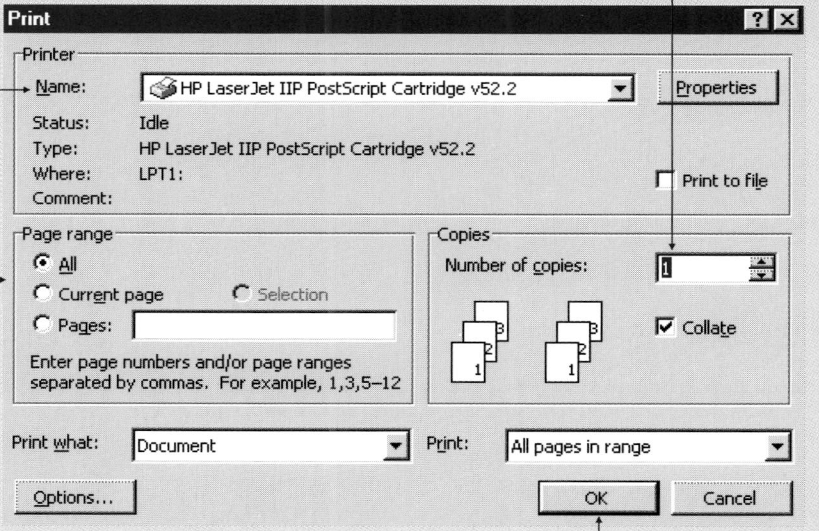

④ Click OK.

While we're on the subject of printing, let me make just a few additional comments. First, remember that if you have a question about some dialog box option, you can click the question mark button (which appears in the upper-right corner of the dialog box) and then click the option you have a question about. If you think you want to use an option on the Print dialog box that I didn't describe in the Step by Step instruction, this is the way you can learn what the option does.

A second thing I'll tell you is that the Print dialog box looks a little bit different for different applications. The illustration in the Step by Step box, for example, shows what Word's Print dialog box looks like. Excel's Print dialog box, not surprisingly, looks a little bit different. And so does PowerPoint's dialog box.

While the Print dialog boxes look a bit different from each other, however, you use them in the same way that I've described here.

Saving Documents

You wouldn't waste your time creating Office documents if they disappeared every time you switched off your computer. In fact, one of the reasons you use a computer is because you know that you can safely store documents you create and then find them again later when you need them. This process of preserving your work is, of course, called *saving*.

Saving a Document for the First Time

The easiest way to save a Word document, Excel workbook, or PowerPoint presentation is to use the Save tool, which appears on the Standard toolbar.

Just click the button, and the Office application displays the Save As dialog box. Then follow the instructions in the "Save a New Document" Step by Step box shown opposite.

Resaving an Office Document

Once you've named and saved your Office document, its new filename will appear in the title bar at the top of the screen. When you want to save the document a second time, and any subsequent times, you do either of the following:

- Choose the File | Save command.
- Click the Save button on the toolbar.

All you'll see is a series of little blue (if you're using the Windows standard color scheme) squares flitting across the status bar at the bottom of your screen and a notice that says, "Saving [your file name]." The Office application saves your file by writing a new copy over the previously saved copy, incorporating any changes you've made.

One final point. If you've made changes to a document since you last saved it, the Office application asks if want to save your document when you choose the File | Close or File | Exit commands, to prevent you from accidentally destroying data.

STEP BY STEP Save a New Document

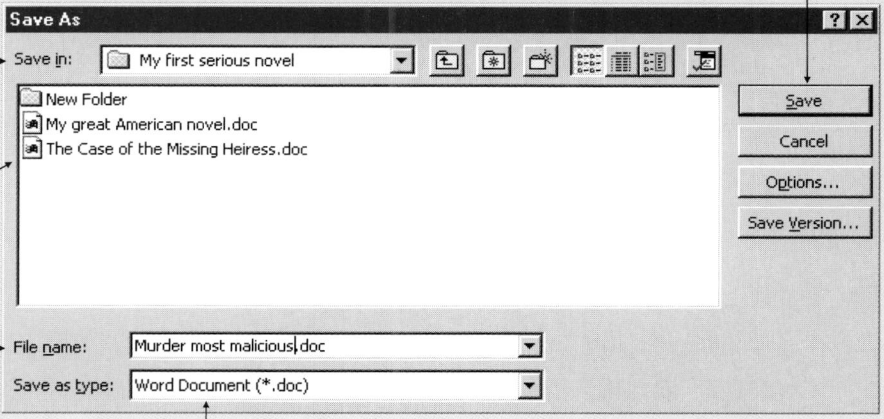

1 Give your document a name using the File Name box. (Remember that you can, in Windows 95 and Windows NT, enter lengthy and very descriptive file names.)

2 If you want, use the Save as Type drop-down list to specify the document format. (To do this, click the downward-pointing arrow next to the Save as Type list and select the file type you want.) You might save something as a different type if you're planning on opening the document in a non-Office application or in a previous version of an Office application.

3 Specify the folder in which you want to save your document, workbook or presentation. The Office application suggests the name of a folder using the Save In drop-down list. In the large list box below the Save In box, the Office application lists any subfolders and files contained in the suggested folder.

4 Click Save.

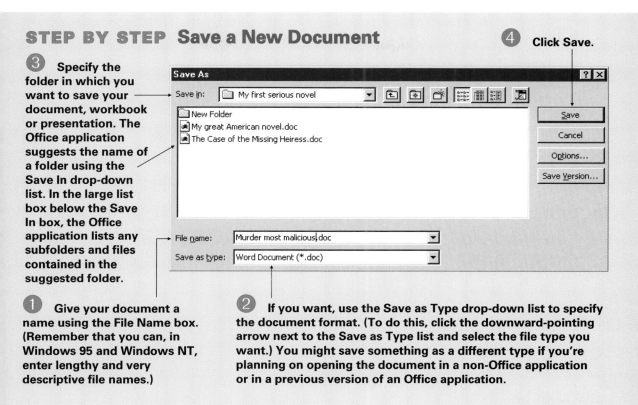

SHORTCUT

You can also use the Save As dialog box to copy a previously saved file onto a floppy disk. Just specify the floppy drive using the Save In box.

Saving a File with a New Name

Sometimes you'll want to save more than one copy of the same document, perhaps so you can experiment with changing the format or information in one copy while leaving the original unchanged, or maybe just as insurance against accidental loss of critical data. (You'll usually want to give each copy a different name or store the copies in different folders to distinguish between them.) To save a document with a different name or in a different location:

1. Choose the File | Save As command.
2. When the Office application displays the Save As dialog box, enter the new name in the File Name text box and/or the new location in the Save In text box.
3. Click Save.

Protecting Your Documents with Passwords

Figure 7.1 shows the Save Options dialog box that Word uses, but the Excel and PowerPoint Save Options dialog boxes resemble it.

If others have access to your files, either on your computer or through a network, you can take precautions to prevent your files from being read or changed without your okay. In the Save Options dialog box, shown in Figure 7.1, Word, Excel, and PowerPoint provide three levels of security, which I'll discuss next.

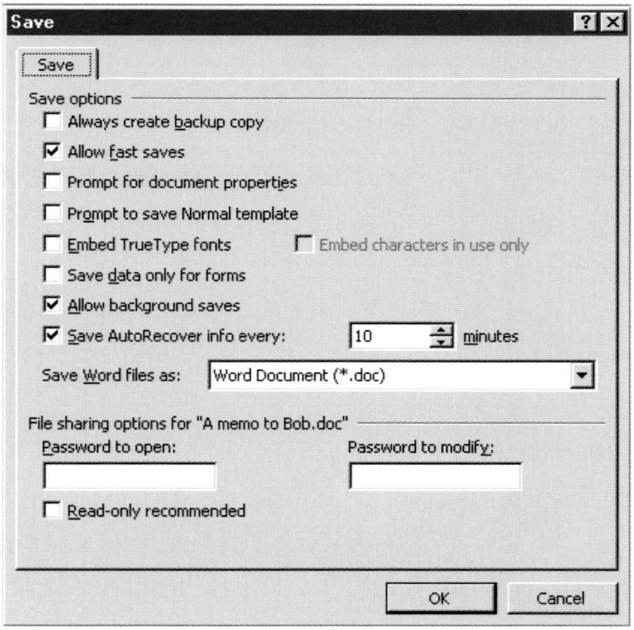

Figure 7.1 You use the Save Options dialog box to turn on Word's password protection

Using the Read-Only Option

The lowest level of security is the Read-Only Recommended option. This option is really just a suggestion that others open your file as a read-only file. Read-only means just what it says: someone opening the file can read it, but not write to and, hence, change it. If you select the Read-Only Recommended option in the Save Options dialog box, someone attempting to open your file will be prompted by the Office application to select the Read Only option in the Open dialog box. If they select that option to open the file, they won't be able to change the file in any way. But note that this read-only status is strictly voluntary. Someone can choose to ignore the suggestion that a file be opened as read-only—and if they do ignore the suggestion, they can rewrite the original file. Needless to say, this strategy works only with nonsensitive data and with people you can trust.

Using a Write Reservation Password

The next higher level of security is the Password to Modify option (also called the Write Reservation option). If you password-protect a file, anyone trying to open it will see this dialog box. If they can't supply the appropriate password, they must choose the Read Only option in order to gain access.

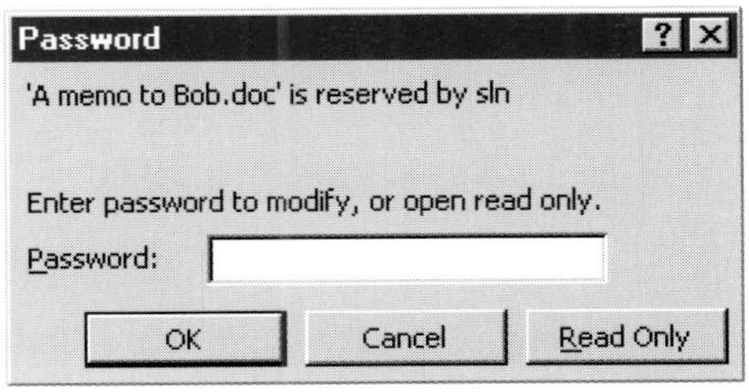

To enable the Password to Modify Option:

1. Enter a password in the Password to Modify text box in the Save Options dialog box. Your password can be up to 15 characters long and is case sensitive. (For instance, if you first enter the password as mAgnOLIA, you must use the same case for letters when reentering the password. Magnolia wouldn't work. Neither would MAGNOLIA.)

2. Click OK. The Office program will ask you to confirm the password you entered, while reminding you of the importance of remembering your password.

CAUTION

I'll do the same reminding here: Don't forget your password. If you do, you're out of luck—you'll never be able to modify that file again.

3. Reenter the password to confirm it, click OK, and click Save.

Using a Protection Password

You get the highest level of security by assigning a Password to Open password (also called a *protection password*). When a file is assigned a Password to Open password, it simply can't be opened—not at all—without the password. This is the way to go for sensitive data or files that you just don't want anyone to mess with, period. The procedure is basically the same as it is for Password to Modify passwords, except you enter the password in the text box marked Password to Open (see Figure 7.1). The same caveat also applies: forget the password at your own peril.

EXPERT ADVICE

You can use both Write Reservation and Protection levels of password protection at the same time. Give those whom you want to have unlimited access both passwords. Give those whom you want to restrict to read-only access only the protection password.

Getting Rid of a Password

To remove a password:

1. Display the Save Options dialog box.

2. Delete the existing password by selecting the Password to Open or the Password to Modify text box and then pressing DELETE.
3. Save the document again.

Opening Documents

Choosing the File | Open command produces exactly the same result as using the Open tool.

Okay—you saved your work successfully last night. Now it's the next morning and time to get back to work. How do you open that document you were working on? Here are three ways:

- Choose the document from the Start menu's Documents submenu. This is the easiest way to open an Office document.
- Use the File menu to reopen any of the four files you used most recently. They are listed at the bottom of the file menu. Just click a file to open it.
- Click the Open tool on the Standard toolbar. You can always use this method if neither of the other options is available to you because it has been a while since you last opened the document.

When you click the Open tool, the Office application displays the Open dialog box. If you know the name and path of the file you want, just type it the File Name text box of the Open dialog box. If, however, you've forgotten where you saved something, you'll need to do a bit of searching. I've laid out a game plan for you in the "Find the Document to Open" Step by Step box on the next page.

An Office application typically lists only those files it created—for example, Excel will display files with the .xls extension, Word will display files with the .doc extention. To display other types of files, activate the Files of Type drop-down list in the Open dialog box and select one of its entries.

Using the Buttons in the Save In and Open Dialog Boxes

You may have noticed those buttons that appear to the right of the Save In box in the Save As dialog box and to the right of the Look In box in the Open

STEP BY STEP Find the Document to Open

1 Activate the Look In drop-down list to display a list of your drives. Then click the drive that contains the file you want.

2 Double-click folders until you locate your document. (Alternatively, you can start looking through the folder hierarchy by clicking the Up One Level button just to the right of the Look In box.)

3 Click your document to select it

4 Click Open.

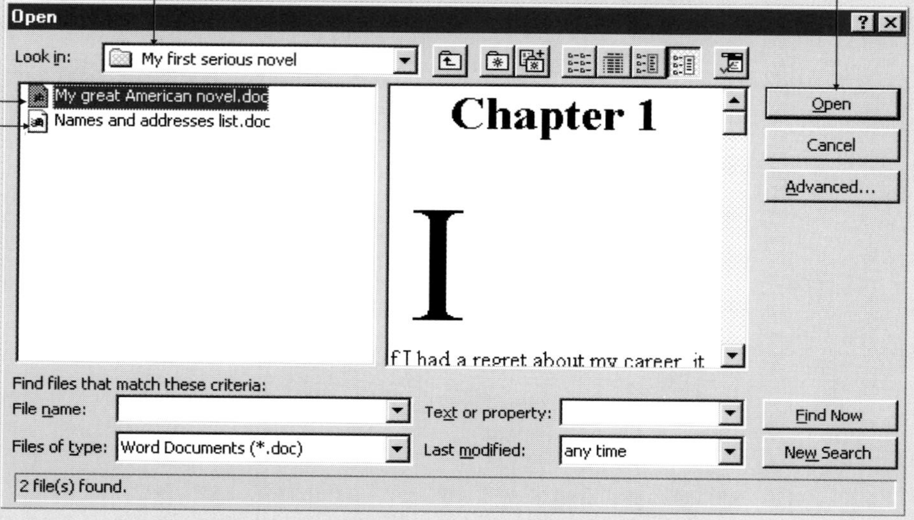

dialog box. You'll want to learn what these buttons do and how to use them. They can save you much time. Table 7.1 shows and describes each button.

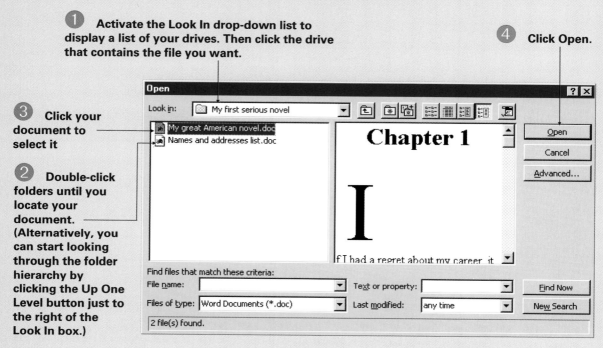

EXPERT ADVICE

Right-click any document listed in the Open or Save As dialog box to display a shortcut menu of commands. You'll find commands to let you view the file without opening it (Quick View), create a shortcut to the selected file, delete or rename the file, send the file to disk, and fax or e-mail the file.

Button	Name	Description	Appears In...
	Up One Level	Moves up one level in the folder tree: to the next higher folder if the active folder is a subfolder, to the folder's disk if the active folder isn't a subfolder, and to My Computer if you're viewing a disk's root directory.	both the Open and Save As dialog boxes.
	Look in Favorites	Makes the Favorites folder the active one. (When you install Microsoft Office, the setup program creates the Favorites folder as a location where you can store frequently used documents.)	both the Open and Save As dialog boxes.
	Add To Favorites	Adds the selected folder or document to your Favorites folder.	the Open dialog box.
	Create New Folder	Displays a dialog box you use to create (and name) a new subfolder in the active folder.	the Save As dialog box.
	List	tells Windows to list just the names of folders and documents.	both the Open and Save As dialog boxes.
	Details	Tells Windows not only to list folder names, but also to describe the documents in more detail by providing information about the file size, type, and last modification date.	both the Open and Save As dialog boxes.
	Properties	Tells Windows to provide document properties information about the selected file: its title, author, creation date, last modification date, number of pages, and so on (if that information is available).	both the Open and Save As dialog boxes.

Table 7.1 Common Save and Open Dialog Box Buttons

Button	Name	Description	Appears In...
	Preview	Tells Windows to display a picture of the first part of the first page of the document (if that's available).	the Open dialog box.
	Commands and Settings	Displays a menu of handy, document-related commands you can use to open a document as read-only, print the selected document, and so on.	both the Open and Save As dialog boxes.

Table 7.1 Common Save and Open Dialog Box Buttons (*continued*)

Creating New Documents

When you want to create a new document, you have several options available. You can start from scratch with a blank slate, or you can take advantage of some of Office's built-in templates to get a head start.

Using the New Document Tool

The easiest way to open a new document—a Word document, Excel workbook, or PowerPoint presentation—is to use the New tool on the Standard toolbar. Just click the button, and the Office application displays a blank document.

Using the File | New Command

Different Office applications display slightly different versions of the New dialog box, but they all work the same basic way.

Choosing the New command on the File menu displays the New dialog box, as shown in Figure 7.2. The New dialog box displays a bunch of different tabs. (Each tab corresponds to a subfolder in the Microsoft Office Templates folder.) And each of these tabs presents one or more templates.

You may recall from Chapter 2 that a template is an Office document that's already partially built. A Word template, for example, might have a lot of formatting already done. An Excel template might have some labels, values, and formulas already entered. A PowerPoint template might have a really snazzy color scheme and design.

To view the templates, click the various tabs.

To use a particular template, double-click it. Office then creates a new document based on the template.

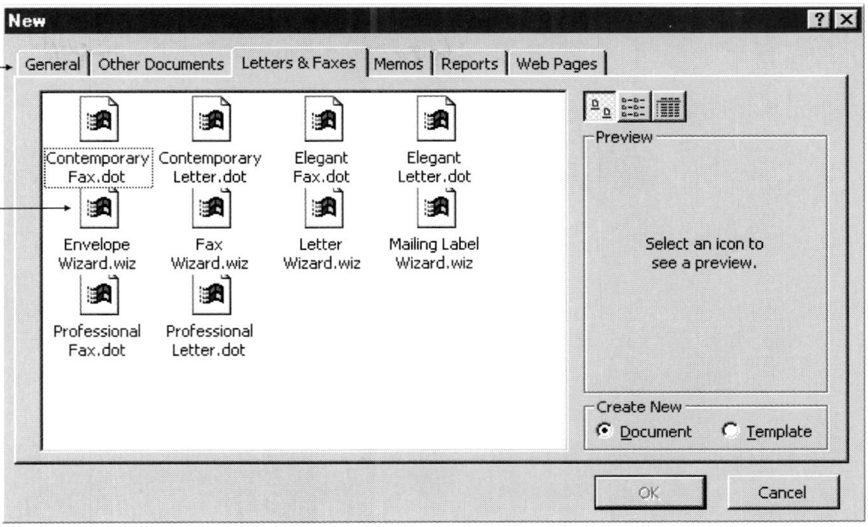

Figure 7.2 Word displays the New dialog box so that you can describe what type of new Word document you want to create

Searching for Lost Documents

Everyone's had this experience at one time or another: you know for sure there's a file somewhere on your hard disk that has the information you need, but you just can't, for the life of you, remember where it is. (Maybe you can't even remember what it's called.) You could try just browsing through your disk in Explorer—and sometimes that will work—but there are much more powerful tools available to you.

Using the Find Feature

Your first line of attack is using the Find options at the bottom of the Open dialog box, under the heading "Find files that match these criteria." To find a file, follow the instructions in the "Search for a Lost File" Step by Step box shown next.

STEP BY STEP Search for a Lost File

3 Select the folder where your file is located (if you know where it is located), using the Look In drop-down list. (You can search your entire disk drive by selecting it in the Look In drop-down list, or even all of the drives on your computer by selecting My Computer.)

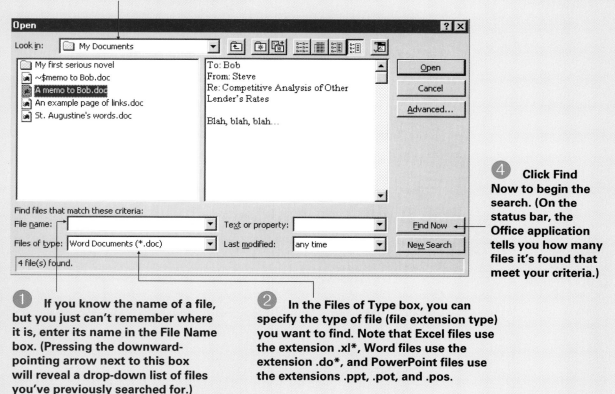

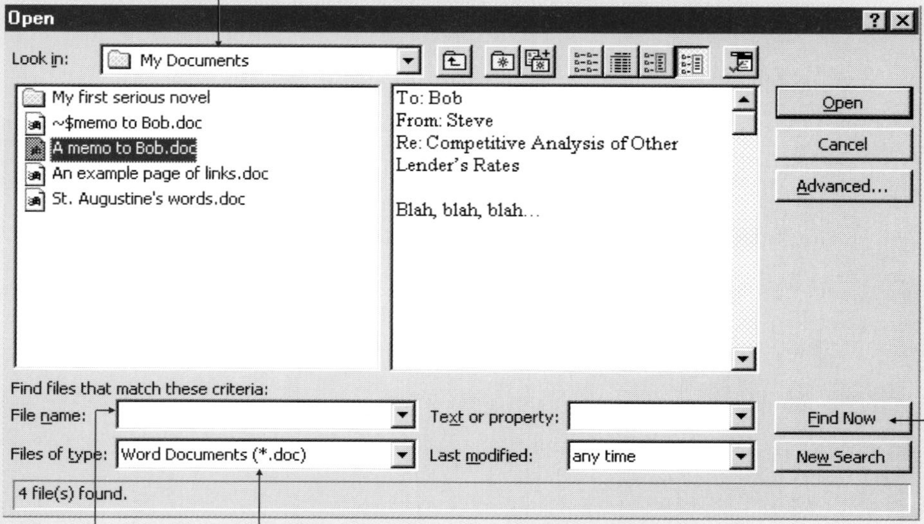

4 Click Find Now to begin the search. (On the status bar, the Office application tells you how many files it's found that meet your criteria.)

1 If you know the name of a file, but you just can't remember where it is, enter its name in the File Name box. (Pressing the downward-pointing arrow next to this box will reveal a drop-down list of files you've previously searched for.)

2 In the Files of Type box, you can specify the type of file (file extension type) you want to find. Note that Excel files use the extension .xl*, Word files use the extension .do*, and PowerPoint files use the extensions .ppt, .pot, and .pos.

Searching for Specific Text or Properties

If you can't remember the name of a file, but you can remember some specific words or text in the name, enter whatever items of text you recall in the Text or Property box. (The drop-down list "remembers" previously searched-for text.) If you know when you last opened and modified the file, enter that information in the Last Modified box. The default is Any Time, but you can click the arrow and select from other time frames, such as Today or Last Month. Click Find Now to start the search. (Click New Search to erase criteria from a previous search and start over.)

Using the Advanced Button

Now it's time to bring out the heavy guns. If you can't find a document using the simpler techniques described in the preceding paragraphs, you can try an Advanced search. To do this, first display the Open dialog box and then click the Advanced button to display the Advanced Find dialog box, as shown in Figure 7.3.

If you know the folder in which your file is located, enter it in the Look In box. Select the Search Subfolders option if you want to widen the scope of your search. (If you do, then use the Details view of file listings in the Open dialog box to pin down exactly where any files the search finds reside.)

You can add more criteria to your search using the Define More Criteria section. The Property list box includes a drop-down list of the document properties

Any search criteria that you already specified in the Open dialog box will be carried over into an Advanced search.

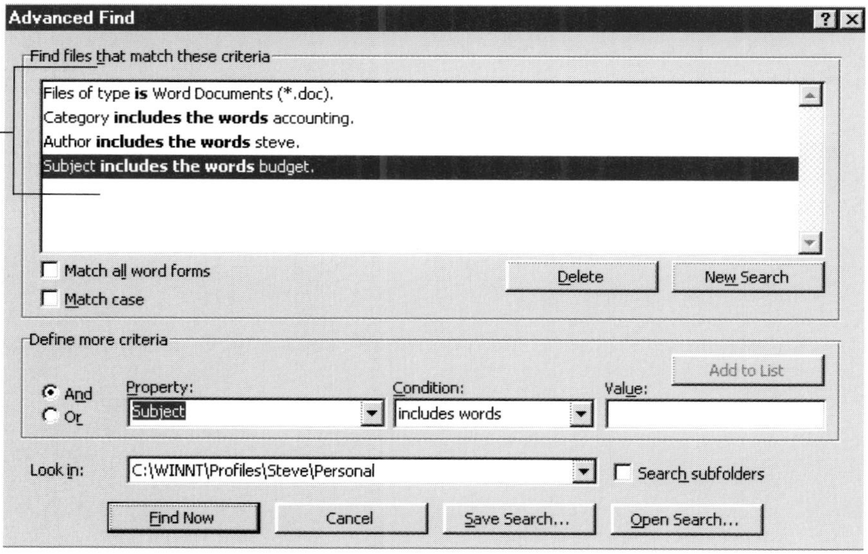

Figure 7.3 Use the Advanced Find dialog box to narrow down a file search

you might have specified using the File | Properties command. For example, using the File | Properties command, you can describe a document as dealing with a subject such as "budget," having an author such as "Steve," or falling into a category such as "accounting."

The Condition box allows you to specify an additional condition to zero in on the property you entered. The listings in the Condition box change depending upon the property you select. For example, conditions that modify the Size property are limited to those that express numerical relationships such as "more than" or "equal."

In the Value box, you can enter either text or numbers to further define the criteria you chose in the Condition and/or Property boxes.

It's Windows 95 or Windows NT that performs the actual search—not the Office application.

Use the And and Or buttons to tell Windows whether each new criteria that you add is in addition to or instead of the previous criteria. Windows will sometimes change And to Or if it finds a contradiction in the criteria you select.

If you want to delete a criterion, select it and click Delete. Clicking New Search clears the entire list box of all criteria, except for the File of Type criterion, which is there by default. You can further define your search using the Match Case option, in which you can specify the case of the letters in the word you seek; and the Match All Word Forms option, which searches for words that merely have some of the same letters as the word you enter in the Value box.

When you have entered all the criteria you want and you are ready to search, click Find Now.

Saving Advanced Search Criteria so You Can Use Them Again

Occasionally, you may need to repeat a search. Using the Save Search and Open Search buttons, you can save and revisit previous searches, saving yourself much time.

To save a search:

1. Click Save Search. The Office application displays the Save Search dialog box.

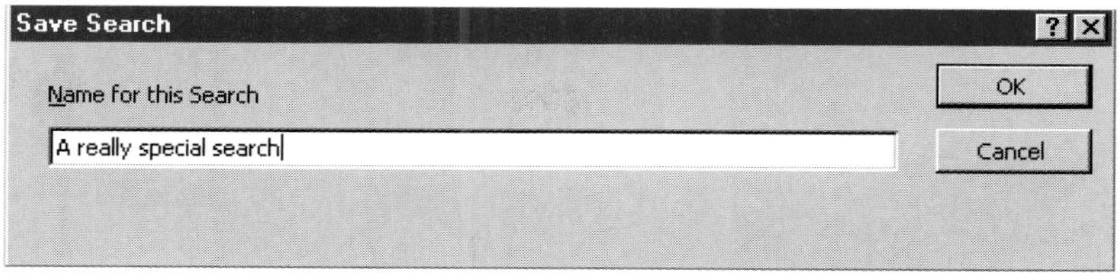

2. Enter a name for the search and click OK.

To open a saved search:

1. Click Open Search to display the Open Search dialog box.

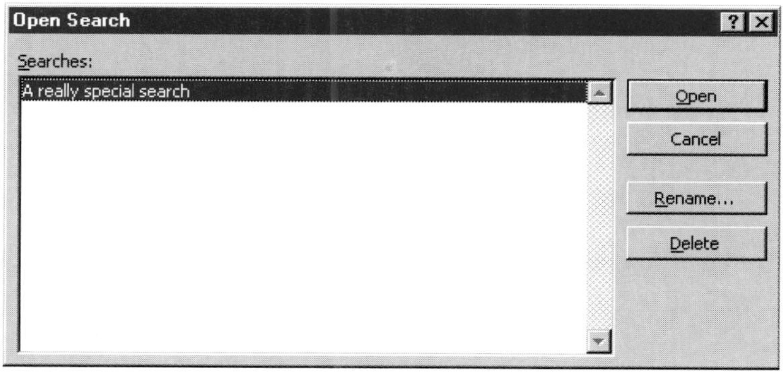

2. Select the search you want and click Open.

You can delete and rename saved searches in this dialog box as well. You can also access saved searches on the Saved Searches submenu of the Commands and Settings menu, which appears when you click the Commands and Settings button in the Open dialog box.

Sharing Files Electronically

One of the neat things about a personal computer, and especially about a personal computer that's connected to a network, is this: it's possible to share your files—your documents—electronically. To make it easier for you to perform this sharing, the File menu on most Office applications provides a Send To command that displays a submenu of commands, as shown here.

I'm not going to go into great detail about any of these commands here. But I do want to just briefly describe what they do—so you'll know what options you have available for sharing:

Chapter 10 explains what Outlook is and how it works.

- The Mail Recipient command starts your e-mail program and creates an e-mail message with the active Office document attached to the message. All you have to do to send the message (and therefore the attached document file) is address the message to the recipient and then transmit the message. (If you use Microsoft Exchange or Microsoft Outlook as your e-mail program, you transmit the message by clicking the Send button.)
- The Routing Recipient command also lets you send an e-mail message, but it gives you more control over how and when the message is transmitted. The Routing Recipient command, for example, lets you create a routing list that your e-mail server software (which runs on a network server someplace—not on your computer) uses to pass an e-mail message about your office.
- The Exchange Folder command lets you post a copy of a document to a folder where it can be viewed by a large number of recipients without your having to route it to each one of them. (Your network needs the Exchange server software to do this.)
- The Fax Recipient command starts the Microsoft Fax Wizard so you can fax a copy of the active document to someone.

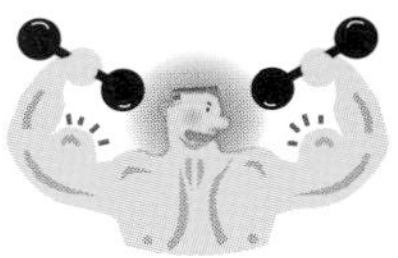

DEFINITIONS

Server: *A network computer that isn't specifically used by one user, but instead runs programs for the benefit of all network users. Some network servers just print documents sent to the server by other, so-called client computers. And some network servers perform the actual work of transmitting e-mail messages over a network.*

Server software: *A program that runs on a network server. Server software typically works in tandem with client software (which runs on users' desktop computers). For example, in the case of an e-mail system, users create and read e-mail messages with client software, but server software does the work of actually delivering messages.*

CHECKPOINT

This chapter describes how you work with the documents that Word, Excel, and PowerPoint create: how you print these documents, save them, later open them, and even share them. Learning how to do this stuff is really essential to your productivity. Fortunately, however, it's also very easy. What's more, once you learn how to print, save, or open a document in Word, you also know how to print, save, and open Excel workbooks and PowerPoint presentations.

While I've alluded to sharing objects between different Office applications—plopping an Excel chart down into a Word document, for example—I still haven't actually described how you create these sorts of compound documents. The next chapter remedies this deficiency by explaining how you share objects among applications and how you use the binder to create compound documents.

CHAPTER

8

Sharing Information

INCLUDES

- Sharing between applications
- Using Microsoft Binder
- Importing and exporting Office documents
- Moving documents between Word and Excel
- Sharing documents with the Apple Macintosh

FAST FORWARD

Embed an Object ➤ pp. 166-167

	A	B
1	Sales	125000
2	Expenses	75000
3	**Profits**	50000

To embed objects, follow these steps:

1. Open the document in which you want to place the shared information.
2. Open the document with the information you want to share.
3. Select the information you want to copy.
4. Press and hold down the CTRL key and then drag the selected information to the document in which you want place the information.

Link an Object ➤ pp. 167-169

To: Alfred
Fr: Buck

Here's the income statement:

Sales	125000
Expenses	75000
Profits	50000

To create linked objects, follow these steps:

1. Open the document in which you want to place the shared information.
2. Open the document with the information you want to share.
3. Select the information you want to copy.
4. Choose the Edit | Copy command from the source document's application window.
5. Place the insertion point in the compound document at the exact location where you want the linked object.
6. Choose the Edit | Paste Special command from the compound document's application window. When the Office application displays the Paste Special dialog box, click the Paste Link button and then OK.

Share New Objects ➤ pp. 169-170

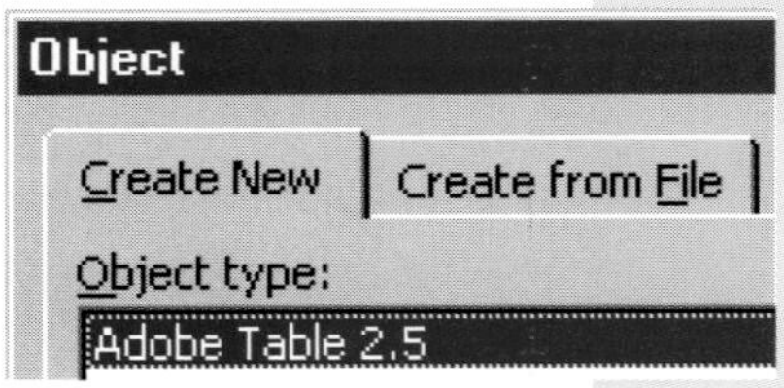

To share a new object:

1. Choose the Insert | Object command.
2. Use the Insert Object dialog box to create the object.
3. Click OK to insert the object in a document.

Use Microsoft Binder ➤ p. 171

Use Microsoft Binder to create compound documents. To start Binder, click the Start button and choose Programs | Microsoft Binder.

Add Sections to a Binder ➤ pp. 172-173

- To add a blank, empty section, choose the Section | Add command.
- To add an existing Office document to the Binder as a section, choose the Section | Add from File command.

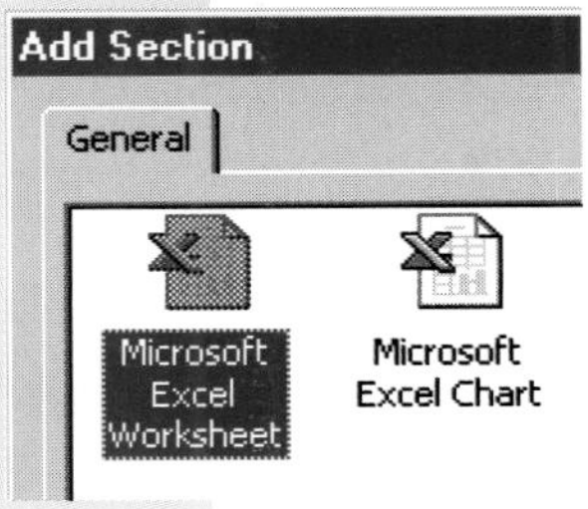

Work with Binder Sections ➤ pp. 173-174

To work with a particular section—remember this is a just an object—simply click the section icon. When you do, Binder replaces its usual menu bar with the menu bar of the server, or section, application.

Save and Open Binders ➤ pp. 174-175

- To save a binder for the first time or to rename an existing binder, choose the File | Save Binder As command.
- To resave a binder, choose the File | Save Binder command.
- To open an existing binder, choose the File | Open Binder command.

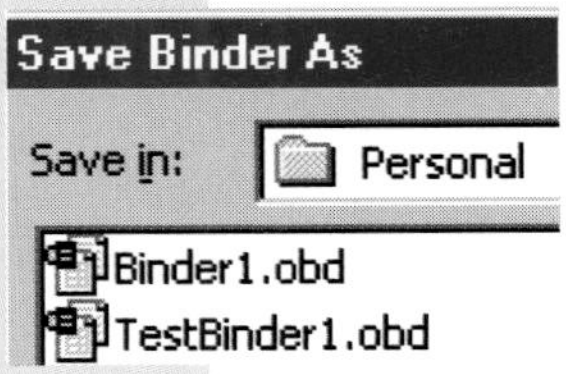

Import Documents ➤ *pp. 176-177*

To import a document into an Office program from another, non-Microsoft program:

1. Select the File | Open command.
2. Use the Files of Type drop-down list to indicate the type of file you're trying to import.

Export Documents ➤ *pp. 177-178*

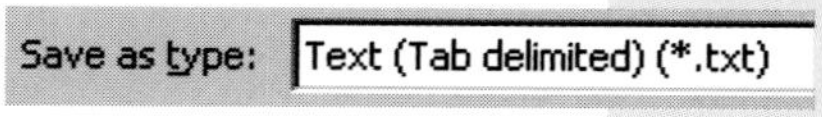

To export a document from an Office program to another, non-Microsoft Program:

1. Select the File | Save As command.
2. Use the Save as Type drop-down list to indicate the type of file you're trying to export.

Share Documents with the Apple Macintosh ➤ *p. 182*

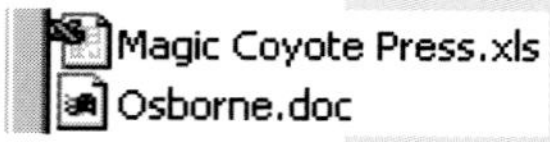

You can transfer Microsoft Office files between PCs and Macintosh computers running Office simply by saving the Office document in a format that the other version of Microsoft Office understands—and by using a 3.5-inch floppy disk formatted by Windows or MS-DOS.

Microsoft Office makes it easy to share information between applications. You can create objects—basically just chunks of Office documents—and then use those objects in other documents, even those created with other applications. For example, you can place Excel workbooks in Word documents and Excel charts in PowerPoint presentations. These documents are referred to as compound documents. You can also easily import and export documents to and from other, non-Microsoft Office applications. For example, you can share Word documents with co-workers or friends who use WordPerfect—and vice versa. And you can easily move workbooks between Excel and, say, Lotus 1-2-3. This chapter explains how you share information in these ways.

DEFINITION

Compound document: *A document, workbook, or presentation that includes objects you've created in other applications—for example, a Word document that includes a chunk of some Excel worksheet.*

Sharing Objects Between Applications

I could spend a lot of time explaining all sorts of fancy-schmancy ways you can share objects between applications. (An object is just a document chunk—Excel workbook selections and charts, parts of Word documents, and PowerPoint slides—that you copy or move between documents.) But let's minimize your reading and head-scratching. What I'll do here is strip away all the clutter that writers usually use to describe how this stuff works—and just cut to the chase.

Embedding an Object

When you embed an object, you make a copy of the object and then plop the object into some other document. The procedure is described in the following "Embed an Object" Step by Step box.

STEP BY STEP Embed an Object

1 Open the document in which you want to place the shared information.

2 Open the document with the information you want to share. (You may want to arrange the two document windows so that both are visible on your screen.)

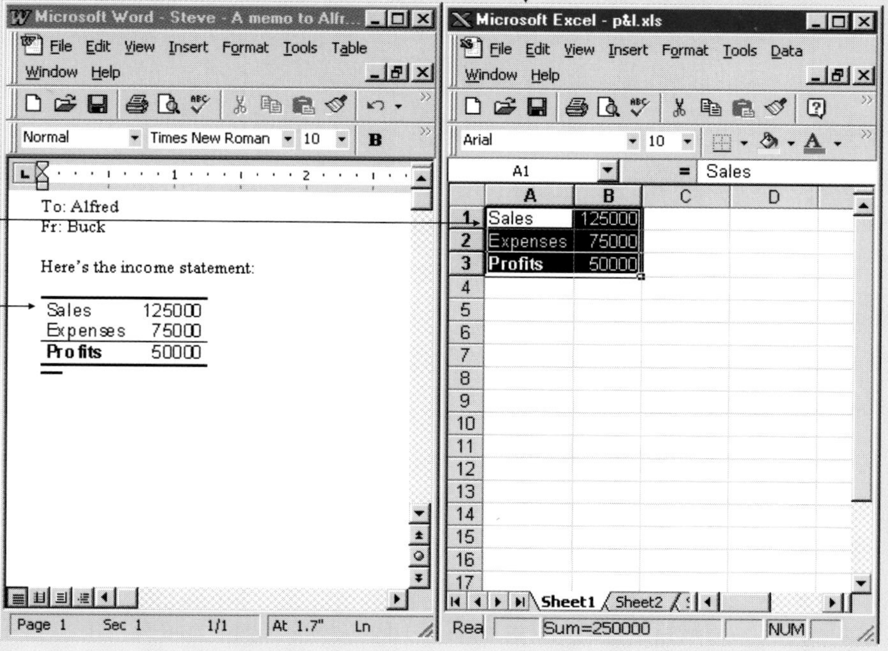

3 Select the information you want to copy. (You can probably do this either by clicking or by clicking and dragging.)

4 Press and hold down the CTRL key and then drag the selected information to the document in which you want to place the information. Release the mouse button when the mouse pointer rests at the exact location where you want the selected information placed.

You now know how to share information between documents and even between applications. Pretty neat, right? No, really. Think about it for a minute. You can easily drag a worksheet range or chart from an Excel document window to a Word document or PowerPoint presentation if you want to use a nicely formatted table or slick-looking chart. And you can use, for example, PowerPoint slides in Word documents and Excel workbooks.

EXPERT ADVICE

If you want to move the selected object from the source document to the compound document—rather than simply copy it as I've described here—don't hold down the CTRL key in step 4.

Linking an Object

When you link an object, you also make a copy of the object and then plop the object into some other document—but the copied object stays *linked* to the source document. By default, all links are "automatic" when they are created, meaning that Windows automatically updates the copied object (stored in the compound document) when you make changes to the source document. The "Link an Object" Step by Step box shown next provides the instructions for you to follow.

Embedding versus Linking

Okay, now that you understand what embedding is and what linking is, let me give you a bit of information you can use to choose between the two techniques.

The advantage of an embedded object—as compared to a linked object—is that the new, compound document you create has all your information. If you

STEP BY STEP Link an Object

1. Open the document in which you want to place the shared information.

2. Open the document with the information you want to share.

3. Select the information you want to copy, then choose the Edit | Copy command from the source document's application window.

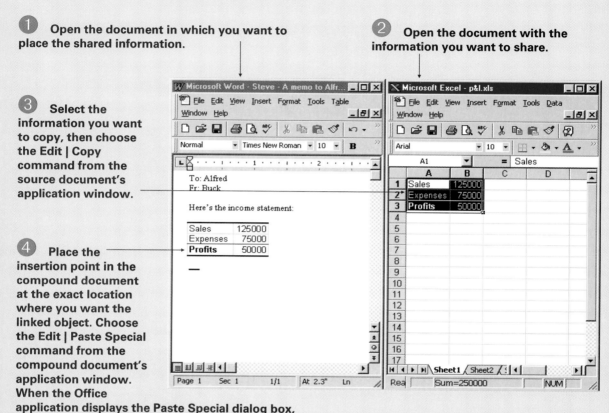

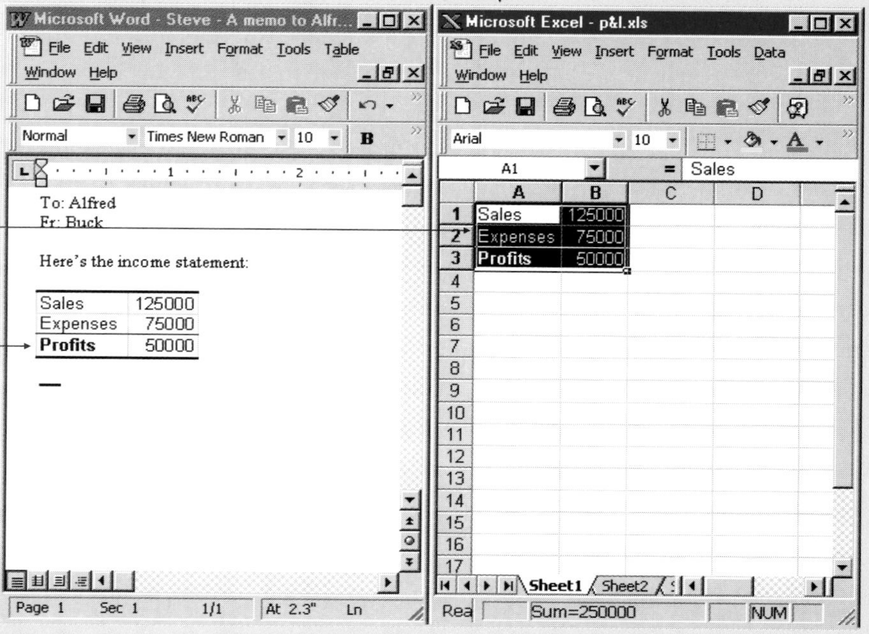

4. Place the insertion point in the compound document at the exact location where you want the linked object. Choose the Edit | Paste Special command from the compound document's application window. When the Office application displays the Paste Special dialog box, click the Paste Link button and then click OK.

have any updates to make, you only have to enter them into this one document. The disadvantage of embedded objects is that embedded objects make your compound documents big. Sometimes really big.

The advantage of a linked object—as compared to an embedded object—is that the compound document is smaller in size, and linked objects can come from source documents you share with lots of other people. The disadvantage of linked objects is that if you want to make changes to the linked object in the compound document, you need to have the source document handy. For this reason, for example, you can't just grab a copy of the compound document and take it home for a weekend of work. You need to remember to grab all of the source documents, too.

Sharing New Objects

The sharing methods I've just described work well when the object you want to embed or link already exists. But what if you need to create the object? Office makes it easy by providing you a menu of objects to choose from. Here's how you do it:

1. Choose the Insert | Object command. The Office application will display the Object dialog box, shown here, which lists various possible types of embeddable objects available on your computer. (The types of objects you can embed depend on which programs you have installed.)

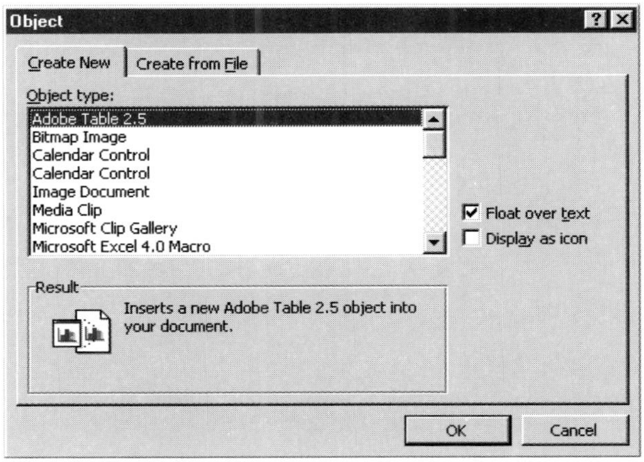

2. Select the type of object you want to embed. The Office application you're working with will open the appropriate application to enable you to create that object.

3. Click OK in the dialog box and then create the object you want to embed.
4. When you've created the object you want, choose Update on the File menu to return you to the compound document.

EXPERT ADVICE

To edit an embedded object, just double-click it. Windows opens up the application you used to create the object, and you can use it to make your changes.

Understanding OLE or ActiveX

I think that Microsoft renamed their newest version of OLE "ActiveX" for marketing reasons related to their Internet strategy.

Now that you know how to embed and link existing objects and how to create new objects, let me quickly point out one more thing. To perform all of this object sharing, Microsoft Office applications support a feature that used to be called OLE (OLE stood for object linking and embedding) and that is now called ActiveX. To share objects, the applications that you're moving objects between need to be OLE-aware, or ActiveX-aware, applications. Does that make sense? Good.

Okay, here's the next thing you'll benefit by knowing. The application program in which you create the source document is called the *server*, and the application program in which you create the compound document is called the *client*. So if you embed data from an Excel worksheet range into a PowerPoint presentation—perhaps to use as a table in a slide—Excel is the server, or server application, and PowerPoint is the client, or client application.

Here's why understanding this stuff is important. Not all of the programs and tools in Microsoft Office work as both server applications and client applications:

- Word, Excel, PowerPoint, and Outlook can function as both server and client applications. This means, basically, that you can use Word, Excel, and PowerPoint objects in compound documents and that Word, Excel, and PowerPoint will all create compound documents.

- Access functions only as a client application. This means you can use Access to create a compound document—sort of—but that you can't place Access objects into other compound documents.
- Finally, most of the Office tools (the Drawing tool, WordArt tool, Graph tool, and Organization Chart tool) function only as server applications. This means you can plop Drawing, WordArt, Graph, and Organization Chart objects into compound documents but that you can't use these applications to create compound documents.

Using Microsoft Binder

You start Binder the same way you start other Office applications. For example, you can click the Start button and then choose Programs | Microsoft Binder.

Now that you understand what compound documents are, you have the basic knowledge required to use the Microsoft Binder, a tool for creating compound Office documents. When you first start Binder, it displays the window shown in Figure 8.1.

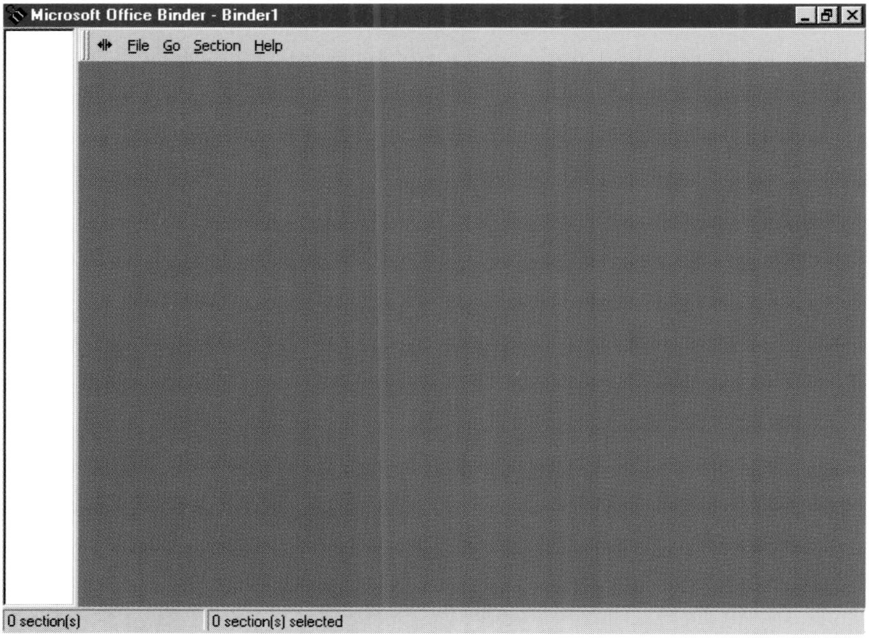

Figure 8.1 The first window of Microsoft Binder, a tool for creating compound documents

Adding Sections to a Binder

To create your compound document, you need to add sections. Each section corresponds to an object. To add a blank, empty section:

1. Choose the Section | Add command and Binder displays the Add Section dialog box.

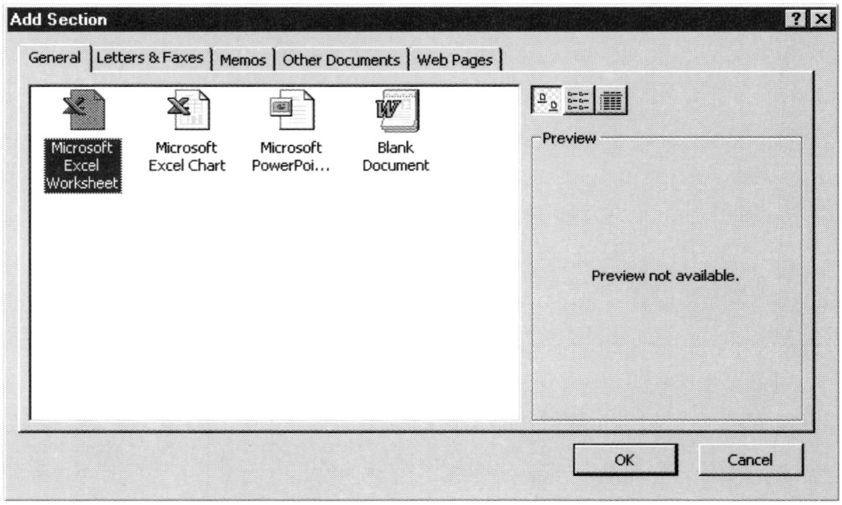

2. Click the tab that provides the document template you want to use for the section. Alternatively, click the General tab to just use a blank Excel Chart or Workbook, Word document, or PowerPoint presentation.
3. Double-click the document you want to use for the section. Binder adds a new section to the binder.

If you want to add an existing Office document to the binder as a section:

1. Choose the Section | Add From File command and Binder displays the Add From File dialog box, shown here.

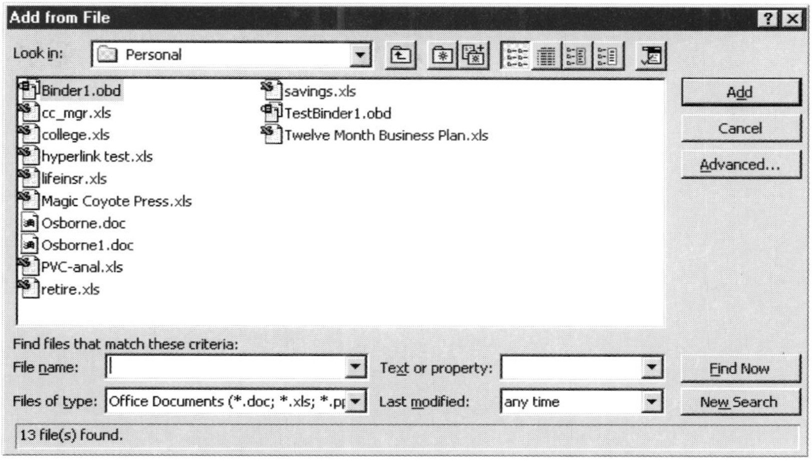

2. Specify the location of the document using the Look In drop-down list.
3. When you see the document name in the list, double-click it. Binder plops the document into the binder as a new section.

SHORTCUT

If you erroneously add a section to a binder, select the section and then press the DELETE key or choose the Section | Delete command.

Once you've added a section to the binder, Binder adds an icon for the section to the Section bar, as shown in Figure 8.2.

Working with Binder Sections

Actually, Binder refers to server applications as section applications, but why complicate matters here?

To work with a particular section—remember this is just an object—simply click the section icon. When you do, Binder replaces its usual menu bar with the menu bar of the server application. (Recall that the server application is the one that supplies, or originally creates, the object and is the one you use to make changes to the object.) At this point, you work with the object or section in the usual way. You work with Word sections, for example, in the same manner as you

The Section bar (with Excel workbook and Word document sections)

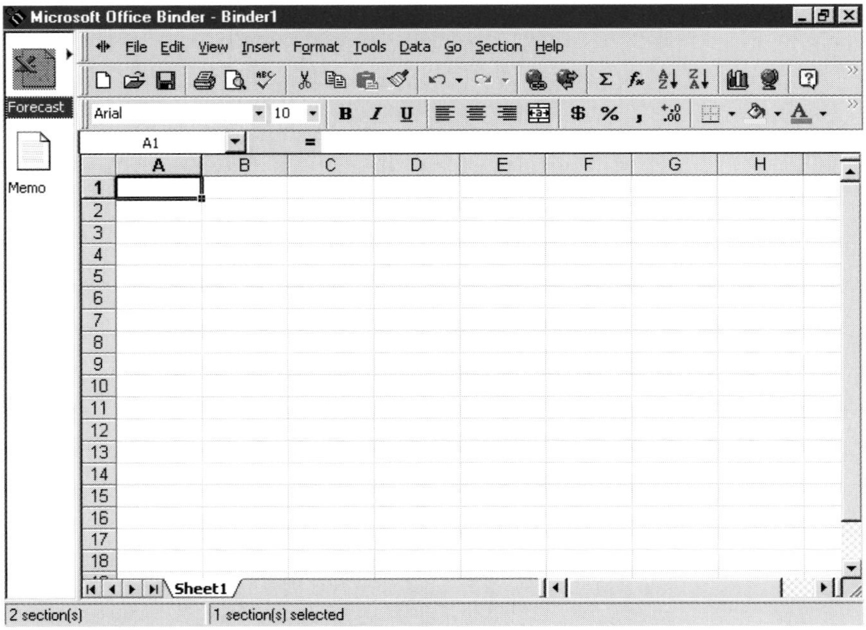

Figure 8.2 The Binder window after a couple of sections have been added

work with regular Word documents. You work with Excel sections in the same manner as you work with regular Excel workbooks.

Saving and Opening Binders

You save and open binders in a fashion very similar to that used for saving and opening Office documents. To save a binder for the first time or to rename an existing binder, choose the File | Save Binder As command. You provide the filename and location in the Save Binder As dialog box, shown in Figure 8.3, that is displayed.

SHORTCUT

You can rename a section by clicking the section name (in the Section bar) and then typing your new, replacement name.

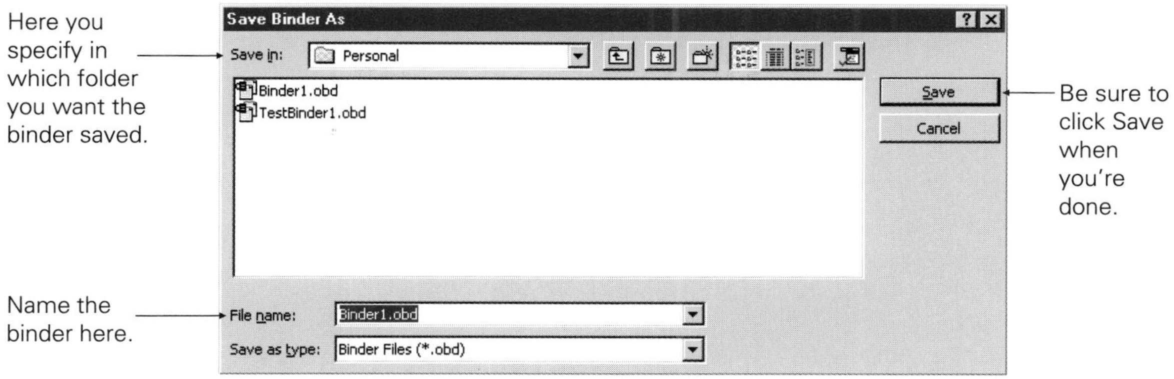

Figure 8.3 Saving a binder

To save a binder subsequent times, choose the File | Save Binder command or click the Save toolbar button.

To open a binder, choose the File | Open command or click the Open toolbar button. You provide the filename and location in the Open Binder dialog box, shown in Figure 8.4, that is displayed.

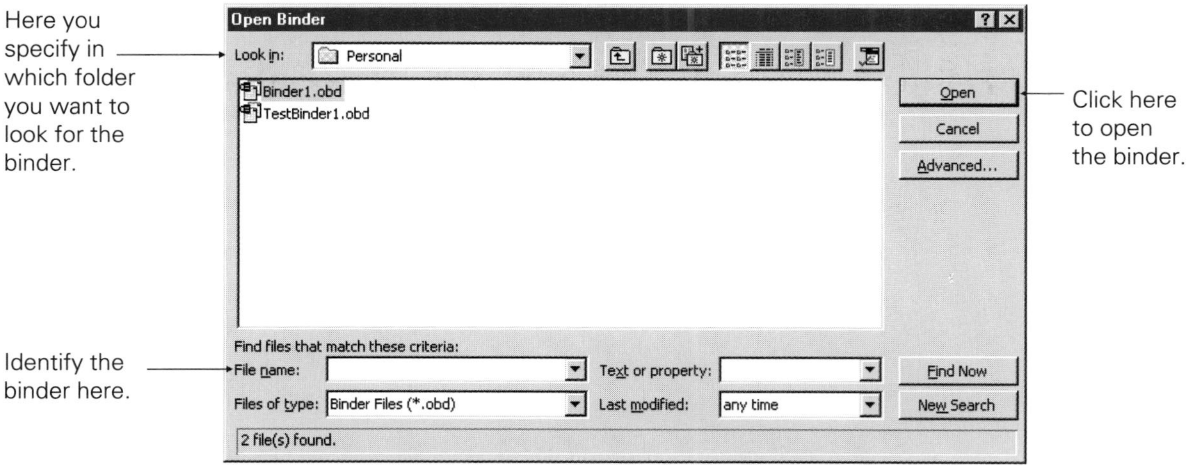

Figure 8.4 Opening a binder

Printing Binders

To print a binder—which really means printing each of the document objects, or sections, within the binder—choose the File | Print Binder command or click the Print toolbar button. If you choose the File | Print Binder command, Binder displays the Print Binder dialog box, shown in Figure 8.5. You can use it to specify which sections are printed (the default is for all sections to be printed) and how they are printed.

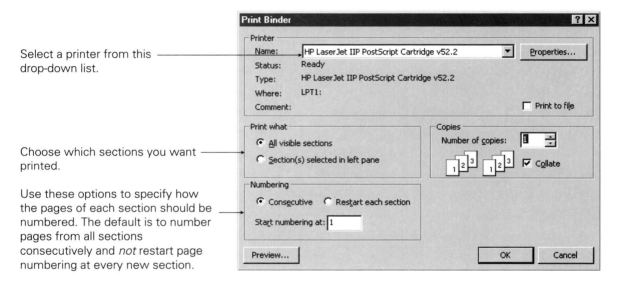

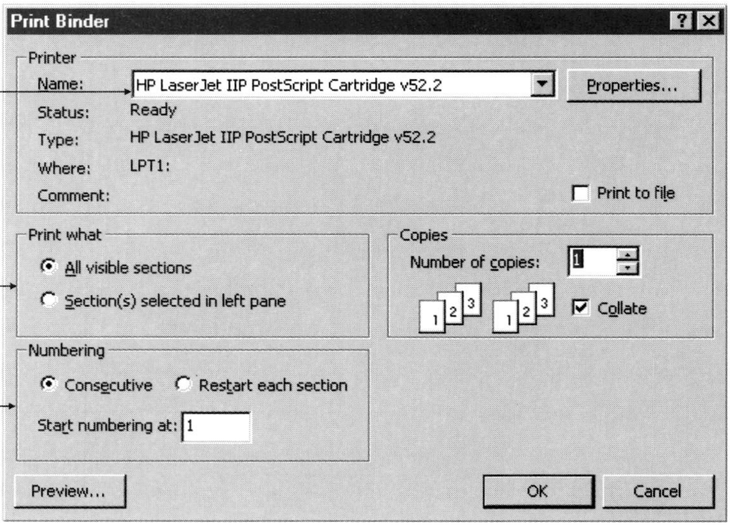

Figure 8.5 Printing a binder

Importing and Exporting Office Documents

Another one of the great things that Microsoft Office has going for it is the ease with which it allows sharing of documents with other vendors' programs. Both Word and Excel, for example, include file format converters for many popular competing products. You can, therefore, easily move Microsoft Office documents between Microsoft programs (such as Word and Excel) and other competing products (such as WordPerfect and Lotus 1-2-3).

Importing and exporting documents in Office is easy because you do it with the help of two old friends: the File | Open and File | Save As commands and their associated dialog boxes. We covered these in Chapter 6, so I'll briefly review here the procedures for using these commands.

Importing with the File | Open Command

To import a document from another, non-Microsoft program, first start the equivalent Microsoft Office program. (If you're trying to import a WordPerfect document, for example, you start Word. If you're trying to import a Lotus 1-2-3 workbook, you start Excel.) Then follow these steps:

1. Click the Open button on the Standard toolbar or choose Open on the File menu.
2. Enter the name of the workbook, document, or presentation file in the File Name box. If you don't remember the file's exact name, you can browse your hard disk using the Look In box and Up One Level button, or you can search for it using the Find Now and Advanced buttons.
3. Narrow your search by selecting the appropriate file extension in the Files of Type drop-down list. Click the downward-pointing arrow to display a list of file types that the Office application recognizes and select the one that matches your file.
4. Once you locate the file you want, click Open, and the Office application opens it for you.

For more information about how the File | Open command works, refer to Chapter 6.

Exporting Files with the File | Save As Command

To save a Microsoft Office document so it can be used by a non-Microsoft Office program, first open the document you want to export. Then, once you've done this, follow these steps:

1. Choose the File | Save As command to open the Save As dialog box.

2. Click the downward-pointing arrow next to the Save as Type box and scroll through the list of file types to find the one you want; then select it.
3. In the File name text box, enter the name under which you want to save the file.
4. Open the file in the other application. (The other application may need to convert the file.)

For more information about how the File | Save As command works, refer to Chapter 6.

Moving Documents Between Word and Excel

You can rather easily move documents between Word and Excel by first converting into a text file any document you want to move. I know this may sound like something you would never want to do, but here's what I'm thinking. Maybe you've always known Word pretty well and, because of that knowledge, you've used Word to create documents that really would work better as Excel workbooks. Or maybe the reverse is true: maybe you've used Excel to create workbooks that should really be Word documents. And now that you know all of the Office applications quite a bit better (I'm assuming you've actually read some of the preceding chapters), maybe you're wondering whether you can transform an Excel workbook into a Word document, or vice versa. Fortunately, the answer is "Yes."

Converting an Excel Worksheet to a Word Document

The process to convert an Excel worksheet to a Word document is threefold: save the Excel worksheet as a text file, open the text file in Word, then save as a Word document. Here's the nitty-gritty.

1. Save the Excel worksheet in the usual way, but with one minor twist: activate the Save Files as Type drop-down list and select the Text (Tab delimited)(*.txt) entry, as shown here. This saves the active worksheet as a text file.

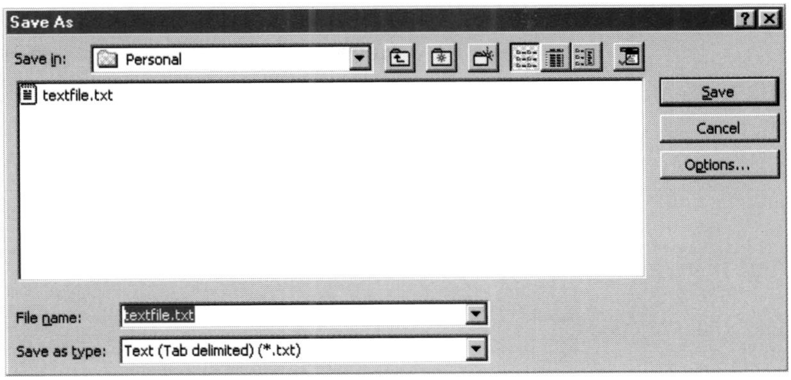

EXPERT ADVICE

When you save a worksheet, you'll actually be creating a text file that is equivalent to the Excel worksheet. The new text file won't be a worksheet any more, so you won't be able to use it for calculating and recalculating formulas. However, it will be a text document that you can easily work with in Word.

2. Once you've created a text file using Excel, close the file in Excel and then open it using Word. To do this, start Word, choose the File | Open command, specify the file name (including the .txt extension) and location using the Open dialog box's boxes and buttons, shown here, and click Open.

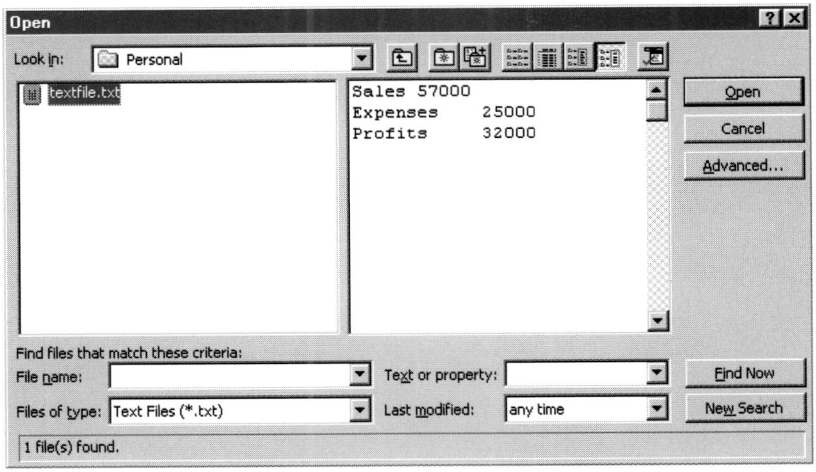

Once you've opened a text file using Word, make whatever changes you want. (Perhaps you want to add formatting, for example.) If you converted more than one worksheet from Excel so that you have more than one text file, you might want to combine the text files into one Word document by cutting and pasting. Then save the text file as a regular Word document.

Converting a Word Document to an Excel Workbook

The beginning of this process is similar to Excel to Word, as described earlier. But there are a few more steps needed at the end:

1. Save the Word document in the usual way with one minor difference: activate the Save Files as Type drop-down list and select the Text Only[*.txt] entry.
2. After you've created a text file using Word, close the file in Word and then open it using Excel. To do this, start Excel, choose the File | Open command, and then specify the file name, type, and location using the Open dialog box's boxes and buttons.
3. Excel next displays the Text Import Wizard - Step 1 of 3 dialog box, shown here. In the Original Data Type section, select the option that describes your data.

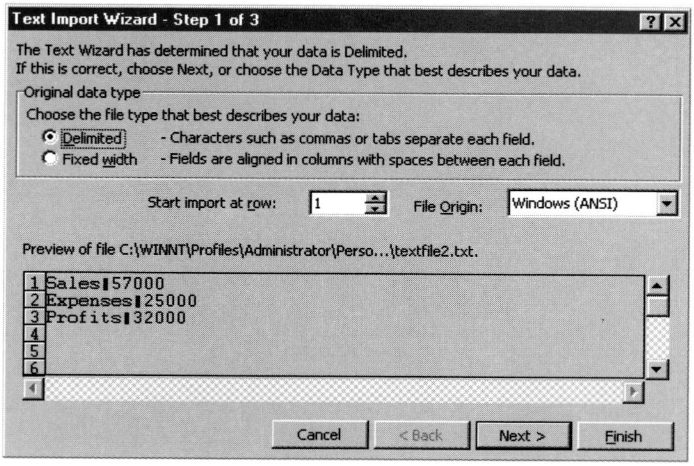

4. Click Next, and Excel will display the Step 2 dialog box. Check to make sure the Wizard's choice of delimiters is correct.

Use the Data Preview area to confirm that Excel understands how you've delimited, or organized, your data into columns.

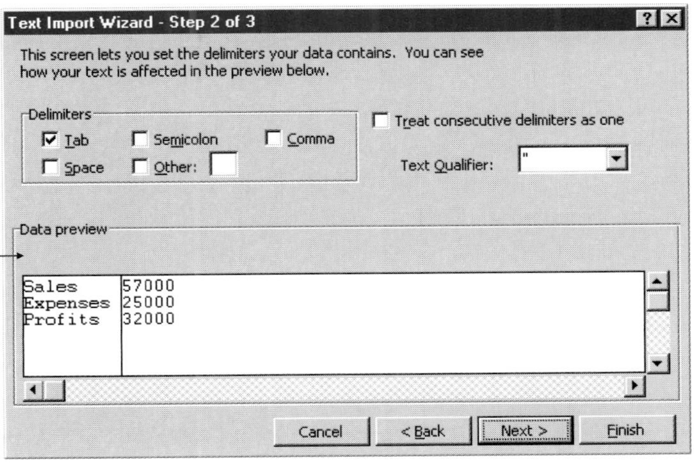

5. Click Next to display the Step 3 dialog box. Choose the formatting you want for each data column and click Finish. The Wizard will import your data into Excel.

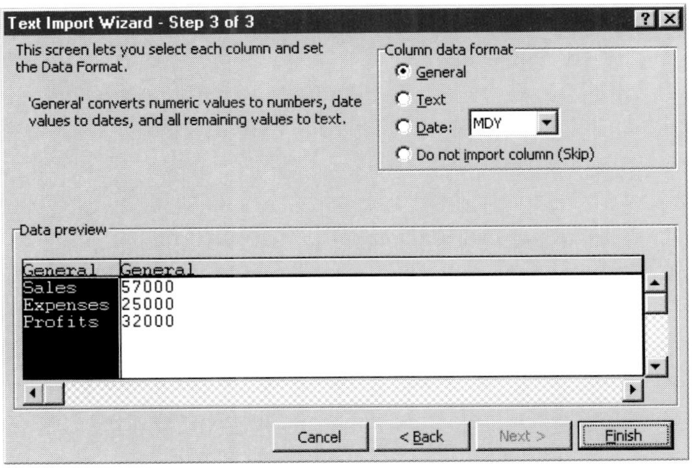

EXPERT ADVICE

Excel also imports text files created by applications other than Word. For example, you can import a text file created by an accounting system.

Sharing Documents with the Apple Macintosh

Microsoft Office 97 for Windows applications are highly compatible with their older cousin, Microsoft Office for the Macintosh. You can transfer Microsoft Office files between PCs and Macintosh computers simply by saving the Office document in the format of your other version of Microsoft Office. Once you've done this, you can copy the document to a 3.5-inch floppy disk formatted by Windows or MS-DOS. (The Apple Macintosh can both read and write to floppy disks formatted by Windows or MS-DOS.) To open the Office document on the "other" computer, start the appropriate Office program and then issue the File | Open command in the usual way.

This chapter describes how you share the information that you create or want to manipulate using the Microsoft Office applications: how to share information between applications, how to use Microsoft Binder to create compound documents, how to import and export Office documents, and how to move Excel workbooks to Word and Word documents to Excel. Fortunately, none of this sharing is difficult. And the ease with which it's possible to share information means that you should be able to work with your information in exactly the way you want.

With the newest version of Office, you aren't limited to the very local, rather provincial sharing described in this chapter. You can also share information using the Internet. Chapter 9 describes how you do this.

CHAPTER

9 Office and the Internet

INCLUDES

- Understanding what the Internet and World Wide Web are
- Using hyperlinks in Office documents
- Understanding what uniform resource locators (URLs) are
- Publishing web documents with Office
- Using an Internet search service

FAST FORWARD

What Is the Internet? ➤ pp. 186-187

The Internet is a network of networks. Using the Internet, people can easily share information (such as messages and files) and hardware (such as storage disks and printers).

What Is the World Wide Web? ➤ pp. 187-189

The World Wide Web is a simply a collection of multimedia documents connected with hyperlinks.

Use Hyperlinks in Office Documents ➤ pp. 189-195

You can insert a hyperlink in an Office document by choosing the Insert | Hyperlink command. If you click the hyperlink, you move to the web page described by the hyperlink.

What Are Uniform Resource Locators? ➤ pp. 190-192

The uniform resource locator, or URL, is the address of an Internet resource—such as a web server or web page. There are three parts to the URL, or address:

- The service name
- The server name
- The document, or file, name

Create HTML Documents in Word ➤ pp. 196-199

To create an HTML document in Word:

1. Start from one of the Word Web Design templates. This tells Word to create a fill-in-the-blanks HTML document already formatted to appear a certain way.
2. After you finish the HTML document, use the File | Save As command to save it to your disk.

Create HTML Documents in PowerPoint ➤ *pp. 199-200*

To create HTML documents with PowerPoint:

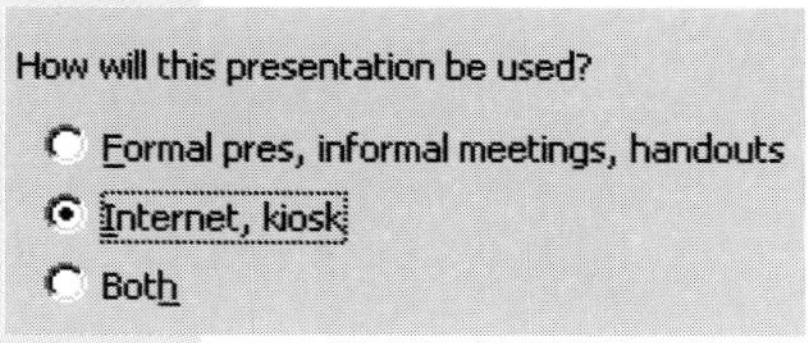

1. Tell the AutoContent Wizard that you're creating a presentation for use as a set of web pages.
2. When you finish creating the HTML document using PowerPoint (say by adding text, hyperlinks, and graphic objects), save the HTML document using the File | Save As command.

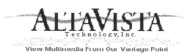

Use Internet Search Services to Find Content ➤ *pp. 200-202*

If you're looking for specific content on the Internet, use AltaVista search service, or a similar search service, by following these steps:

1. Start your web browser, enter the search service URL into the Address box, and press ENTER to connect to the search service.
2. Enter the word or phrase that best describes the content you're looking for.

Many of the neatest new features in Office 97 relate to the Internet. For this reason, I wanted to clump all of this information together in one chapter, where it will stand out. I'll start off by reviewing what the Internet is and what the World Wide Web is. (Experienced Internet users can skip this discussion.) Next I'll explain what hyperlinks are, how you use them, and why you create them. Then I'll explain how you browse the World Wide Web from within Microsoft Office applications. After that, I'll explain how you can use Microsoft Word and Microsoft PowerPoint to publish web documents. Finally, at the end of the chapter, I'll describe (ever so briefly) how to use a search service to find stuff on the Internet.

Understanding What the Internet Is

Let's start this discussion by defining what the Internet is. Actually, it isn't all that special. It's just a bunch of computers—thousands and thousands of them—that are connected together. By connecting computers together, people can easily share information (such as messages and files) and hardware (such as storage disks and printers). You can easily send information to other computers (such as those your friends have at home), for example, and you can easily retrieve information from many of the computers that make up Internet's networks.

The neat feature of the Internet, therefore, isn't the technology. It's the information: articles on just about any subject, pictures of anything you'd want look at (and many that you wouldn't want to look at), useful programs and utilities, and a lot of other stuff as well.

Understanding What the World Wide Web Is

The Internet provides a bunch of different ways, or "services," for sharing information. For example, electronic mail, or e-mail, is one way, or service, to share information. But the most popular and talked-about way to share information is the World Wide Web. In a nutshell, the World Wide Web is simply a collection of multimedia documents connected by hyperlinks. You may already know what this means, but let me quickly define these three terms—documents, multimedia, and hyperlinks—to make sure we (you and I) work from a common set of definitions.

A *document* is just, well, a document—such as a Word document, an Excel workbook, or even a PowerPoint presentation. Most documents you create by hand use words and numbers to communicate their information, but if you use a computer to create a document, you aren't limited to a single medium, or method, of communication. You can create documents (and you know this if you've read the preceding chapters) that use words and numbers, pictures, sounds (such as music), animation, and anything else you can store as a file on a computer. In other words, you can create *multimedia* documents—documents that use multiple mediums, or methods, of communication.

A *hyperlink* is just a piece of text or a picture in one of these multimedia documents that, when clicked on, moves you to another multimedia document. Once there, you'll almost always see other hyperlinks. By clicking these, you can move to still other multimedia documents. Figure 9.1 shows the web page for Microsoft Corporation. As you can see, it contains text and pictures.

DEFINITION

Web pages: *The multimedia documents—documents that use multiple mediums, or methods, of communication—that make up the World Wide Web.*

What isn't so apparent upon first examination is that if you click many of the text chunks and any of the labeled pictures on Microsoft Corporation's web page, you move to other web pages. For example, if you click the MSNBC hyperlink, you see the new web page shown in Figure 9.2.

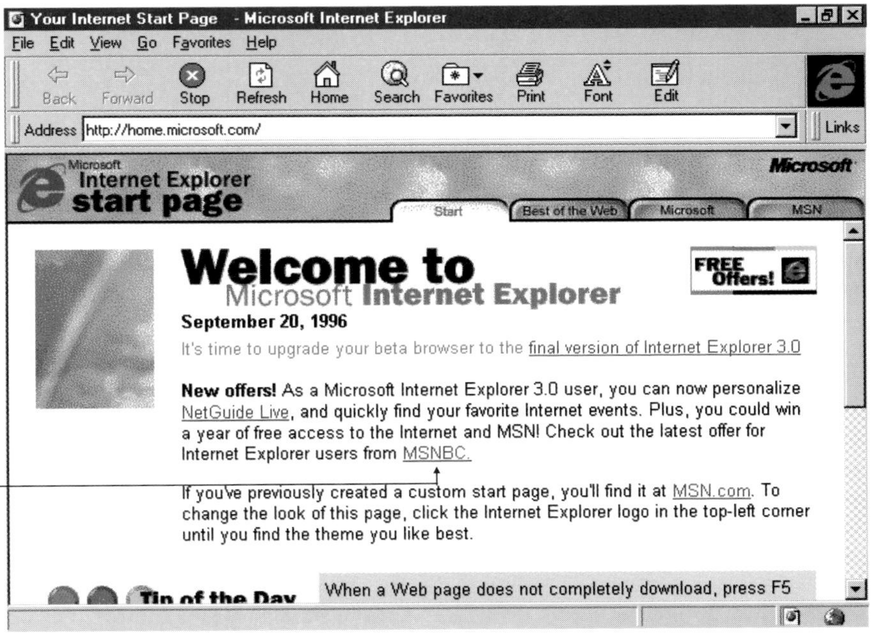

Figure 9.1 The web page for Microsoft Corporation has hyperlinks to other web pages describing the Microsoft Corporation and its products

This picture is also a clickable hyperlink.

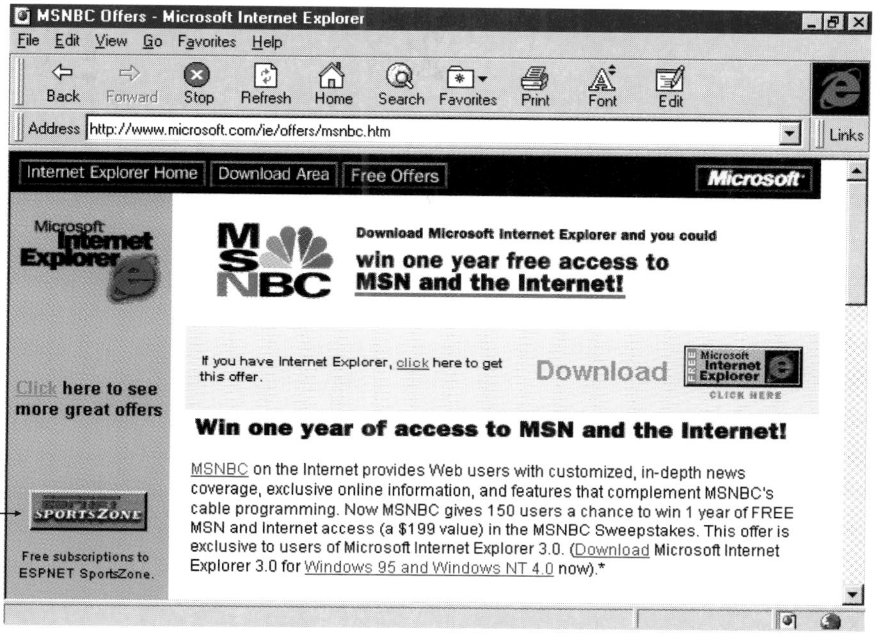

Figure 9.2 The MSNBC web page provides clickable hyperlinks to yet other web pages

Boiled down to its essence, then, the World Wide Web is just a collection of multimedia documents connected together with clickable hyperlinks.

EXPERT ADVICE

You can move backward and forward to previously viewed web pages by clicking the Back and Forward buttons, which appear on the Internet Explorer toolbar.

Using Hyperlinks in Office Documents

Now that you know a bit about the Internet and, in particular, about the World Wide Web, you might be interested to know that you can insert hyperlinks in Office documents. For example, you can insert a hyperlink in a Word document. These hyperlinks work the way I explained in the preceding paragraphs. If you click the hyperlink, you move to the web page described by the hyperlink.

Understanding What Uniform Resource Locators Are

You've already encountered uniform resource locators if you've looked carefully at Figures 9.1 or 9.2 or browsed the World Wide Web even a little bit. The uniform resource locator, or URL, is the address of a web server or web page, and it appears in the Address box at the top of the Internet Explorer window.

CAUTION

A URL never ends with a period or comma, so if you see a URL in this book (or anywhere else) that looks like it ends with period, don't include it. The period is only there to punctuate the sentence.

There are three parts to the URL, or address:

- The service name
- The server name
- The document, or file, name

Other services use different service names. For example, the file transfer protocol— a service that lets you move files between Internet networks—uses the prefix ftp://.

For example, in Figure 9.2, the first chunk of the URL, *http://*, identifies the service as hypertext transfer protocol. The hypertext transfer protocol—http—is the service that the Internet uses to share information across the World Wide Web.

The second part of URL names the server—in this case, a web server. In the case of a web server, this part of the URL starts with the three letters *www* and then is followed by the name of the domain, or computer network, of which the web server is a part. For example, in Figures 9.1 and 9.2, which show the Microsoft web server's home page, the web server's name is *www.microsoft.com*, which means the domain name is *microsoft.com*.

You can identify the type of organization that operates a domain by looking at the domain suffix. Here's a table to provide a quick summary (these are just general rules—and you can find exceptions to most of them—but they do give you a general idea about who operates a particular web server):

Suffix	Indicates That the Domain Is...
com	a commercial network operated by a business.
gov	operated by the government.
edu	operated by a school or university.
mil	operated by the military.
org	operated by a nonprofit organization.
net	operated by an administrative network connecting other networks.

The last part of the URL names the actual web page and identifies its location on the web server. In Figure 9.2, for example, the web page location and name is */ie/offers/msnbc.htm.* The */ie/offers/* part identifies the web server directory holding the web page. The *msnbc.htm* part names the web page. By the way, if you don't specify a web page in your URL, the web server typically loads the default web page for that web site, which is often referred to as a *home page.* (This page frequently is named *index.htm* or *welcome.htm.*)

Web page names always end either with html or htm. HTML is an acronym that stands for hypertext markup language. HTML is what people use to create Web pages. (Later in this chapter I describe how you can create HTML documents using Microsoft Word or Microsoft PowerPoint.)

SHORTCUT

If you know a web page's URL, you can type it directly into the Address box. What's more, although you can start the URL with the http:// acronym, you don't have to. If you leave it out, your web browser adds it for you.

Once you understand how URLs work, it's usually easy to remember them. Take a look at the following URLs, which I gleaned from a couple of computer magazines I was reading just last night:

http://www.microsoft.com
http://www.apple.com
http://www.ibm.com

Do you see the repetition? They all start the same way—with *http://www.* And they also all end the same way—with the *com* domain name suffix—because these are all commercial web servers. So really, all you need to remember when you see a URL that you want to remember or later visit is the part of the URL that's between the *http://www.* part and the *.com* part.

Once you know how URLs are constructed, you can often guess what the URL for a site is. For example, if you wanted to browse Compaq Computer's web server, you might be able to guess that the web server's URL is *http://www.compaq.com.* If you wanted to browse Toshiba's web server, you might correctly guess that the web server's URL is *http://www.toshiba.com.*

Using the Insert Hyperlink Tool

Chapter 10 describes Microsoft Outlook.

Hyperlinks may seem like a crazy idea, but by adding them to an Office document, you connect the document to the Internet and its information—and that can be pretty neat. A Word document or an Outlook e-mail message that describes, for example, how you handle employee business expenses might contain a hyperlink to the Internal Revenue Service web document that describes the deductibility of employee business expenses. (See Figure 9.3)

Fortunately, once you understand what URLs are and how they're constructed, it's painless to create hyperlinks.

1. Select the picture, text chunk, or worksheet range that you want to make into a clickable hyperlink
2. Choose the Insert | Hyperlink command or click the Insert Hyperlink tool and the Insert Hyperlink dialog box appears, as shown here:

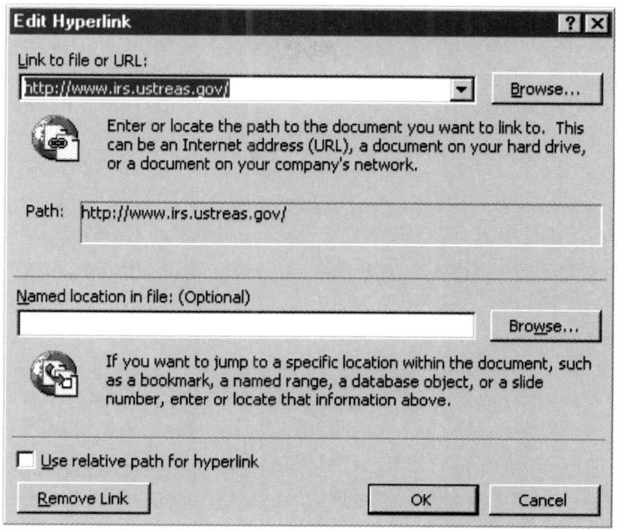

3. If you are creating a hyperlink to a World Wide Web document, enter the appropriate URL in the Link to File or URL box.
   If you are creating a hyperlink that jumps to a file on your computer or local area network, you also use the Link to File or URL box to enter the full path and filename. In addition, you need to specify in the Named Location in File box a location within the file to which the hyperlink connects (for example, bookmarks in Word documents, named ranges in Excel workbooks, or slide numbers in PowerPoint presentations).
4. Click OK. The Office application inserts the hyperlink.

EXPERT ADVICE

If you don't know the name of the file or file location that you want to connect to using a hyperlink, you can click either of the Insert Hyperlink's Browse buttons. The Office application displays a dialog box you can use to view the contents of the disks and folders on your computer and network.

If you enter something that looks like a URL, Office applications may automatically convert your entry to a hyperlink.

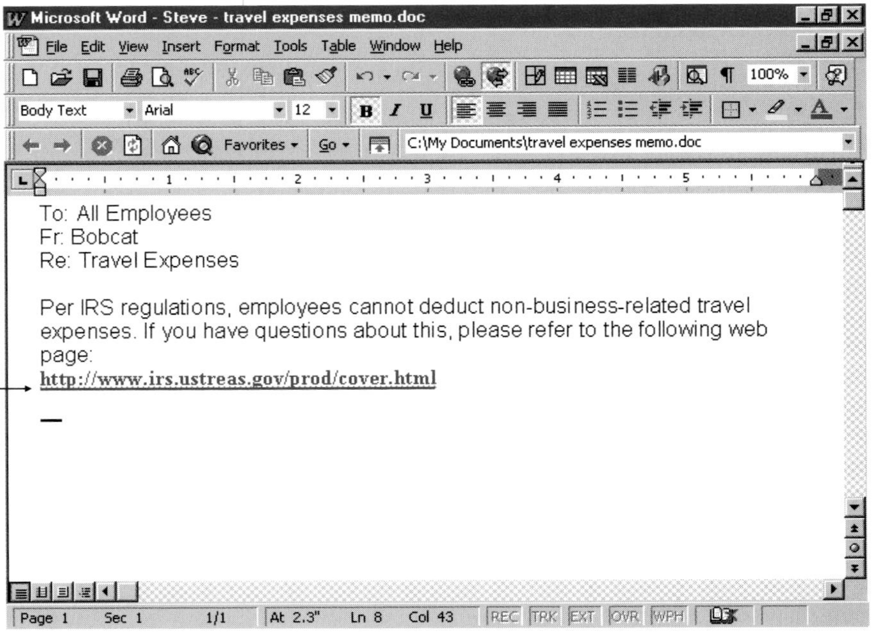

Figure 9.3 This memo includes a hyperlink that a reader can click to move to a relevant IRS publication

Using a Hyperlink

To use a hyperlink you've created, you may need to first connect to the Internet. If you're using a dial-up networking connection, for example, you probably need to make that connection first. (You can do this by first connecting to your Internet service provider in the usual way or by starting Windows 95's or Windows NT's dial-up networking feature.) If your computer connects to a local area network, or LAN, in your office or building for example, and the LAN connects to the Internet using something like a T1 line, you probably won't have to do this. (Ask your network administrator for details.)

Once your computer is connected to the Internet, you simply click the hyperlink to use it. Windows starts your web browser and displays the web page (or other resource) described by the hyperlink's URL. Figure 9.4, for example, shows the IRS web page referenced in the memo shown in Figure 9.3. To move between web pages, you click hyperlinks or enter a new URL in the Address box.

Figure 9.4 The IRS home page is where you'd wind up if you clicked the hyperlink in the Word document shown in Figure 9.3

Okay. Now it's time for a true confession. I wish I could be more specific about how you browse the Web from Microsoft Office applications. But I can't. Unfortunately, this area of the programs' functionality continually changes. As Microsoft continues to refine and expand its web browser, the Internet Explorer, this area of Office's functionality and operation will undoubtedly change. So don't expect your screen to look exactly the way the figures in this chapter look. Microsoft will probably have a new version of its Internet Explorer out by the time you read this.

Web Publishing with Office

Both Microsoft Word and Microsoft PowerPoint let you create HTML documents, which you or others can then view using a web browser such as Internet Explorer. In essence, all you really do is save your document in the HTML format. Once you've done this, you can open the new HTML document with any web browser, including Internet Explorer.

Creating HTML Documents in Word

While the instructions I gave in the preceding paragraph accurately describe the general process for creating HTML documents with Word, let me give you just a bit more information about how the process works. If you want to create an HTML document in Word, you'll want to start from one of the Word Web design templates. You can see these by choosing the File | New command and then clicking the Web Pages tab, as shown in Figure 9.5. Your best bet is to double-click the Web Page Wizard template. This tells Word to create a fill-in-the-blanks HTML document already formatted to appear a certain way.

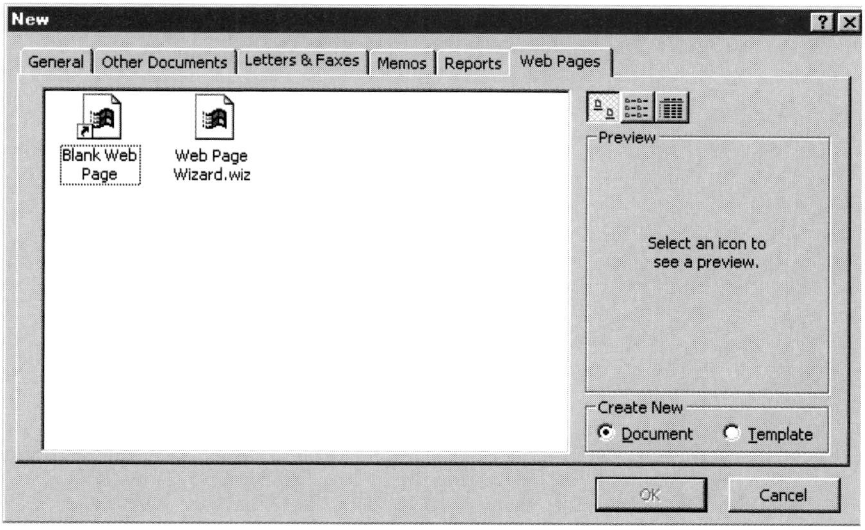

Figure 9.5 Word's Web design templates are available on the Web Pages tab of the New dialog box

When you choose the Web Page Design Wizard template, Word asks you a couple of questions using dialog boxes: what kind of web page you're creating and what design, or look, you want for your web page. You answer the questions by clicking your choices, and when you've finished, Word displays a rough-draft of your web page, as in Figure 9.6.

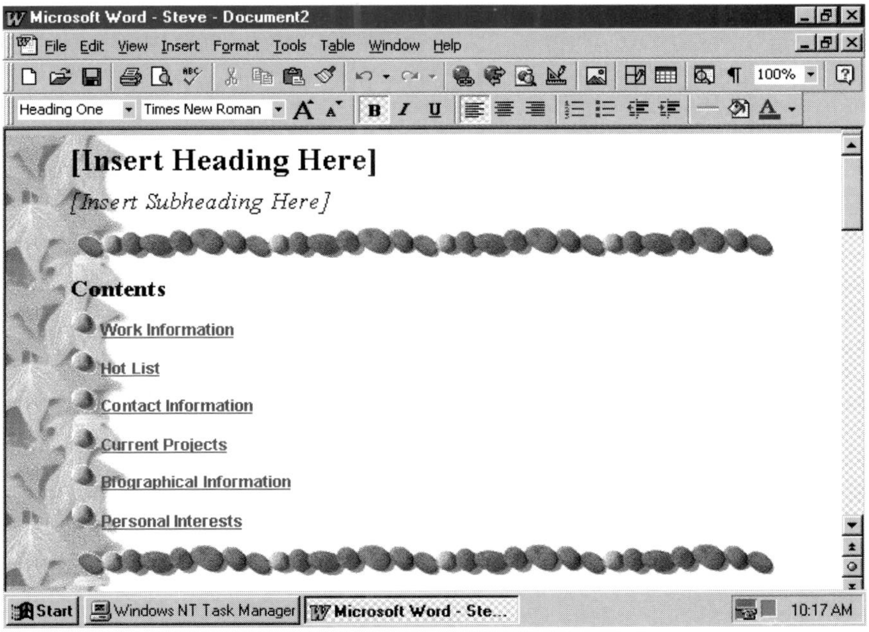

Figure 9.6 A draft web page created by the Web Page Wizard

All you need to do to complete the web page is replace the existing text by selecting it and then typing the replacement text. If you want to create a hyperlink for any of the blue, underlined text fragments, select the text and then choose the Insert | Hyperlink command. Figure 9.7 shows a sample web page I created by modifying the template shown in Figure 9.6.

Saving HTML Documents in Word

To save an HTML document, you just choose the File | Save command if you've created the document using a web page template. Alternatively, if you've

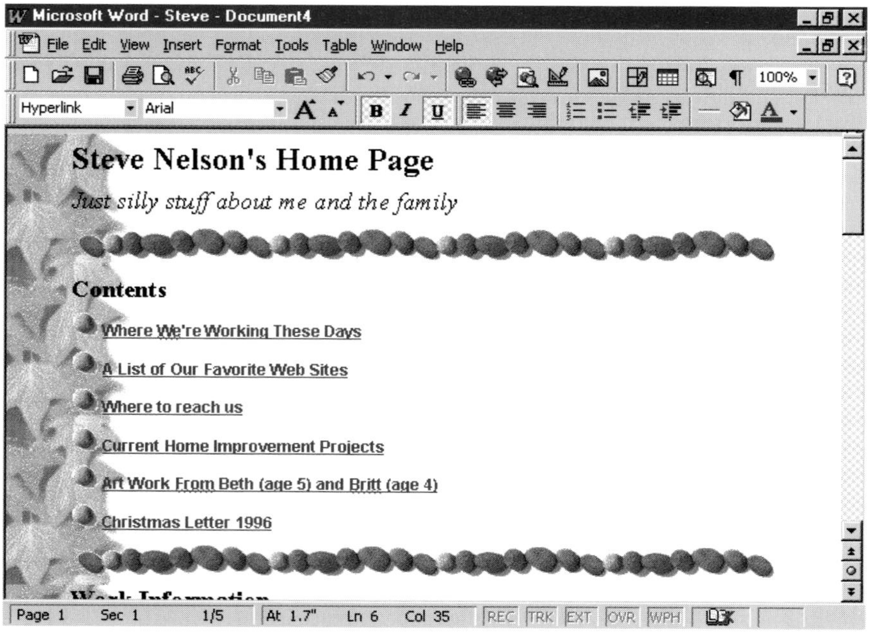

Figure 9.7 A simple web page

created the document using some other template, you choose the File | Save as HTML command. Word displays the Save As dialog box:

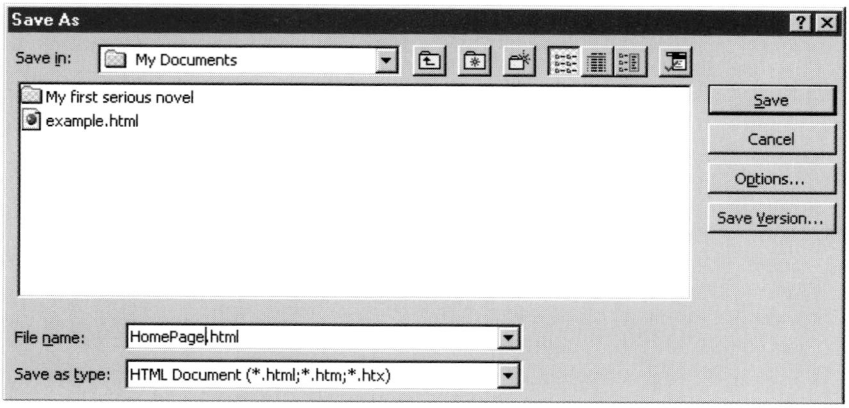

1. Use the File name box to give the HTML document a name.
2. Verify that the Save as Type drop-down list displays HTML Document.
3. Click Save.

Creating HTML Documents in PowerPoint

PowerPoint is probably more useful than Word for creating web pages because of the attractive design templates it lets you use. The only trick is to tell the AutoContent Wizard that you're creating a presentation for use as a set of web pages. For example, after you start the AutoContent Wizard and click Next in the first dialog box, the first question the wizard asks is what type of presentation you want. If you're creating either a corporate home page or a personal home page, you would simply select one of these options from the list box.

Then, when the AutoContent Wizard asks its second question—how you will show your presentation—you select the Internet, Kiosk option (see Figure 9.8).

If you do choose the Internet, Kiosk option—and you should if you're creating web pages—the AutoContent Wizard also asks for information it can use and reuse in your presentation: a copyright notice, an e-mail link, and so on. You make these choices by checking the options in this dialog box.

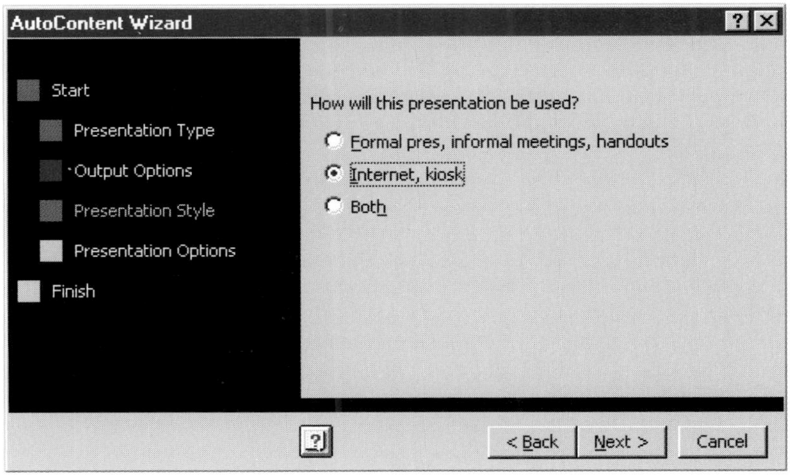

Figure 9.8 The AutoContent Wizard lets you identify your presentation as one you'll use to create HTML documents

For information on how to add pictures and drawing objects to your documents, refer to Chapters 4 and 6. For information on using the Insert | Hyperlink command, see the section "Using Hyperlinks in Office Documents."

When you finish running the AutoContent Wizard, you're ready to add your actual content to the PowerPoint presentation. To do this, edit or replace the boilerplate text that the AutoContent Wizard provides with your own information. Add pictures and drawing objects in the usual way. To create a hyperlink, use the Insert | Hyperlink command.

When you finish creating the presentation and want to turn it into a set of web pages, choose the File | Save as HTML command. This command starts the Internet Assistant for PowerPoint. All you need to do is follow the on-screen instructions.

Using an Internet Search Service

Before you wrap up your reading here, I want to briefly talk about what Internet search services are. This material doesn't fit all that neatly into a discussion of Office. But search services are important, nonetheless. What search services do is let you find information on just about any subject on the Internet.

There are, by the way, two basic means of searching the Web: using a directory, or using an index. I'll briefly describe both techniques here.

Using a Web Directory

Web directories work like your local yellow pages directory. You pick a category or subcategory, and then you look through the entries in the category or subcategory. Yahoo! is probably the best-known, and probably also the best, directory service.

To use Yahoo!, enter its URL into your web browser's address box. Then, when the Yahoo! web server displays its home page, you use the list of categories that appears (you may have to scroll down the page a bit) to find the information you want. (See Figure 9.9.)

You just keep narrowing your search—going from categories to subcategories to sub-subcategories—until you find web pages with the information you want.

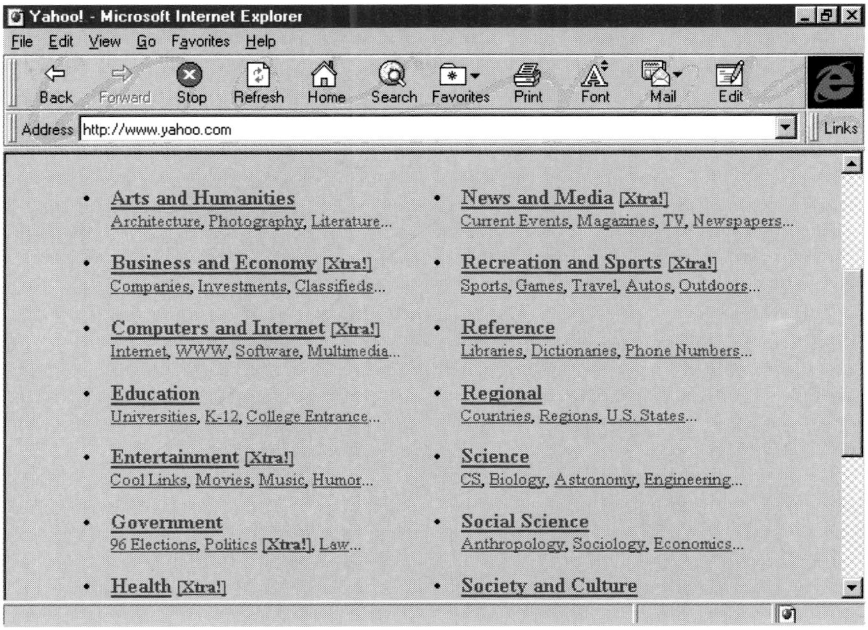

Figure 9.9 If you click any of these categories, Yahoo! displays another directory of subcategories within the selected category

Using an Index

The popular Internet search services (including Yahoo!) usually also have huge indexes of web content that they maintain. You can search these indexes for a word or phrase, and, in my experience, this is usually the way you want to find information. Perhaps the most powerful Internet search service at the time I'm writing this is AltaVista.

To use AltaVista, enter its URL into your web browser's address box. When the AltaVista home page appears, enter the word or phrase you want to look for into the text box and then click the Submit button. When you do, AltaVista builds a list of web pages that use whatever word or phrase you typed (see Figure 9.10).

You can do more with search services than I've described here. And, in fact, in my book *The World Wide Web for Busy People* (Osborne/McGraw-Hill, 1996), I spend an entire chapter talking about how search services work and what to do when they don't.

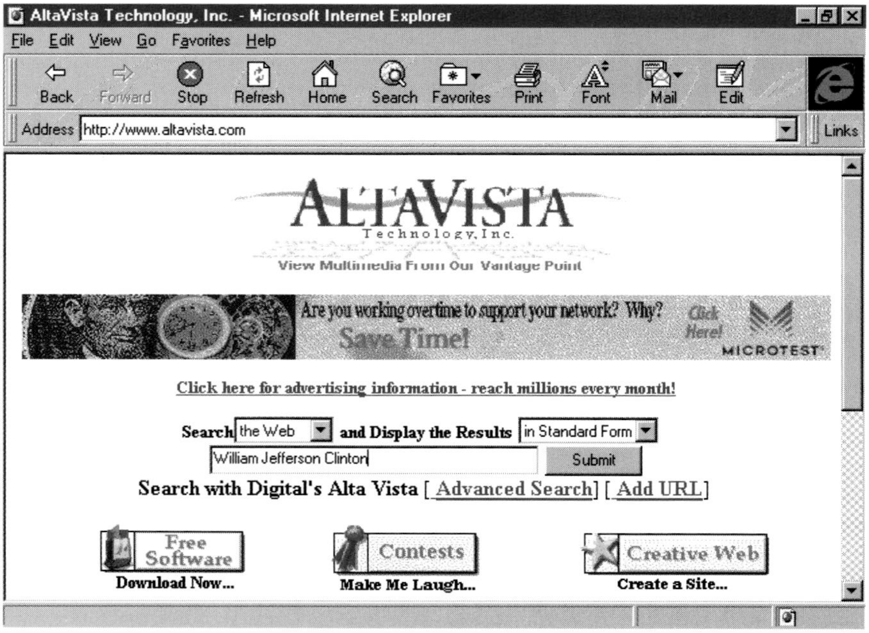

Figure 9.10 Web indexes like AltaVista let you build huge lists of web pages that use a specified word or phrase

I wish I had more time to talk about search services. But I don't. So, in conclusion, I just want to say that they are tremendously useful. If I have one piece of advice for Internet users, however, it is that you take a few minutes to experiment with a good service (like AltaVista) so you know how they work.

Because the newest version of Microsoft Office tightly intergrates with the Internet, this chapter describes what the Internet and World Wide Web are, how to use hyperlinks in Office documents, what uniform resource locators (URLs) are, how to publish web documents with Office, and how to use an Internet search service. If you've reviewed this chapter, in fact, you now know the basics of doing all of this stuff.

This and the earlier chapters of this book focus on the three main components of Microsoft Office 97: Word, Excel, and PowerPoint. Before I wrap up the regular chapters of this book, however, I want to give you a birds-eye view of the other two programs that come with Office: Outlook and Access. Outlook amounts to a personal information manager and e-mail client, and I describe it in Chapter 10. Access is a database program; I describe how it works in Chapter 11.

CAUTION

CHAPTER

10 Outlook Basics

INCLUDES

- Setting up Outlook
- Sending and receiving e-mail
- Keeping track of your contacts
- Organizing your tasks
- Managing your schedule

FAST FORWARD

Write an E-Mail Message ➤ pp. 211-216

To write an e-mail message:

1. Click the New Mail Message toolbar button to open the New Message form.
2. Enter a recipient, a subject, and your message text.
3. Click Send.

Read Your Mail ➤ pp. 216-217

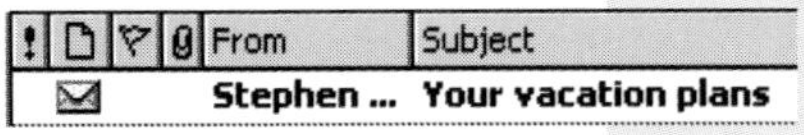

To read your e-mail:

1. Click the Inbox icon.
2. Double-click any messages that appear in bold type.

Reply to a Message ➤ pp. 217-218

To reply to a message:

1. Double-click the message in the Inbox message list.
2. Click the Reply toolbar button.
3. Type your reply.
4. Click Send.

Forward a Message ➤ pp. 217-218

To forward a message:

1. Double-click the message in the Inbox message list.
2. Click the Forward toolbar button.
3. Type any comments you want to pass along.
4. Click Send.

Add a Name to Your Contacts List ➤ pp. 218-220

To add a new name to your contact list:

1. Choose the File | New | Contact command.
2. Fill in the blanks in the New Contact dialog box.
3. Choose File | Save.

Add a Task to Your Tasks List ➤ pp. 222-223

To add a task to your Tasks list:

1. Click Tasks in the Outlook bar.
2. Click the top line of the Subject column.
3. Type the task.
4. Press TAB.
5. Type the due date.
6. Press ENTER.

Schedule an Appointment ➤ pp. 226-227

To schedule an appointment:

1. Choose the File | New | Appointment command.
2. Fill in the blanks in the New Appointment dialog box.
3. Click Save and Close.

Outlook is a personal information manager, or PIM. It combines messaging, scheduling, contact management, and a host of other functions into one package. Outlook lets you stay in touch, via e-mail, with business associates, friends, and relatives. Outlook also gives you the means to stay on top of your schedule, your phone and address book, and your to-do list.

upgrade note

Microsoft Outlook replaces Microsoft Exchange, Microsoft Mail, and Microsoft Schedule+, programs that were part of earlier versions of Office and Windows.

Setting Up Outlook for E-mail and Scheduling

Okay, first things first. If you want to use Outlook for e-mail or group scheduling, it's a bit more complicated to set up than the other Office programs. The reason for this is that Outlook becomes one piece—the client piece—of a client-server application. As I mentioned in Chapter 7, with client-server applications, you have two different computers running two different programs that work together. E-mail, for example, is a client-server application. You use an e-mail client such as the Outlook program to create and read e-mail messages, but you use (or rather, your network uses) an e-mail server—another program—to transmit messages. The e-mail client runs on your desktop or laptop computer. The

The group scheduling feature of Outlook is also a client-server application.

e-mail server runs on a network server—which is another computer someplace else (maybe down the hall or maybe across the country).

Because there are these two pieces to the puzzle, the first time you start Outlook, Outlook runs the Inbox Setup wizard. It asks you specific and, in some cases, rather detailed questions about the server programs that Outlook is supposed to work with. Outlook does this so it can set up a profile, or detailed description, of the messaging services you want to use. Outlook needs to know what you want it to do.

In some cases, answering the Inbox Setup Wizard's questions is easy. If you're working on a Windows 95 computer and you only want to use e-mail with your Microsoft Network account, you click a few buttons (to tell Outlook this is all you're doing), and you're done. If you're working on either a Windows 95 or Windows NT computer connected to a local area network, you only need to know the computer name of the network server that's running the Exchange server software. (You will need to type in the Exchange server's name at one point during the running of the Inbox Setup wizard.)

If you want to do any more than what I described in the preceding paragraph, however, things get mighty complicated—and you probably won't want to run the Inbox Setup wizard yourself. For example, you'll want help—from a network administrator or consultant—if you want to use e-mail with the Microsoft Network on a computer running Windows NT, or if you want to use e-mail on any computer with any Internet service provider.

EXPERT ADVICE

If you don't want to use Outlook's e-mail or its group scheduling feature, you still need to "set up" Outlook, but the setup is really easy. All you do is tell Outlook you don't want to use e-mail or group scheduling.

Starting Outlook

You start the Outlook program in the usual way. You can, for example, double-click the Outlook shortcut icon, which appears on the Windows desktop.

Alternatively, you can click the Start button and then choose the Programs | Microsoft Outlook 97 command.

After you start Outlook, you'll see the Outlook window, as shown in Figure 10.1. Initially, the Outlook window shows the Inbox. The Inbox is Outlook's message center. It's where you create messages you want to send, get notified of messages you've received, read your incoming messages, and store messages you want to save.

EXPERT ADVICE

As mentioned earlier in this chapter, the first time you start Outlook, it runs the Inbox Setup Wizard so you can set up a profile. Depending on the way you run the Inbox Setup Wizard, Outlook may ask you which profile you want to use.

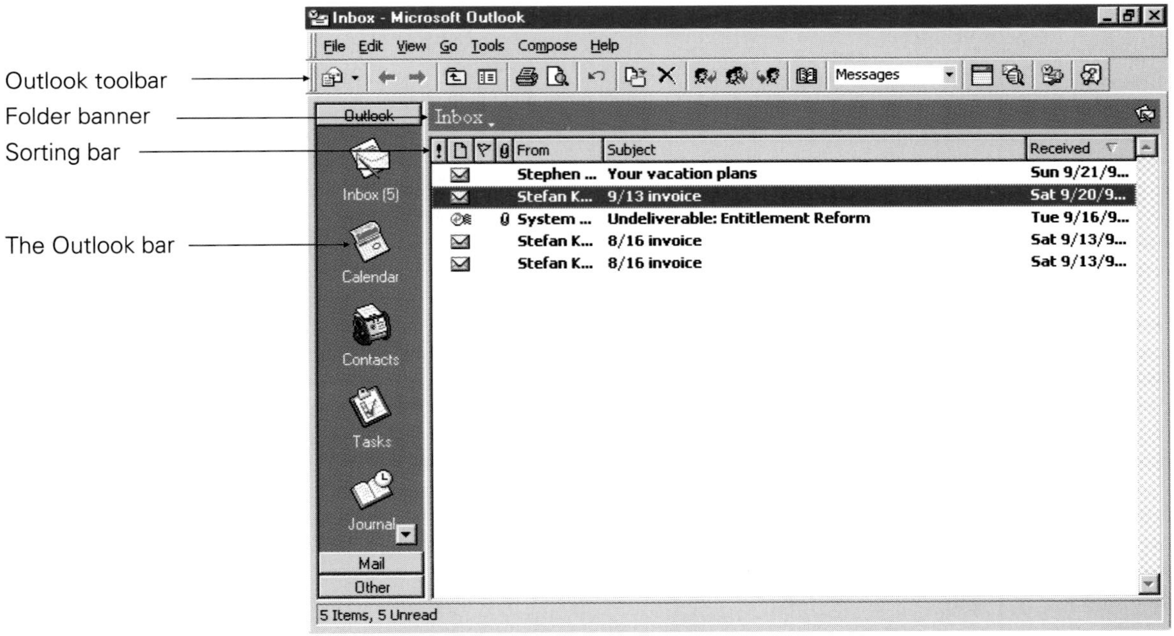

Figure 10.1 The Microsoft Outlook window

Creating E-mail Messages

To create a new message, click the New Mail Message toolbar button and Outlook will open the new Message window. The rest of the procedure is explained in the "Create an E-mail Message" Step by Step box that follows here.

STEP BY STEP Create an E-mail Message

4 Use the Formatting toolbar buttons to add text font formatting, just as you would in Word.

1 Type the recipient's name, or click the To button and select a recipient name from the Select Names dialog box.

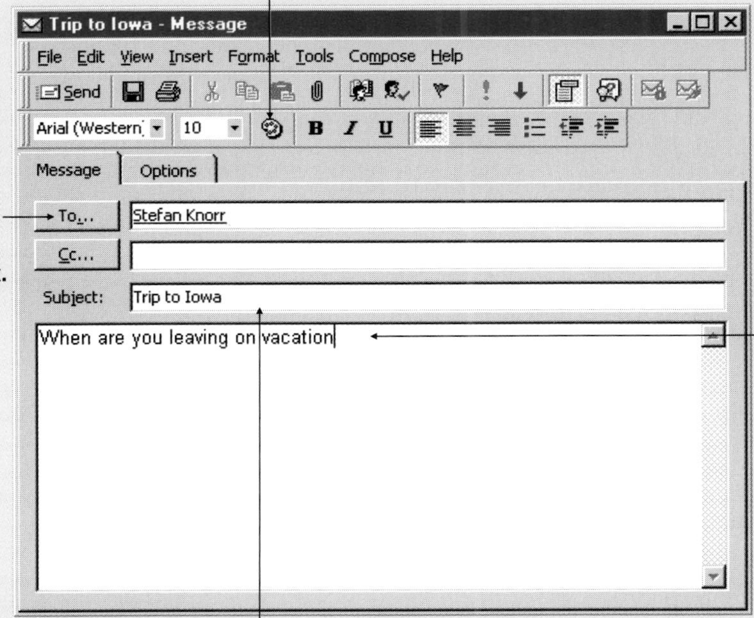

3 Click here and then type your message.

2 Describe the message subject.

You can also send a copy of your message to anyone. (This is referred to as "Cc-ing" and is a holdover from the days of typing with carbons.) Type their name in the Cc box, or click the Cc button and then select a name from the list in the Select Names dialog box.

Working with Your E-Mail Address List

In the preceding section, I noted that you can either type a person's e-mail name (if you know it) in the To box, or click the To button to display the Select Names dialog and then grab the right e-mail name from the list. The Select Names dialog box, shown in Figure 10.2, lists the e-mail names and addresses available on your Global Address List and, if you're connected to the Internet, your Personal Address book.

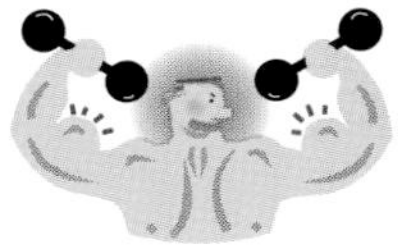

DEFINITIONS

Global Address List: *The list of e-mail names and addresses you use to send messages to other users on your local area network.*

Personal Address Book: *The list of Internet e-mail names and addresses you've recorded manually.*

Choose Global Address List to see all the e-mail names and addresses available on your network, or Personal Address Book to see the Internet e-mail addresses you've added manually.

Double-click the e-mail name you want to use.

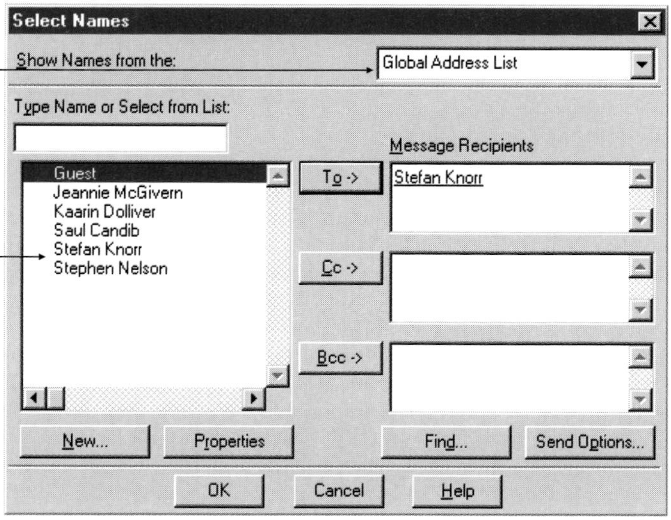

Figure 10.2 Choose e-mail names from the Select Names dialog box

To add an Internet e-mail address to your Personal Address Book, follow these steps:

1. In the Select Names dialog box, click New.
2. When Outlook displays the New Entry dialog box, shown next, select the type of address that corresponds to the method you want to use to send the message (fax or Internet, for example) and click OK.

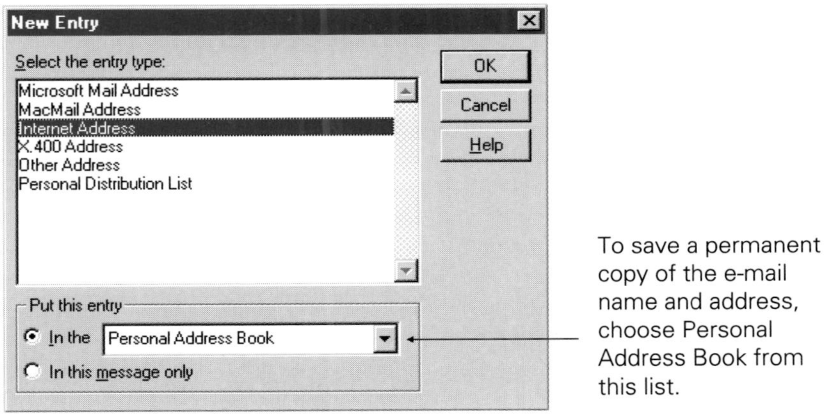

3. When Outlook displays the New Internet Address Properties dialog box (see Figure 10.3), use it to describe the e-mail address.
4. Click OK to address the message and add the name to the Select Names list.

EXPERT ADVICE

You should be able to get a person's full e-mail name, including both the name and the domain, from the person. You should also be able to give your full e-mail name, including both the name and domain, to other people. If you don't know your e-mail name, ask your network administrator or ask the online service or Internet service provider's technical support department.

Enter the person's name here.

Enter the person's full e-mail name and address here using the form *name@domain*.

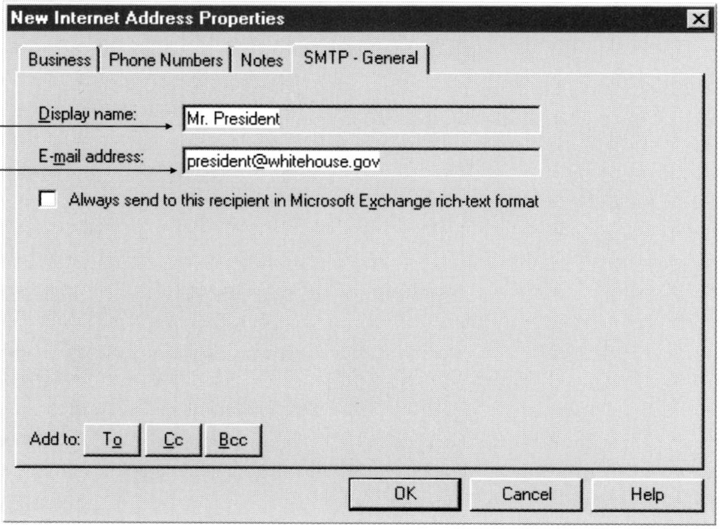

Figure 10.3 Use the New Internet Address Properties dialog box to record addresses for your e-mail lists

Adding a File to a Message

One of the nicest features of e-mail is the ability to send files along with your messages. At least in theory, you can include not only text files, but graphics and even video and sound clips in your e-mail messages. Unfortunately, you may find that you get inconsistent results when you attempt to send anything too fancy. E-mail delivery systems seem to vary dramatically in their ability to deliver anything more than simple text files.

To insert a file in a message:

1. Click the Insert File toolbar button. Outlook will display the Insert File dialog box, shown here:

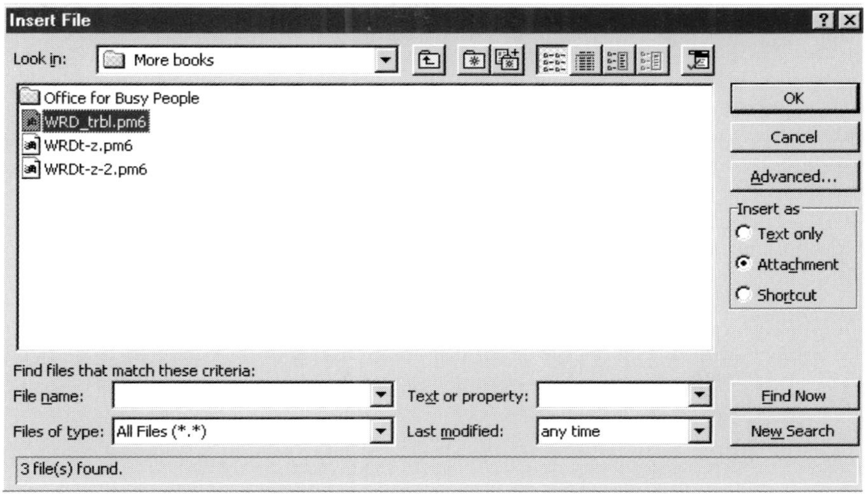

2. Use the Look In drop-down list to find the folder where you've stored the file.
3. Once you find the file, double-click it to add it to the message.

Sending and Delivering a Message

When you're satisfied that your message contains all the information you want to include and you like the way it looks, click Send.

If you're connected to a network, your message is sent instantly. You can expect a reply shortly.

If, however, your message is to be sent over the Internet or via an online service, clicking the Send button sends it to a temporary holding area called the Outbox. You must take one more step to actually deliver the message. Choose the Tools | Check for New Mail command or simply press the F5 key. If you've configured your profile properly, Outlook will dial up your online or Internet

Don't ask me why there's no Deliver command—there just isn't.

service provider, supply your account information and password for verification, and connect with the service to send your message. It will disappear from the Outbox and show up in the Sent Items folder.

To see what's in the Outbox (see Figure 10.4), click the Outbox icon in the Mail section of the Outlook bar. The Folder banner will display the word "Outbox." To view the Sent Items folder contents, click the Sent Items icon on the Outlook bar.

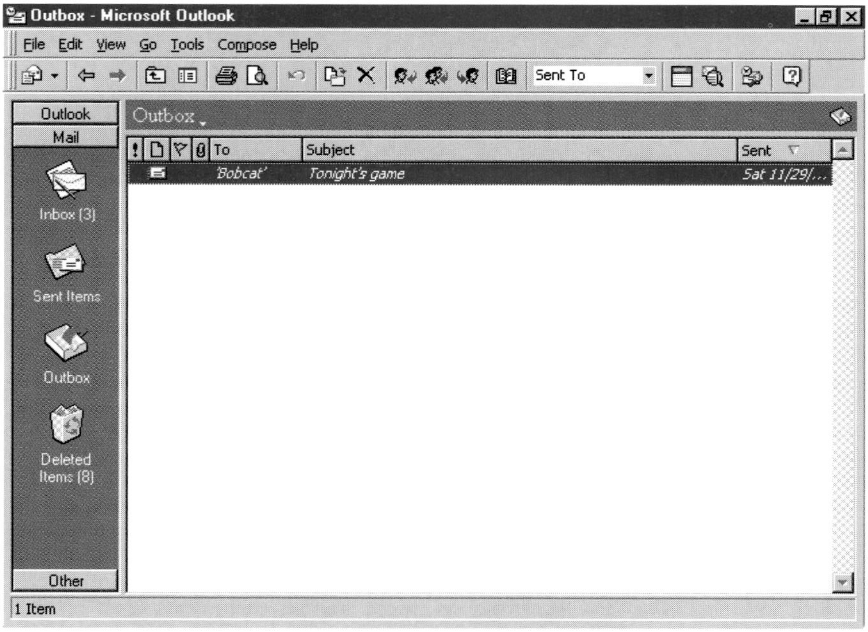

Figure 10.4 The Outbox holds any outgoing message items you've created but haven't yet delivered

Reading Your E-mail

To read your e-mail, just open the Inbox and double-click a message you want to read. The Message window appears, as shown in Figure 10.5, which you use to view the message item.

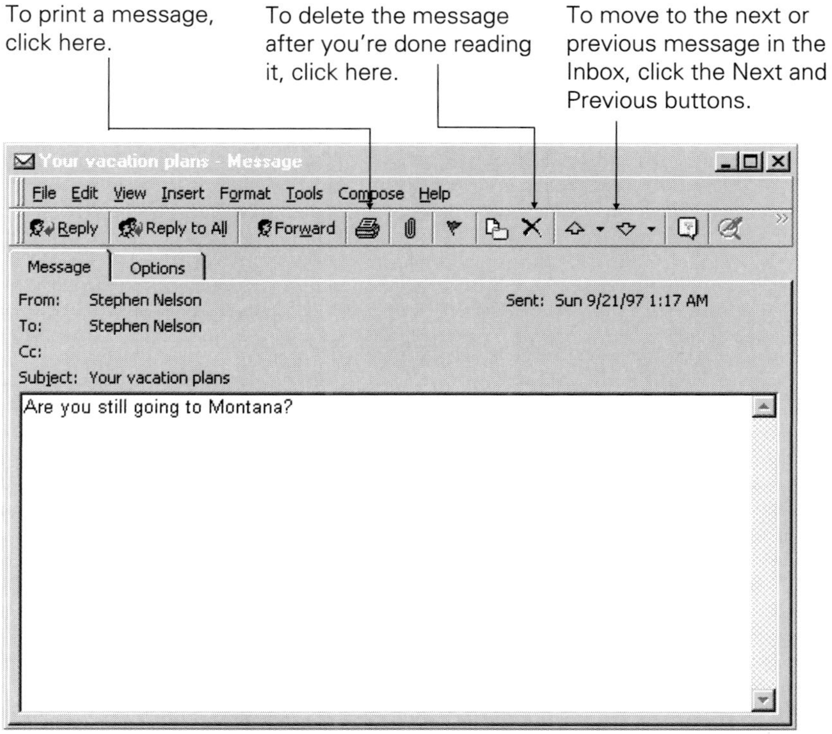

Figure 10.5 This message window shows the text of the first message listed in Figure 10.1

By the way, it's very simple to rearrange your incoming messages:

- To sort Inbox messages by earliest-to-latest or latest-to-earliest date, click the Received column heading button on the Sorting bar.
- To sort Inbox messages by sender name in alphabetic or reverse alphabetic order, click the From column heading button on the Sorting bar.

Replying to and Forwarding Messages

It's easy to reply directly to the sender of a message you receive:

1. Click the Reply button, which appears at the top of the Message window. Outlook opens a Reply message window that contains the

original message you were sent, but now addressed to its sender. (If you click the Reply to All button, Outlook addresses the reply message to all of the original message's recipients rather than to just the original message's sender.)

2. Type your reply above the original message text and click Send.

Forwarding a message is nearly the same as replying to a message:

1. Click the Forward toolbar button, which also appears at the top of the Message window, and Outlook opens the FW (Forward) message window.
2. Address the message by entering the e-mail name of the person you want to send the message to in the To box.
3. Add a comment if you like and then click Send.

You can forward messages to more than one person. Add as many names as you like in the To box, separating them with semicolons.

Creating a Contacts List

A Contacts list is like a high-powered address book. Like any address book, Outlook's Contacts list lets you keep track of the names, addresses, and phone numbers of your business contacts, friends, relatives, and acquaintances. But for each contact, Outlook provides space for 20 additional phone numbers, two additional addresses, three e-mail addresses, a web page address, notes and comments, and much more. Furthermore, you can assign contacts to categories for easy retrieval.

Adding a New Contact to Your Contacts List

The New Item button is one of those toolbar buttons whose name changes depending on the last item you chose from its drop-down list.

To add a new contact to your list, click the down arrow next to the New Item button on the toolbar. This displays a drop-down list.

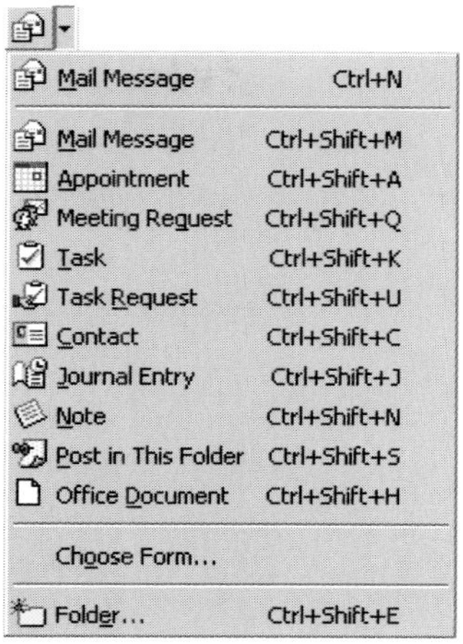

Choose Contact from the list. Outlook will display a new Contact form, shown in Figure 10.6.

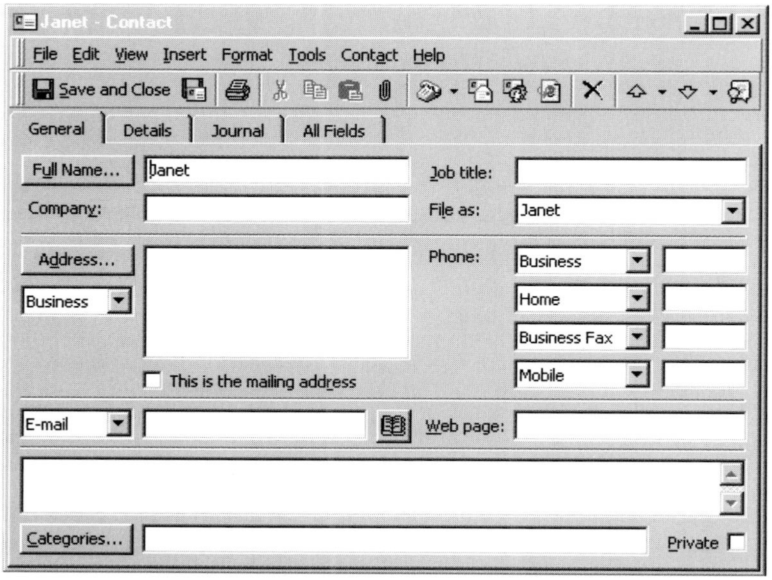

Figure 10.6 Enter information about a new contact on this form

1. Click the Full Name button to display the Check Full Name dialog box. This is a good place to enter name information—just fill in the blanks, using the TAB key to move from box to box. Click OK when you are done.
2. Next, click the Address button and use the boxes of the Check Address dialog box to enter address information; then click OK. (The address you enter is, by default, a business address. To enter a home address instead, or in addition, click the down arrow next to Business and select Home from the list. Fill in the other boxes as necessary, depending on how much information you have about your contact.)
3. To assign the contact to a category, click the Categories button. Check as many boxes as you want in the Available Categories list, or add a new category of your own. Then click OK.
4. When you've finished entering all the information about your contact, click the Save and Close button. To add another contact, click the Save and New button.

Looking Up a Contact in Your Contacts List

To look up a contact in your Contacts list, click the Contacts folder icon in the Folder list or on the Outlook bar. Outlook displays the Contacts list. You can view the Contacts list as a Rolodex-like display of address cards (the default view, shown in Figure 10.7) or in table form. To look up an address card, use the card index on the right side of the window. To find a contact whose last name begins with T, for example, click the *t* index button. You may need to scroll left or right if you have a lot of *t* listings.

EXPERT ADVICE

If you can't remember a contact's name, but you can remember, say, the company the person works for, choose Tools|Find Items to display the Find dialog box. Use its boxes, buttons, and tabs to describe the contact. Then click Find Now.

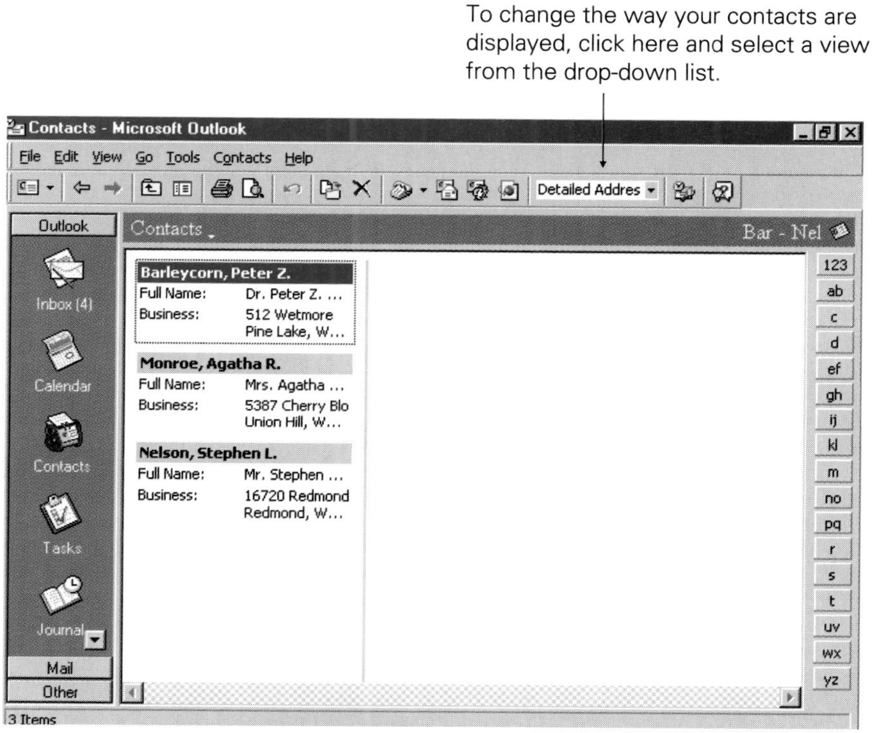

Figure 10.7 A Contacts list, shown in the default view format

Grouping Your Contacts

To group contacts by company or some other criterion:

1. Choose the View | Current View command.
2. When Outlook displays the Current View submenu, choose one of the groupings listed.

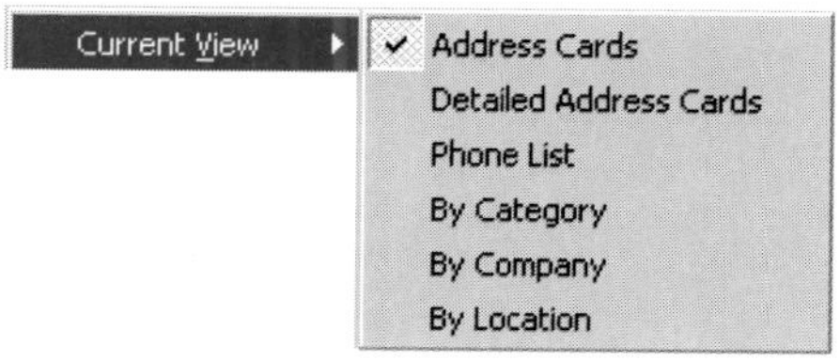

Printing Your Contacts List

To print your Contacts list:

1. Choose the File | Print command to display the Print dialog box.
2. Choose a style from the Print Style list. The Print Style list just offers a bunch of different ways that you can print out your contact information: on cards, in a phone-directory-style list, in a memo, and so forth. If you have questions about how any of these Print Styles look or work, just experiment.
3. Click Page Setup to set print options. When you're done, click OK in the Page Setup dialog box.
4. Click Preview to get a sneak peek of your printed copy. Then click Print if all is to your liking.

Once you've set up print options the way you want them, you can just click the toolbar Print button to print the Contacts list.

Creating a Tasks List

Few of us want to be reminded of the things we have to do. Still, attacking tasks in an organized manner is the most efficient and painless method of getting them behind us. The first step is keeping track of the tasks you need to accomplish and Outlook gives you the tools to do it.

Adding Tasks to Your List

Click the Tasks icon on the Outlook bar or in the Folder list to display the Tasks list, as shown in Figure 10.8.

To add simple, to-do list type tasks (call the dentist, pay the phone bill):

1. Click the top row of the Subject column, where it says "Click here to add a new task." Type the name of the task and then press TAB and type a due date for the task. (Overdue tasks will appear in red in the Tasks list.)
2. Press ENTER to add the task to the list and clear the top line for adding another task.

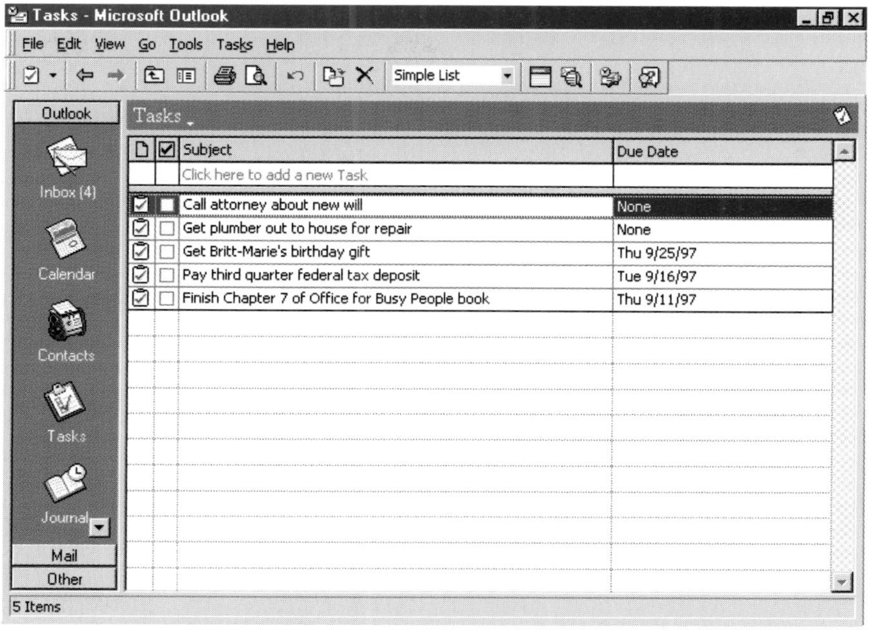

Figure 10.8 The Tasks list itemizes any to-do lists you've described

For more involved tasks, follow these steps:

1. Double-click the top line of the list (the "Click here to add a new task" line) to open the New Task dialog box.
2. Use the buttons, boxes, and tabs of this box to describe the new task in detail. Note that all you really need to do here is describe the task in a few words (such as "call Janet to say Happy Birthday") and provide a due date (such as "5/26/97").
3. Click Save and Close when you're done.

More About Tasks

For more information about the Calendar module, see "Managing Your Schedule" later in this chapter.

Tasks can be sorted, grouped, filtered, and categorized just like messages and contacts. You can print the Tasks list, too. A smaller version of the Tasks list, called the TaskPad, appears in the Calendar module to remind you of your outstanding tasks while you're checking or arranging your schedule.

EXPERT ADVICE

You can create a category for a project and then assign all the tasks that pertain to the project to that category. You'll then be able to view them more easily.

Marking a Task Complete

When you've completed a task, click to put a check in the box to its immediate left. Outlook crosses the task off your list, but leaves the canceled task listing in place.

To completely remove a task from the list, select the task and press DELETE.

Managing Your Schedule

If you're a busy person—and who isn't these days—it's important to manage your schedule. Outlook's Calendar module is a great place to do just that. Use it to track appointments, events, tasks, and meetings or just to keep a record of birthdays and anniversaries.

Here's how.

DEFINITION

Event: *An all-day "activity," such as your mom's birthday, that doesn't necessarily take time out of your schedule. Events appear as a banner at the top of the daily calendar.*

Viewing the Calendar

To view the Calendar, click the Calendar folder icon on the Outlook bar or in the Folder list. The Calendar pops up in Day, Week, Month view, as shown in Figure 10.9.

You'll see the daily calendar in the center of the view. The daily calendar is divided into half-hour segments, so you can schedule multiple appointments on

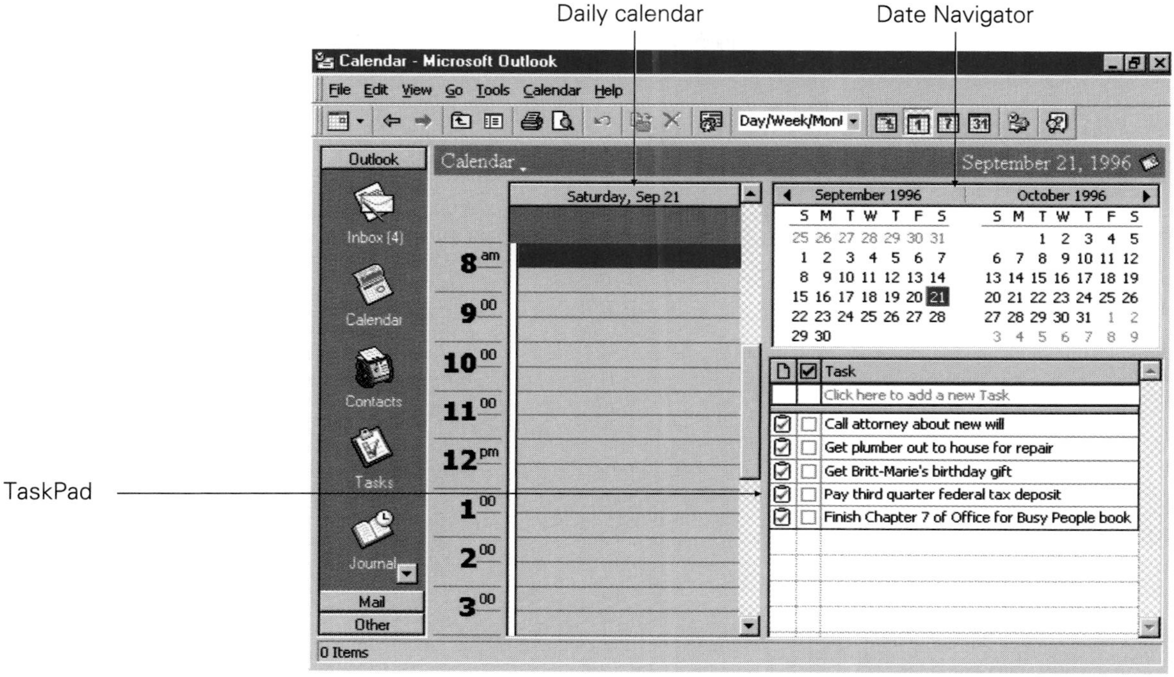

Figure 10.9 The default view of the Calendar module

any given day. (You can even schedule simultaneous appointments, if you can do two things at the same time.) The calendar shows your local time.

EXPERT ADVICE

You can change the work hours and work days shown on your calendar using the Calendar tab in the Tools | Options dialog box.

Navigating the Calendar

The small calendar in the upper right is called the Date Navigator. Date navigation works like this:

- Click a date in the Date Navigator to display its schedule in the daily calendar.

- Click the left and right arrows in the Month bar atop the Date Navigator to move one month forward or backward.
- Click the Month bar and select a month from the list to go to that month.
- Choose Go | Go to Date to open the Go to Date dialog box and then enter the date you want to display in the calendar.

- Click the Go to Today toolbar button to return to today's schedule.

Changing the Calendar View

Instead of viewing the calendar one day at a time, you can view an entire week or month. Click the Week or Month toolbar button. Week and Month views are, obviously, better for getting an overview than for checking details.

Scheduling an Appointment

Here is how you schedule an appointment:

- To schedule a half-hour appointment, double-click a time slot on the calendar.
- To schedule a longer appointment, click and drag to select the time period you want the appointment to cover. Then hold down the SHIFT key and double-click the selected period.

Outlook opens the Appointment dialog box. Now all you do is follow the instructions in the "Schedule an Appointment" Step by Step box.

STEP BY STEP Schedule an Appointment

4 Click Save and Close to place the appointment on your calendar.

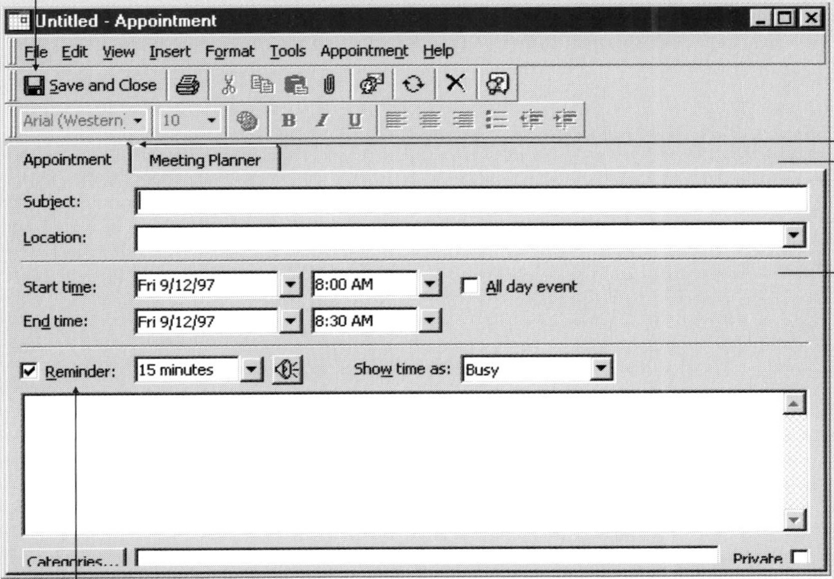

1 Click the Appointment tab.

2 Enter the details of the appointment.

3 Check the Reminder box if you want to be reminded of the appointment shortly before it occurs.

Other Outlook Features

I don't have room here to explain all the rest of Outlook's features—there are quite a few. Try experimenting on your own. Knowing what you know now, you'll find the other features quite intuitive.

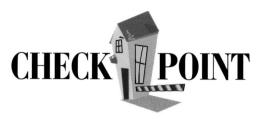

CHECK POINT

You now know everything you need to know about using Outlook, Microsoft Office's new personal information manager. You know how to send and receive e-mail messages, how to keep a contacts list, how to use Outlook to maintain a to-do, or tasks, list, and how to use Outlook for keeping your appointment calendar. Sure. Outlook provides a few other whistles and bells. But you know how to do all of the important stuff.

You're almost done if you've been reading since Chapter 1. There's only one more chapter left—Chapter 11. It describes how you use the Access database program.

CHAPTER

11

Access Basics

INCLUDES

- Exploring a sample database
- Creating a database
- Entering data into a database
- Finding, sorting, and filtering records

FAST FORWARD

Open an Existing Database ➤ *pp. 234-235*

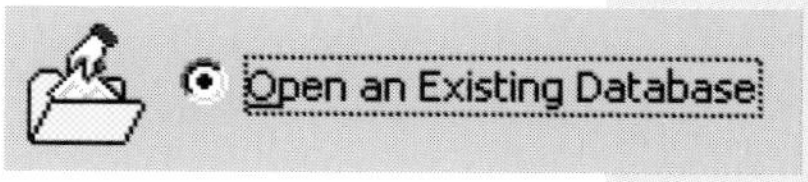

To open an existing database, start Access. Then, in the Microsoft Access dialog box, click Open an Existing Database and follow one of these steps:

- If you see the database you want listed, select it and click OK.
- If you don't see the database you want, double-click More Files. In the Open dialog box, browse the folders on your hard disk to find the database you want. Click Open.

Create a New Database ➤ *pp. 234-235*

To create a new database, start Access. Then, when Access displays the Microsoft Access dialog box, use it to describe what you want to do:

- To create a blank, or empty, database, mark the Blank Database option button and click OK.
- To use the Database Wizard to create your new database, mark the Database Wizard option button and click OK.

Use the Database Wizard ➤ *pp. 243-245*

To create a new database using the Database Wizard, start Access and click the Create a New Database Using the Database Wizard button. When the Wizard starts, follow these steps:

1. In the first Wizard dialog box, click Next.
2. In the next dialog box, choose the fields you want to include in the various tables of your database.
3. Decide whether you want sample information included. Then click Next.
4. Choose the graphic style of database forms you want to see on your screen and click Next.
5. Choose the style of printed reports you want and click Next.
6. Name your database and, optionally, choose a picture to include on reports. Then click Next.
7. Click Finish to open the database.

Enter Data in a Form ➤ pp. 245-247

To enter data in a form:

1. Open the form from the Switchboard or the Forms tab of the Database window.
2. Click the New Record toolbar button.
3. Type data in the first field.
4. Press TAB. Continue typing data and tabbing through fields until you've filled all the available fields.

Edit Data in a Form ➤ pp. 247-248

To edit data in a form:

1. Open the form.
2. Find the record you want to edit and double-click the field label to select the first field you want to change. Type in the new data. Repeat this step for any other fields you want to change.
3. Click the Save button to save your changes.

Sort Records ➤ p. 249

To sort records:

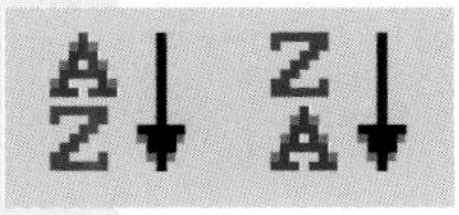

1. Click the field you want to sort by.
2. Click the Sort Ascending toolbar button to sort records in ascending alphabetic or numeric order. Alternatively, click the Sort Descending toolbar button to sort records in descending alphabetic or numeric order.
3. Click the Save toolbar button to save your changes.

Filter by Selection ➤ pp. 249-250

To filter the records in a form or table:

1. Select an entry in a field or column that meets the criterion you want to filter for.
2. Click the Filter by Selection toolbar button.
3. To restore all records, click the Apply Filter toolbar button.

Filter by Form ➤ *pp. 250-251*

You can also filter records using any form or table. To do so, follow these steps:

1. In a form or a table, click the Filter by Form toolbar button.
2. Select an entry in a field or column that meets the criterion you want to filter for.
3. To include records matching a different criterion, click the Or tab.
4. Select an entry that meets another criterion.
5. Continue clicking the Or tab and adding criteria as desired.
6. Click the Apply Filter toolbar button.
7. To restore all records, click the Apply Filter toolbar button again.

Many computer users, even those with a considerable amount of experience using word processing and spreadsheet programs, are intimidated by database programs. Databases, such as Access 97, are often believed to be more work to learn than they are worth or simply too complex to fathom. Happily, neither of these beliefs has much basis in fact. True, databases are intimately associated with programming, and many of the intricacies of a powerful database such as Access are beyond the casual user. But you need not be a programmer to get a lot out of Access. Thanks to its many wizards and other user-friendly features, Access can be effectively employed by anyone who feels comfortable with Word or Excel. In fact, once you see just how easy Access is to use, you'll wish you'd started exploring it sooner.

To prove my point, I'll take you on a brief tour of Access 97. Together, we'll put Access through its paces and see what it can do, or, more to the point, what you can do with it. For the purpose of the tour, we'll use the built-in sample database that comes with Access, called Northwind Traders. Then I'll show you how easy it is to create an entire database of your own using Access's Database Wizard. You'll create a database that you can start using right away to catalog your music CDs and other recordings. Also, I'll cover the basics of using your new database, including entering data, finding lost records, and sorting and filtering records. I think you'll find that once you've experimented a bit, you'll have the confidence to start exploring further on your own.

Exploring a Sample Database

As mentioned earlier, I want to begin by having you explore the sample database that comes with Access. Begin by starting Access and opening the existing sample database:

1. Click the Start button and then choose Programs from the Start menu. You should find the icon for Access 97 in the Microsoft Office folder on the Programs menu.
2. To start Access, click the icon. When Access starts, it will display a blank application window and the Microsoft Access dialog box, shown in Figure 11.1.

This is the Northwind sample database.

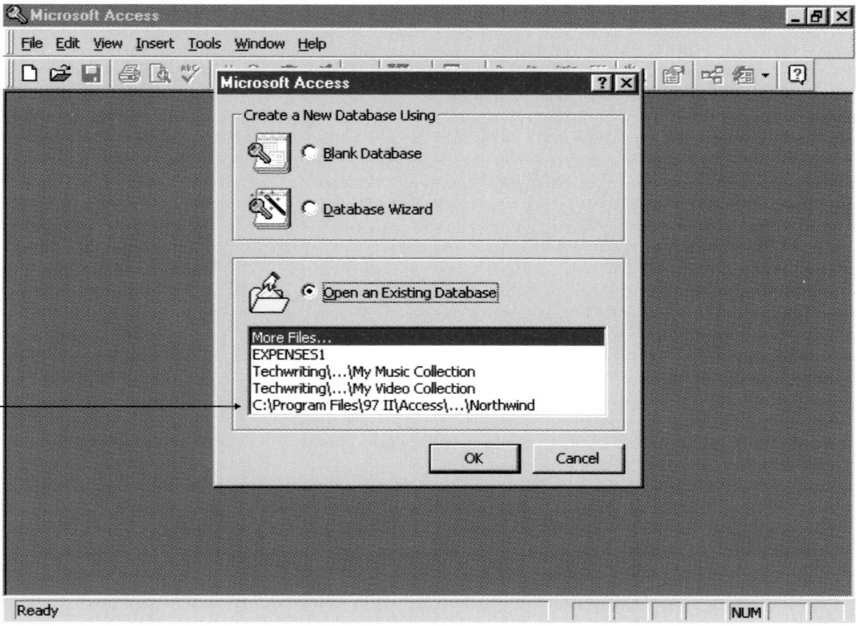

Figure 11.1 The Microsoft Access dialog box is what you see when you start Access

3. You're given three choices: under Create a New Database you can choose either Blank Database or Database Wizard. I'll talk about those choices a little later. The third choice is Open an Existing Database, and that's the one you should choose now. Since the option is already selected by default, all you need to do is click the line that shows the path C:\MSOffice\Access\Northwind Traders and then click OK. If your path is different, that's okay.

Verifying Your Sample Database Installation

If the Northwind Database doesn't show up in your dialog box, you may not have installed it when you set up Office 97. In that case, you have to go back into Office Setup and install it. Here's how:

1. Click Settings on the Start menu.
2. Choose Control Panel from the Settings menu, and in the Control Panel window double-click Add/Remove Programs. The Add/Remove Programs Properties dialog box appears.
3. Select the Microsoft Office 97 Professional item from the list. Then click the Add/Remove button.
4. When prompted, place your Office 97 CD in your CD-ROM drive and click OK.
5. When the Setup program displays the Microsoft Office Professional 97 dialog box, click the Add/Remove button.
6. In the Microsoft Office Professional 97-Maintenance dialog box, select Microsoft Access in the Options list.
7. Click the Change Option button.
8. When the Setup program displays the Microsoft Office Professional 97-Microsoft Access dialog box, check the Sample Databases box in the Options list and click OK.
9. Keep clicking OK, Continue, or Finish until Setup is complete.
10. Restart your computer. You should now be able to open the Northwind Database.

11. When the Northwind database opens, you'll briefly see its Database window, and then the Northwind Traders information and disclaimer screen. Click OK to return to the Database window.

SHORTCUT

Press F11 to open the Database window from anywhere in the database.

Looking in the Database Window

The Database window, shown in Figure 11.2, is the control center of the database. On the various tabs of the Database window are listed all the components (or *objects*, to use database lingo) of the database. These objects fall into six categories, represented by the tabs of the Database window: Tables, Queries,

You'll find all the objects in the database listed on the tabs of the Database window.

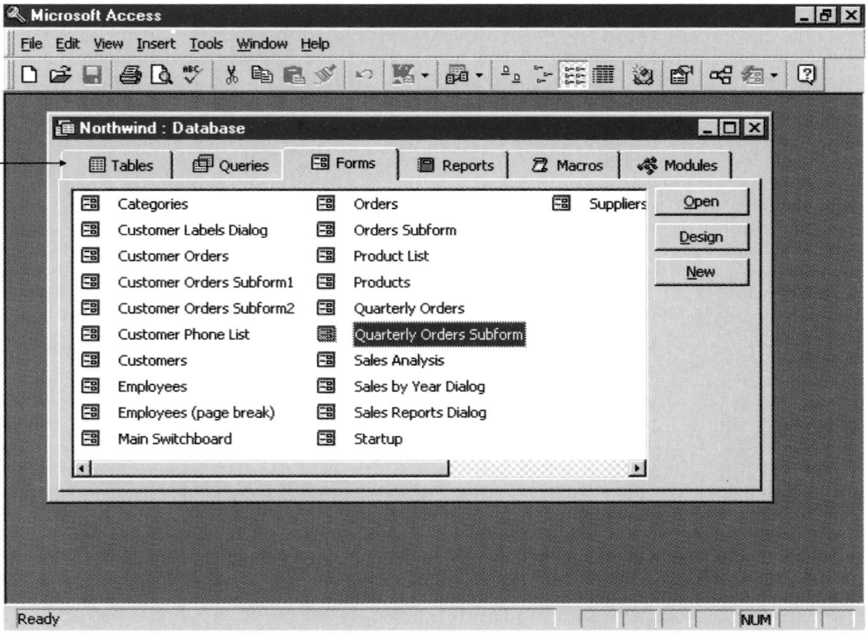

Figure 11.2 The Database window

Forms, Reports, Macros, and Modules. Don't worry about the last two kinds of objects, Macros and Modules—they're better left to programmers. I'll concentrate on the first four kinds of objects, Tables, Queries, Forms, and Reports—they're the ones you'll need to know about to find your way around Access.

Tables

If you've used Excel, or even Word, you're already familiar with tables. In fact, just about everyone gets familiar with tables, starting in elementary school. Click the Tables tab of the Database window. You'll see eight table objects listed. Double-click the Products listing. Access opens the Products table, shown in Figure 11.3.

Using the buttons at the bottom right of the screen, scroll to the right side of the table. Like all tables, this one is organized into rows and columns. The rows of the first two columns contain the ID numbers and names of the products sold by the imaginary Northwind Traders. The rows of the rest of the columns contain

Each column of a record is a separate field.

Each row of a table constitutes a separate record.

Product ID	Product Name	Supplier
1	Chai	Exotic Liquids
2	Chang	Exotic Liquids
3	Aniseed Syrup	Exotic Liquids
4	Chef Anton's Cajun Seasoning	New Orleans Cajun Delights
5	Chef Anton's Gumbo Mix	New Orleans Cajun Delights
6	Grandma's Boysenberry Spread	Grandma Kelly's Homestead
7	Uncle Bob's Organic Dried Pears	Grandma Kelly's Homestead
8	Northwoods Cranberry Sauce	Grandma Kelly's Homestead
9	Mishi Kobe Niku	Tokyo Traders
10	Ikura	Tokyo Traders
11	Queso Cabrales	Cooperativa de Quesos 'Las Cabras'
12	Queso Manchego La Pastora	Cooperativa de Quesos 'Las Cabras'
13	Konbu	Mayumi's
14	Tofu	Mayumi's
15	Genen Shouyu	Mayumi's
16	Pavlova	Pavlova, Ltd.
17	Alice Mutton	Pavlova, Ltd.

Figure 11.3 The Products table lists all the products carried by Northwind Traders

data about these products. The rightmost column of the table is named Discontinued. When a product is discontinued and Northwind Traders no longer sells it, whoever is in charge of such things places a check mark in the Discontinued check box for that product. You'll see why that's of interest shortly.

Scroll back to the left side of the table and click anywhere in the fifth row down. Notice that the little black triangle in the left margin, the row selector, is now pointing at row 5, indicating that the record in that row is selected. Also notice that the Record box in the lower-left corner of the window reflects this fact. Now click the Close button to dismiss the Products table and return to the Database window.

Just about every table in every database looks essentially like this one. Some are a lot bigger, of course, but conceptually they're all the same. Tables are a good place to view a lot of data quickly, at a glance. You can use tables for entering data, too, but you'll find that forms are generally better for that purpose.

Queries

Now let's look at a query. Click the Queries tab. Then double-click to open the Current Product List query, shown in Figure 11.4.

This query looks like, and basically is, another table. The main difference is that no one laboriously entered data in this table, row by row (as someone had to do for the Products table shown in Figure 11.3).

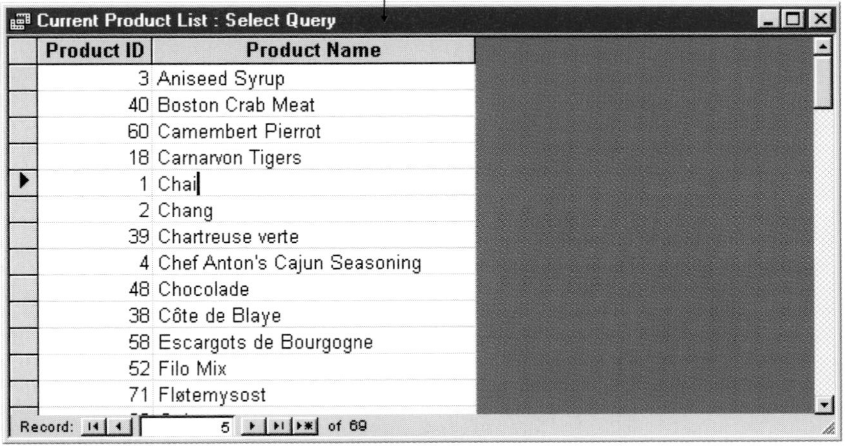

Figure 11.4 The Current Product List window shows the results of a select query

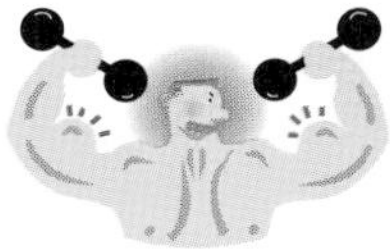

DEFINITION

Query: *A query selects data from one or more tables or other queries in response to a request for that data.*

The information in the Current Product List query was culled, or queried, automatically by Access from the data in the Products table, in response to a request. In plain English that request could be stated, "Please tell me which of the products in our product list have not been discontinued." (Now you see the relevance of the Discontinued column in the Products table mentioned earlier.) Actually, of course, the request wasn't made in English, but rather in what you might call query language. Close the query and return to the Database window.

Forms

Forms represent another database building block. You typically use forms either to enter or view individual records. To learn a bit more about forms, click the Forms tab of the Database window. Since you've already seen the Products table, it will be instructive to take a look at the Products form, so double-click to open it. The Products form is shown in Figure 11.5.

This attractive form is where the Northwind Traders product manager goes to enter data about new products and change data about existing products, including, yes, marking products discontinued. As I'm sure you've guessed, the Products form contains the same information as the Products table, but arranged differently. In a form, you see only one record at a time. However, you see all the data associated with that record at one time. That makes it easy to enter or edit data related to one record. Forms are frequently generated from their associated table.

Notice that record numbers (shown in the text box in the lower-left corner of the form) and Product ID numbers don't necessarily correspond. That's for two reasons: first, through sorting, or by some other means, record order may have been changed since data was first entered into the form; and second, some products may have been removed from the product list. When records are removed from a table, record numbers are reassigned, but ID numbers are not. The number next

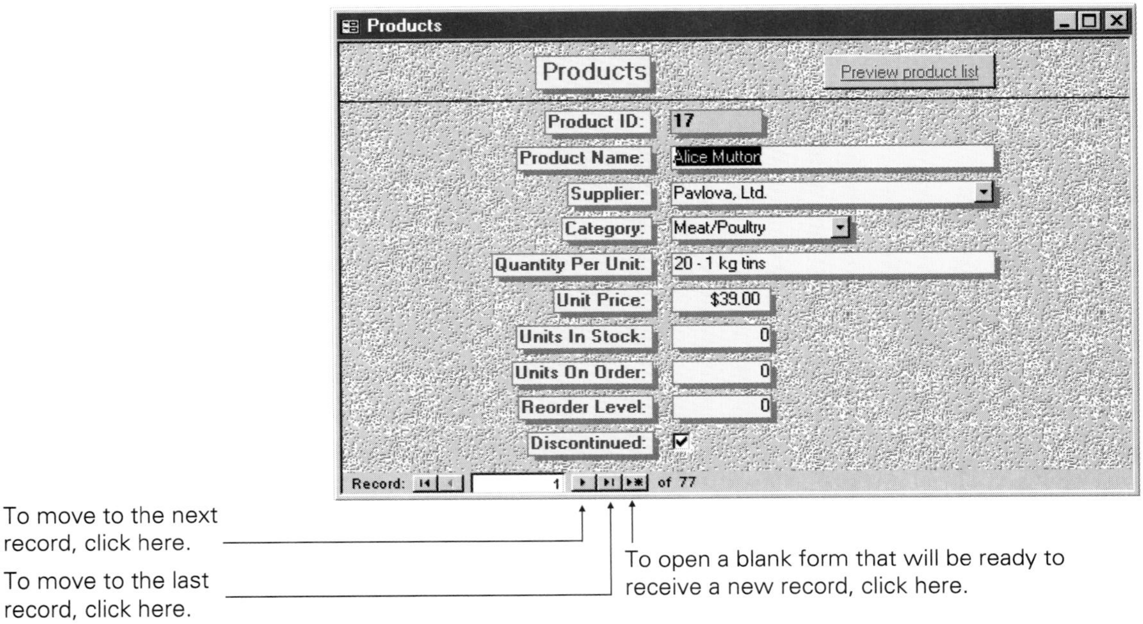

Figure 11.5 The Products form. This form shows the last record listed in the table shown in Figure 11.3

to the Record box accurately reflects the current number of records. Click the Close button to return to the Database window.

EXPERT ADVICE

Don't worry about saving data each time you add a new record: Access does that automatically. It also saves your database when you close it. It doesn't save changes you make to table and form layout unless you tell it to.

You may have noticed that the Alphabetical List of Products report can also be accessed by clicking a button in the Products form.

Reports

Reports summarize database information. To see an example of a report, click the Reports tab of the Database window. Double-click the Alphabetical List of Products report. Access opens the report in a Print Preview window, shown in Figure 11.6.

This report presents the data from the Products table/form (they're two sides of the same coin) in an attractive, readable, printed format.

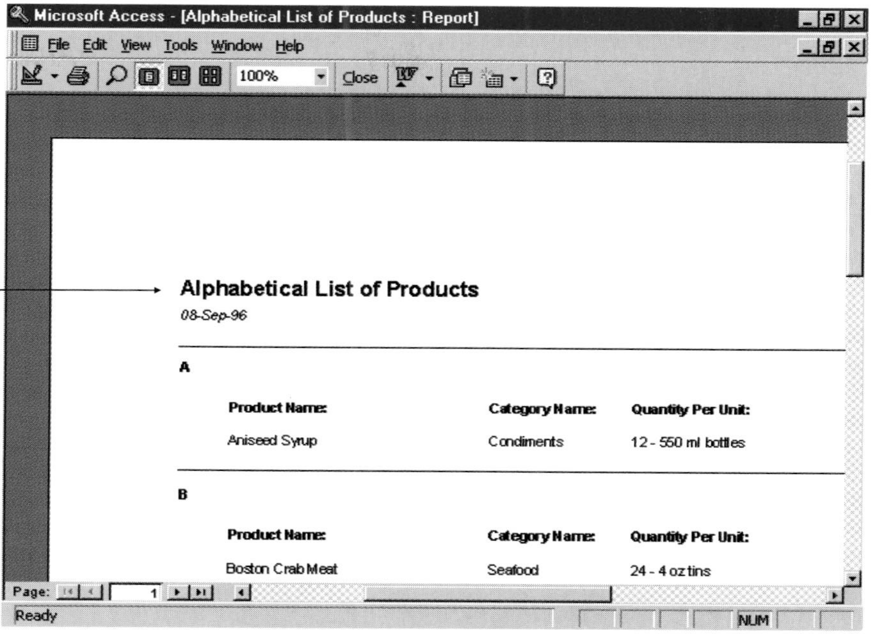

Figure 11.6 The Alphabetical List of Products report

Looking in the Relationships Window

There's one more sort of behind-the-scenes aspect of a database that you should know about. It's called the Relationships window. (Sounds kind of warm and fuzzy, doesn't it?)

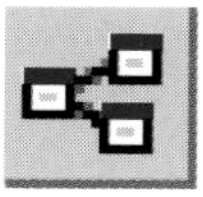

Click the Relationships toolbar button. (If you have a report open, you'll need to close it first.)

Access displays the Relationships window, shown in Figure 11.7. (It doesn't look warm and fuzzy though, does it?)

Because Access is a *relational database*, many of the tables in a database are related to each other by common information. One benefit of this scheme is that information need be entered only once, in one table, to be available to the entire database. Suppose, for example, your company's database contains two tables: one containing records of sales, and another containing records of customers. Furthermore, suppose you have a lot of repeat customers. If the two tables are related, all you have to do is indicate a customer ID number for each sale. Then if you need

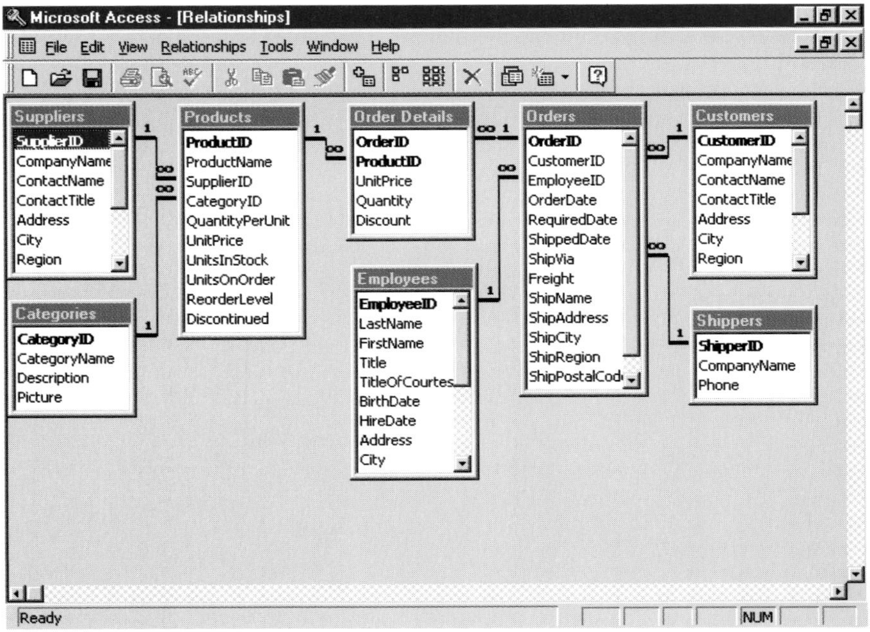

Figure 11.7 The Relationships window shows how all the tables that make up the database are related to one another

to know the customer's address and phone number for a particular sale, you can look up the information for that customer ID in the Customer table. Otherwise, you'd need to repeat customer information for each sale in the Sales table. That would be a waste of time, effort, and money.

EXPERT ADVICE

If you design your own databases, consider carefully how best to organize them to avoid duplication of data—or what database gurus call data redundancy.

Using the Database Wizard to Create a Database

Now that you understand the basic ins and outs of a database, it's time to create one. You'll do it the easy way, using one of Access's built-in templates and the help of the Database Wizard. Using a Wizard is so easy it doesn't take much instruction, but I'll quickly go through the steps with you. I'll use the Music Collection database as an example, but the process is the same for all Access templates.

Click the Close button of the Northwind Database (if it's still open). Then follow these steps to create a new database:

1. Click the New Database toolbar button.
2. In the New dialog box, click the Databases tab, shown in Figure 11.8.

The available database templates are displayed here.

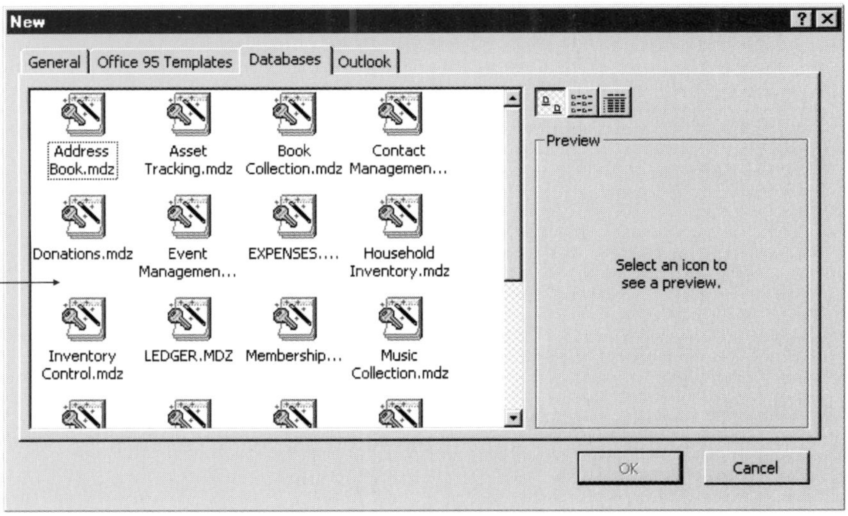

Figure 11.8 The Databases tab of the New dialog box

3. Double-click a template—in this case, select the Music Collection icon.

4. In the File New Database dialog box that appears, tell Access where you want to file your new database and give it a name. (I'm going to call mine "My Music Collection.") Then click Create. You'll briefly see the Music Collection Database window, followed by the first Database Wizard dialog box, which just introduces the database. Click Next.
5. In the next Database Wizard dialog box, shown in Figure 11.9, Access describes the fields it will create in the tables it will include in the database. Then click Next to accept the default table fields.

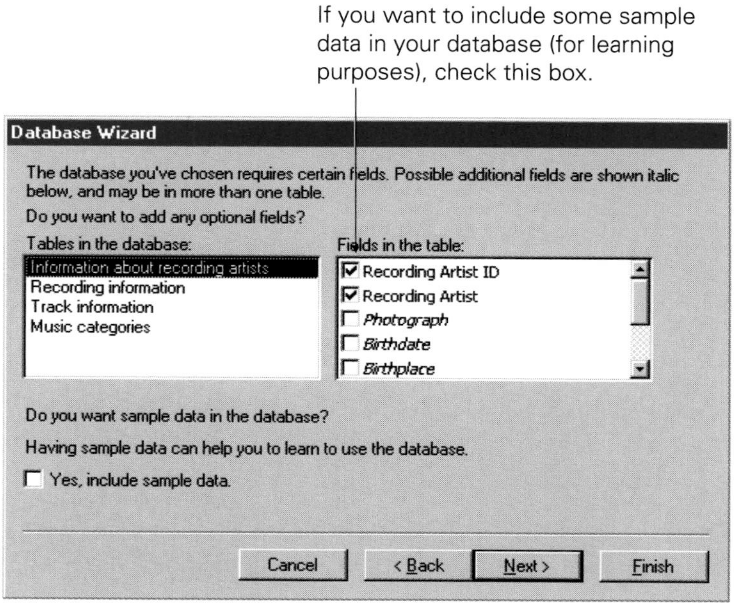

Figure 11.9 The second Database Wizard dialog box

6. In the next Database Wizard dialog box, click the various list items to preview and choose the screen display style you want for your database forms. I'm going to pick Dusk, which looks cool and urbane—suitable for my jazz collection. Click Next again.
7. Choose a style for your printed reports. To avoid appearing like a computer nerd, I'm going to pick Bold. Indicate the database title you want to appear on printed reports, and whether or not you want a

picture on reports. To include a picture, check the Yes I'd Like to Include a Picture box and click the Picture button. Browse your hard drive for the picture you want. I found mine in the Clipart subfolder of the MSOffice97 folder.

8. Click Next and then Finish to tell Access to open your new database. The first screen you see is the Main Switchboard, shown in Figure 11.10.

DEFINITION

Switchboard: *A special form designed to make it easy for database users to get to the most important parts of the database.*

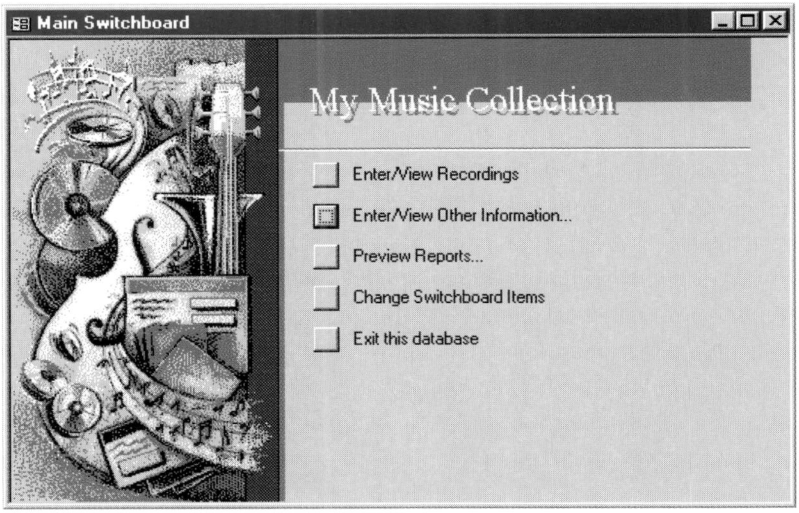

Figure 11.10 The Music Collection database switchboard

Entering Data in a Form

Now let's try entering some data:

1. Back in the Main Switchboard, click the Enter/View Recordings button to display the Recordings form. Click the New Record toolbar button. A blank form appears.

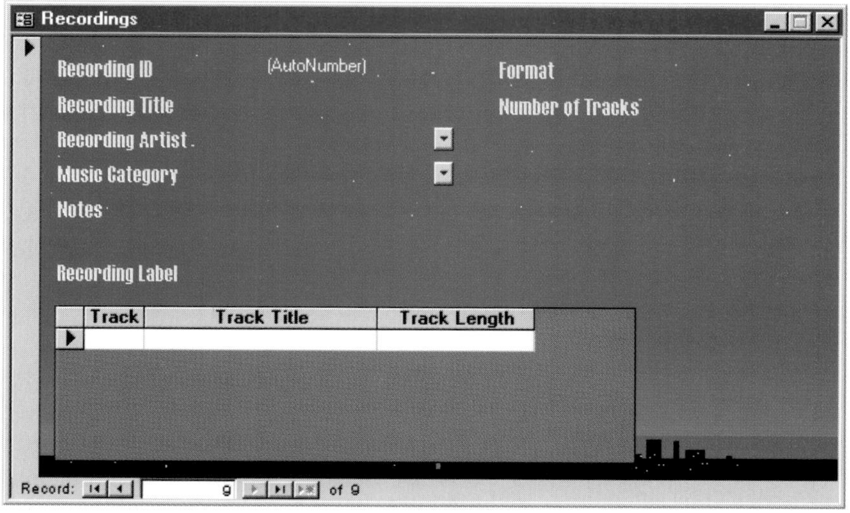

2. In the Recording Title field, type the title. I'm going to enter information about the classic Miles Davis recording, "Someday My Prince Will Come." Notice that as soon as you begin typing the title, Access assigns the new record an AutoNumber. This number will become the ID for the new record, used to identify this record to related tables in the database.
3. Press TAB to move to the next field. If you'd entered a record by this artist before, his name would appear in the drop-down list. That not being the case, just type **Miles Davis**. Because Miles is a new entry, Access asks you to double-click his name. Do so, and Access displays the Recording Artists form, so you can identify the new artist.

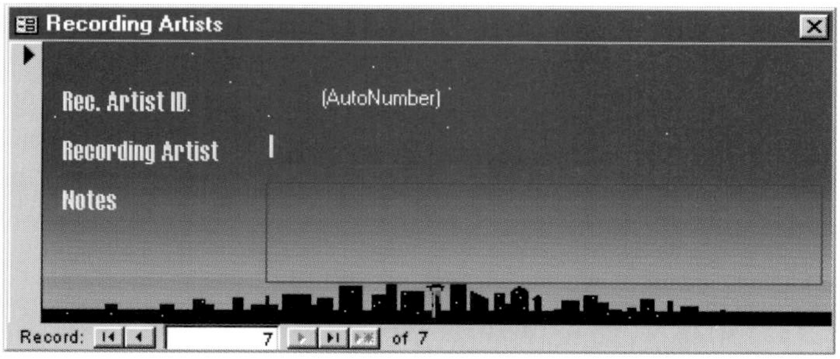

4. Type **Miles Davis**, tab to the Notes field, and type **My favorite horn player**. Click the Close button to return to the Recordings form. Now you can select Miles' name from the drop-down list.
5. Tab to the Music Category field and select **Jazz** from the drop-down list. Tab to the Notes field and type **Classic Miles**. Tab to the Recording Label field and type **Columbia**. Tab to the Format field and type **CD**. Tab to the Number of Tracks field and enter **6**. Then fill out the subform.

That's all there is to it. The completed form is shown in Figure 11.11.

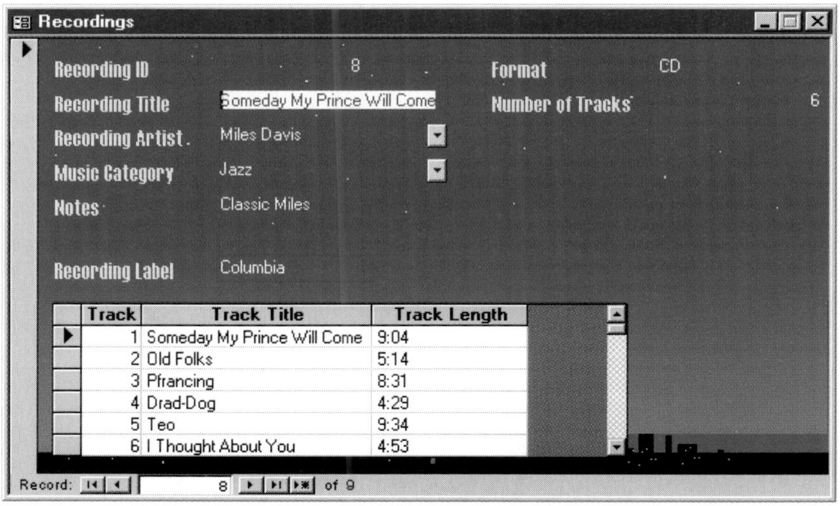

Figure 11.11 The Recordings form after you've added a new entry

Editing Data in a Form

Editing data in a form resembles entering data in a form. First, you open the form that contains the data you want to change. Next you find the record you want to edit. You can do this by paging through the records (as described earlier in the chapter in the section, "Looking in the Database Window") or by finding, sorting, or filtering records (as described later in this chapter in the sections,

"Finding a Lost Record,""Sorting a Table," and "Filtering a Table by Selection"). Then follow these steps:

1. Double-click to select the first field you want to change.
2. Type the new data.
3. Repeat the process for any other fields you want to change.
4. Click the Save button to save your changes.

Finding a Lost Record

If you can't remember the exact name of a particular recording, you can use the Find feature to locate it. Suppose you know that the recording you want contains the word "sounds" in its title. Click the Recording Title field and then click the Find toolbar button. Access will display the Find In Field dialog box. Next, follow the instructions in the "Find a Record" Step by Step box shown here.

STEP BY STEP Find a Record

1 Type the word you are looking for in this box.

2 If you can only remember part of the item, select Any Part of Field in the Match drop-down list.

3 Check the Match Case box if you want whatever you enter in the Find What text box to match the case of the data shown in record fields. (Leave check box unmarked if case doesn't matter.)

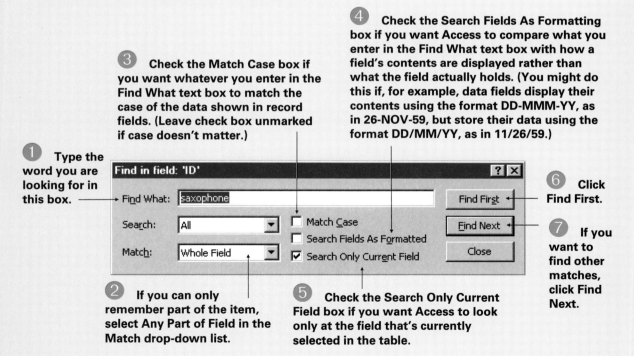

4 Check the Search Fields As Formatting box if you want Access to compare what you enter in the Find What text box with how a field's contents are displayed rather than what the field actually holds. (You might do this if, for example, data fields display their contents using the format DD-MMM-YY, as in 26-NOV-59, but store their data using the format DD/MM/YY, as in 11/26/59.)

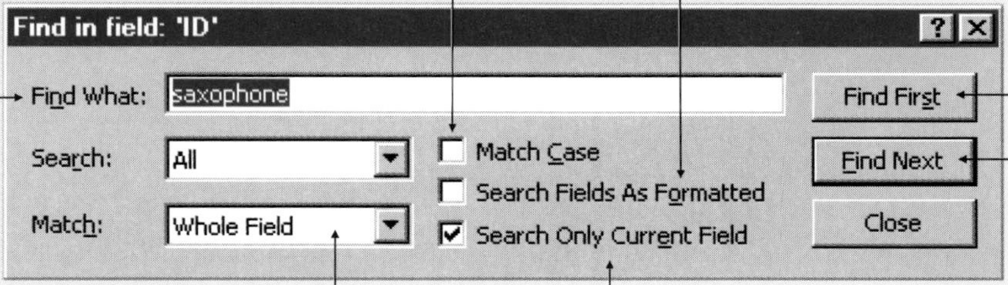

5 Check the Search Only Current Field box if you want Access to look only at the field that's currently selected in the table.

6 Click Find First.

7 If you want to find other matches, click Find Next.

Once you select your options in the Find In Field dialog box, Access searches and then displays the record it locates. Click Close and then click the Close button in the Recordings form to return to the Main Switchboard.

Sorting a Table

Once you've entered several recordings, you might want to put them all in alphabetical order. To do so, follow these steps:

1. Click the Database Window toolbar button. Access displays the Database window. (Remember the Database window shown back in Figure 11.2?) Click the Tables tab and double-click the Recordings object to open the Recordings table.

EXPERT ADVICE

Double-click the column-heading divider between two columns to increase the width of the left column enough to show all data in the column.

2. To sort the table alphabetically by artist, click the column heading of the Recording Artist column to select that column. Then click the Sort Ascending toolbar button. Your table will look like the one in Figure 11.12.

Filtering a Table by Selection

Suppose you want to display only those records containing jazz recordings.

1. Click the word "Jazz" in the Music Category column of the Miles Davis record.

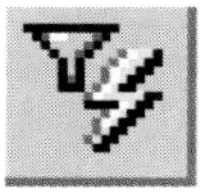

2. Click the Filter by Selection toolbar button. Now only the two records in the Jazz category are displayed.

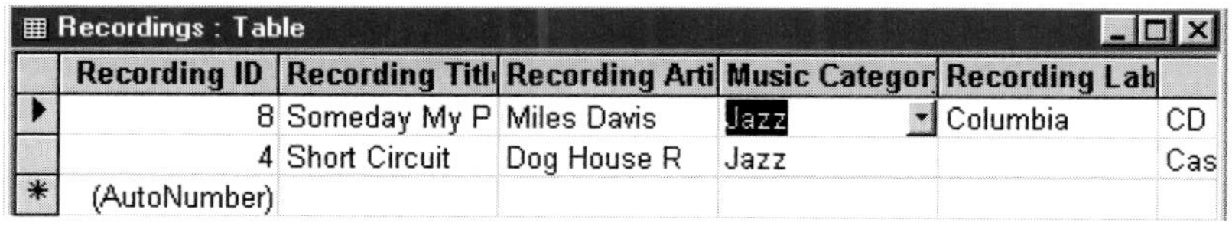

	Recording ID	Recording Titl	Recording Arti	Music Categor	Recording Lab	
▶	8	Someday My P	Miles Davis	Jazz	Columbia	CD
	4	Short Circuit	Dog House R	Jazz		Cas
*	(AutoNumber)					

After sorting, recording artists are listed in alphabetical order.

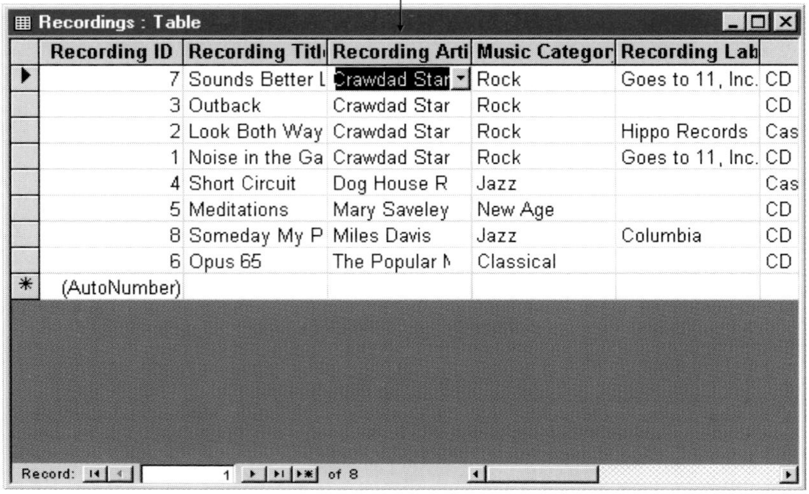

Recordings : Table

	Recording ID	Recording Titl	Recording Arti	Music Categor	Recording Lab	
▶	7	Sounds Better L	Crawdad Star	Rock	Goes to 11, Inc.	CD
	3	Outback	Crawdad Star	Rock		CD
	2	Look Both Way	Crawdad Star	Rock	Hippo Records	Cas
	1	Noise in the Ga	Crawdad Star	Rock	Goes to 11, Inc.	CD
	4	Short Circuit	Dog House R	Jazz		Cas
	5	Meditations	Mary Saveley	New Age		CD
	8	Someday My P	Miles Davis	Jazz	Columbia	CD
	6	Opus 65	The Popular N	Classical		CD
*	(AutoNumber)					

Record: 1 of 8

Figure 11.12 The table with the sorted records

3. To restore the missing records, click the Apply Filter button.

Filtering a Table by Form

Now suppose you'd like to display only those recordings in either the Jazz or Classical category. Filter by Selection is limited to one criterion, so that won't work. You'll use Filter by Form instead:

1. Click the Jazz field again. This time, click the Filter by Form toolbar button.
2. Access displays the Recordings: Filter by Form window. Click the Or tab. Select Classical from the drop-down list. Then click the Apply Filter button. The resulting table displays records in the Jazz and Classical categories only, as shown here:

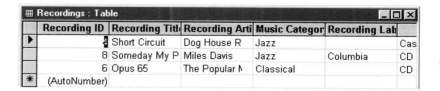

Recordings : Table

	Recording ID	Recording Titl	Recording Arti	Music Categor	Recording Lab	
▶	4	Short Circuit	Dog House R	Jazz		Cas
	8	Someday My P	Miles Davis	Jazz	Columbia	CD
	6	Opus 65	The Popular N	Classical		CD
*	(AutoNumber)					

3. Click Apply Filter again to restore all the records.

EXPERT ADVICE

You can add as many criteria as you like when you filter by form. They can all be in the same column or in as many different columns as you wish.

Exporting a Report to Microsoft Word

You can rather easily export Access data to a Microsoft Word document. First create a report with the data. Then follow these steps:

1. Display the report in a preview window.
2. Click the Office Links toolbar button down arrow and choose Publish It with MS Word.

Access saves the report file in .rtf format and opens it in Word.

Entering Data into a Table

Although you'll probably most often use forms to enter data, you can also enter data directly into a table. Here's how:

1. Open a table if you don't already have one opened. Then click the New record button, either the one in the toolbar or the one at the bottom of the table.
2. Fill in the new, blank row of the table.

I should tell you that while this directly-into-the-table approach isn't a bad one, it often doesn't work very well. Because of an Access feature called *referential integrity*, you need to enter data into a *primary* table before entering data into *subordinate* tables. For example, let's say you've created a two-table database. Furthermore, let's say that one of the tables stores customer information (this will be the primary table), and the other table stores customer orders (this will be the subordinate table). In this example, you wouldn't be able to enter a record into the customer order table unless you've already described the customer by entering a record into the customer table. In essence, what referential integrity does in a situation like the one I've just described is say, "You can't record an order for a customer you haven't first described." The disadvantages of using a table for data entry is that you must remember all this stuff yourself and do all the data entry manually.

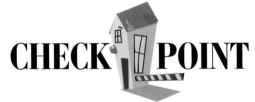

CHECKPOINT

This chapter introduced the Access database program by briefly describing how you create and work with Access databases. One thing I should note again before I close the chapter is that in Access you'll want to perform as much of your work as possible by using Access's wizards. By relying on Access's wizards, you'll find it very easy to do everything described in this chapter—as well as a whole lot more.

This is the last chapter in the book; however, there are a couple of appendixes. Appendix A describes how you install the Microsoft Office programs on your computer. Appendix B explains how you can get some Excel templates from the Osborne/McGraw-Hill World Wide Web site. Appendix C covers the basics of Windows 95 and Windows NT.

APPENDIX

A

Installing Microsoft Office 97

Installing Microsoft Office 97 isn't difficult, but if you are new to either Windows 95 or Windows NT version 4.0 (the two operating systems that Microsoft Office 97 was built for), you'll benefit from the help that I present in this Appendix. Note that for this discussion, I'm going to refer to either of the Windows operating systems as just Windows.

CAUTION

Installing Office on a computer running Windows NT version 4.0 works just like installing Office on a computer running Windows 95. The only difference, really, is that you need to have enough authority to run the installation. (Often, for example, you need to be a network administrator.)

To install Office 97, find the Microsoft Office 97 CD or the first floppy disk. Got it? Good. Now follow these steps:

1. Click the Start button (to display the Start menu) and choose Settings | Control Panel.
2. When Windows displays the Control Panel window, double-click Add/Remove Programs. (See Figure A.1.)
3. When Windows displays the Add/Remove Programs Properties dialog box, click the Install button. Windows will ask you to insert the CD or the first floppy disk. Do this and then click the Next button.

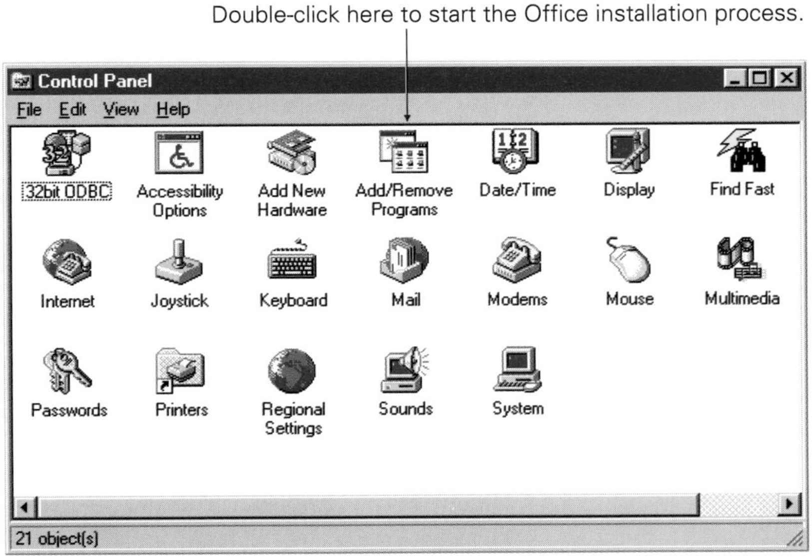

Figure A.1 The Control Panel window provides a special tool for installing new programs

4. When Windows tells you it's found the setup program on the CD or first floppy disk, click the Finish button. The Add/Remove Programs tool installs the Microsoft Office 97 software.

EXPERT ADVICE

You will be asked to make several decisions during the installation. If you're ever unsure of what to do, just accept the default, or suggested, setting.

And that's it.

KING

APPENDIX

B

Companion Office Templates

As I was looking through the components that make up the Microsoft Office 97 product, I realized there was, well, sort of a hole in the product. Office supplies several dozen very handy templates for Microsoft Word and PowerPoint. (A template is just a document that's already set up for you to use.)

What's more, PowerPoint and Access come with wizards that make it really easy to build PowerPoint presentations and Access databases. Excel, on the other hand, doesn't really provide a rich set of spreadsheet templates all set up for you to use—nor does it provide a wizard that helps you build your own spreadsheets from scratch. For this reason, the publisher and I decided to supplement Office 97's template set with a handful of additional Excel templates, which you can retrieve from the Osborne/McGraw-Hill World Wide Web site at *http://www.osborne.com.*

One other thing. I feel sort of sheepish about this, but my editor thinks I should tell you just a bit about myself. You know, to give you an idea about what sort of person created the templates you might just want to use. So here's the scoop. I have an undergraduate degree in accounting, am a certified public accountant, and have a masters degree in business administration in finance. I've worked as a financial systems consultant for Arthur Andersen & Co., the large multinational public accounting and consulting firm, and have been the controller and treasurer of a 50-person, venture capital-funded start-up company. I've also done independent financial consulting, and over the last ten years have written a bunch of books and magazine articles—mostly about how people use personal computers for business and financial management.

Excel Template Descriptions

The Osborne/McGraw-Hill Web site provides nine additional, handy Excel workbooks that are free to the readers of this book. You can use the templates either as they are (without modification) or as building blocks to construct your own, customized Excel solutions.

The Business Templates

I created three business templates: two for forecasting finances over different time periods, and the third to analyze profits versus costs.

12-Month and 5-Year Plans

12moplan.xls

5yrplan.xls

To use the 12 -month and 5-year plan workbooks, you'll need to understand business accounting and financial statement analysis.

These templates forecast a business's profits, cash flow, and financial condition over a 12-month or 5-year forecasting horizon. These two templates also provide common-sized income statements and balance sheets, and they calculate the dozen or so most popular financial ratios. With these workbooks, business owners, managers, and entrepreneurs can more easily and more expeditiously perform short-range and long-range business planning.

CAUTION

Because the 12-month and 5-year templates provide so many functions, both of them are rather large—almost 3 megabytes in size.

Profit-Volume-Cost Analysis

pvcanal.xls

You'll find it easiest to use the profit-volume-cost analysis template if you're familiar with basic managerial accounting techniques.

This template performs profit-volume-cost analysis over a specified range of sales volumes, and it calculates a business's break-even point. It also graphically depicts (using an Excel area chart) the results of this profit-volume-cost and break-even analysis.

The Personal Financial Templates

I have created six personal financial templates: cc_mgr.xls, college.xls, homebuy.xls, lifeinsr.xls, retire.xls, and savings.xls. You don't need to be a financial wizard to use the personal financial templates. Just download a template, open it, and follow the on-screen instructions.

Credit Card Balances

cc-mgr.xls

If you or someone you know has gotten in over his or her head with credit cards, you need to map out a path back to financial sanity. Use this template to calculate how long it will take to repay a credit card balance.

Future College Expenses

college.xls

This template lets you calculate how much you need to save to pay for a child's future college expenses. Note that this template is most useful to parents of children who won't be attending college in the near future. If college is right around the corner and you can't easily pay for junior's college expenses out of your annual salary (and who can?), you probably just need to be saving as much as you possibly can.

Buying a Home

homebuy.xls

This template lets you calculate how expensive a home you can afford based on your financial condition and standard mortgage-qualification rules. By the way, I've set up this template so that it initially uses my best guesses as to your lender's mortgage qualification rules. But before you start looking seriously at homes, you'll want to corroborate and possibly update three numbers in the template: the down payment percentage (I set this at 10 percent, but your lender may require a larger or smaller down payment than this); the debt service percentage (I set this at 33 percent—meaning your debt service payments must be equal to or less than 33 percent of your income); and the housing expenses percentage (I set this at 28 percent—meaning your total housing expenses must be equal to or less than 28 percent of your income).

Life Insurance Coverage

lifeinsr.xls

Nobody likes to think about his or her own mortality, but if you have family members who depend on your income, you need life insurance. By using this template, you can estimate how much life insurance you'll require in order to replace your income over a specified number of years. Forget about those vague rules of thumb that life insurance agents and naïve financial writers suggest and instead use the power of your computer and Excel to make a really robust estimate of your insurance needs.

Retirement Savings

retire.xls

If you haven't figured out how much you need for retirement (and you *do* want to retire some day), don't do anything else until you first use this template—you can estimate how much you need to save to provide a specified level of retirement income.

General Savings

savings.xls

Need to make a down payment on a new house or on a new car? Use this template, which resembles the retirement and the college savings templates, to estimate how much you need to save to accumulate the money necessary for those major purchases that are certain to come along.

Using an Excel Template

To use one of the Excel templates, first start your web browser and enter **http://www.osborne.com** as the URL, and follow the Busy People hyperlinks. You'll eventually see a list of the templates I've just described. To download a template, double-click it and follow the on-screen instructions provided by your web browser. You want to save the template in your Excel templates folder. (This is probably c:\msoffice97\templates\spreadsheet solutions.)

For the personal financial templates, I also documented each of the template calculation results with cell comments.

Once you've saved a template, you can begin using it:

1. Start Excel.
2. Choose the File | New command, and click the Spreadsheet Solutions tab.

3. When Excel displays its list of your Excel templates, double-click the template you downloaded to create a new Excel document based on the template. (See Figure B.1.)

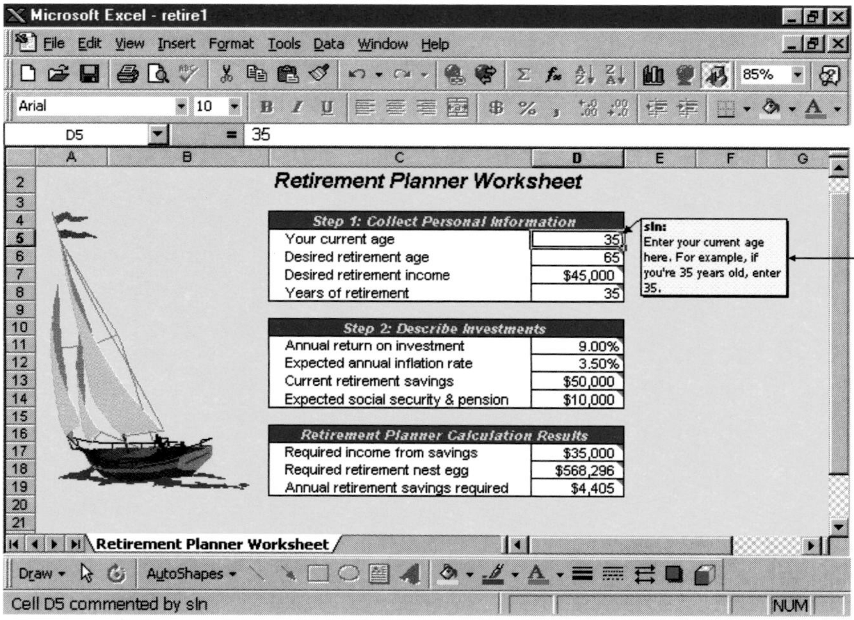

Figure B.1 The retirement planning template lets you estimate how much you need to save to provide a specified level of retirement income

APPENDIX

C

The Basics of Windows

This book assumes that you've already learned the basics of Windows (either Windows 95 or Windows NT), and have perhaps read *Windows 95 for Busy People* or *Windows NT for Busy People* (Osborne/McGraw-Hill, 1996). But if you haven't, this appendix should help you get started.

All of Microsoft's Office 97 programs (Word, Excel, PowerPoint, Outlook, and Access) were especially designed to take advantage of the Windows (either Windows 95 or Windows NT) operating system. If you know your way around Windows, you have a leg up on getting the most out of these and many other programs.

The Desktop

Windows starts when you turn on your computer. You don't need to type anything first, but you might be asked for a password once or twice. If you don't know one of the passwords, try pressing the ESC key (you should be able to use Windows but you might not have access to your network or to e-mail; so if passwords are required, you should contact your network administrator to set one up). After Windows starts, it displays a screen called the desktop. Figure C.1 shows a typical Windows desktop. Yours might look different. That's perfectly OK.

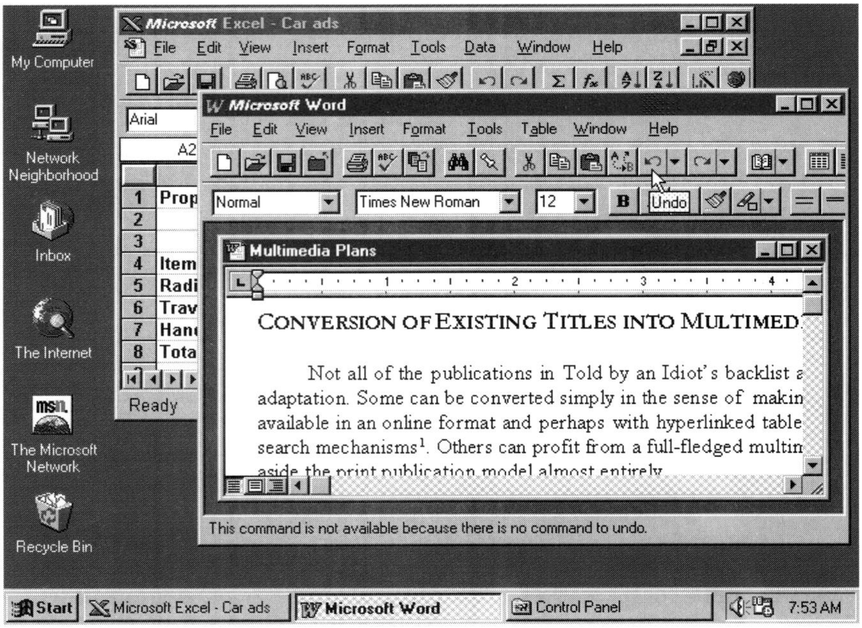

Figure C.1 A typical Windows desktop

The desktop contains small pictures of items like disk drives, a recycle bin, and so on. These little pictures are called icons. At the bottom of the Windows desktop you'll probably see the Taskbar, which will be discussed later in this appendix. Windows also displays windows. These windows are the spaces in which you do your work. Program windows contain programs (like Word, or Excel, or whatever) and can also contain other windows, often called document windows or child windows. So, for example, you might have a Word window on your desktop with one or more word processing document windows inside it. Any time you double-click a folder icon (or an icon representing a disk drive), it will open up a window on the screen (and a button on the Taskbar), showing the contents of the folder (or drive).

Mouse Basics

You use the mouse to point to objects on the desktop. (Incidentally, some computers have trackballs or other pointing devices, but all of these devices share some common characteristics: each has at least two buttons, and each lets you point to things.) As you move the mouse or other pointing device, a corresponding pointer moves on the desktop. Sometimes the shape of the pointer changes to give you a clue about what you can do next, because what you can do depends on what you're pointing to.

You can also make choices with the mouse (such as choosing a menu option), and you can use it to move and resize objects. You do this by pointing to something and clicking, which usually selects the object or causes something to happen. Clicking is accomplished by pressing and releasing a mouse button. Double-clicking is the act of pressing and releasing a mouse button twice in rapid succession. Dragging is the act of clicking on an object (a window, an icon, or whatever) and moving your mouse while holding down the button.

Most computer pointing devices (mice, trackballs, and so on) have two buttons. If the buttons are side by side, and if you have not modified Windows' default mouse settings, you will use the left button for clicking to select things and initiate most actions. You will also use the left button to drag objects around on the desktop and to change the size and shape of things. (Lefties and others who like to customize their environments can switch the functions of the right and left mouse buttons.)

Windows makes extensive use of the right button as well. Clicking the right button (also called right-clicking) on almost any screen element will pop up a shortcut menu full of useful options. For example, you can change the appearance of your desktop by right-clicking just about anywhere on the desktop and choosing Properties from the menu that pops up. Many programs, including Excel, will display shortcut menus when you use the right mouse button. Examples of right-clicking appear throughout this book.

There is one more mouse technique worth mentioning. It is called hovering. Frequently, if you slide the mouse pointer over an object and leave it there for a second, a little message called a tool tip will pop up that will tell you something about the object. In Figure C.1, for example, Word is telling you that the button under the mouse pointer is for activating the Undo feature.

The Taskbar

The Taskbar lets you easily run programs and switch from window to window. (If you don't see the Taskbar at the bottom of the desktop, slide your mouse pointer down to the bottom of the screen. The Taskbar should appear.) On the left end of the Taskbar you will always see the Start button. If you have opened windows or started programs (or if Windows has started them for you), your Taskbar will also contain other buttons. See "Taskbar Tips," later, for an explanation of how these buttons work.

The Start Menu

Let's begin with a look at the Start button and the Start menu that is displayed when you click on it. This is the menu from which you start programs, change Windows settings, retrieve recently used documents, find lost files, and get Windows help. You point to items in the Start menu to choose them.

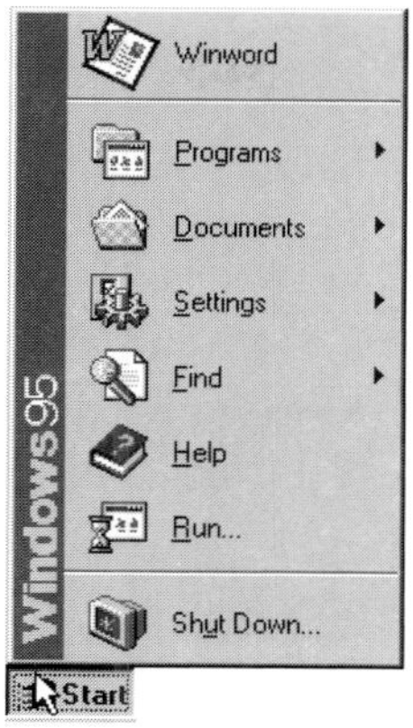

Everyone's Start menu looks a little different, particularly when you scratch the surface. (You can also add shortcuts to programs to the Start menu, such as the Winword item at the top of my menu, shown above.) The Start menu often reveals additional levels of menus called submenus. Let's look at the primary Start menu choices.

Programs

Roughly equivalent to the old Program Manager program groups in earlier versions of Windows, the Programs item on the Start menu pops up a submenu of programs and special Start menu folders. The folders themselves open sub-sub-menus, and so on. You can run any properly installed program in Windows by clicking on the Start button, then clicking on the Programs choice in the Start menu, and then clicking on the desired program (or perhaps on a folder and then on a program in the folder).

Documents

The Start menu remembers the last 15 documents you've opened and displays their names in the Documents menu. (However, be forewarned that programs designed prior to Windows often fail to add documents to the Documents menu.) When you want to work with a recently used document again, click on its name in the Documents menu. The document will appear on your screen in the program in which it was created. If the program is not already running, Windows will launch it for you automatically.

Settings

To change the various settings for your computer, such as the way the Start menu looks or how your screen saver works, choose Settings from the Start menu and then choose Control Panel from the Settings submenu. From the resulting Control Panel window, a part of which is shown here, you can exercise centralized control over all of your computer's settings.

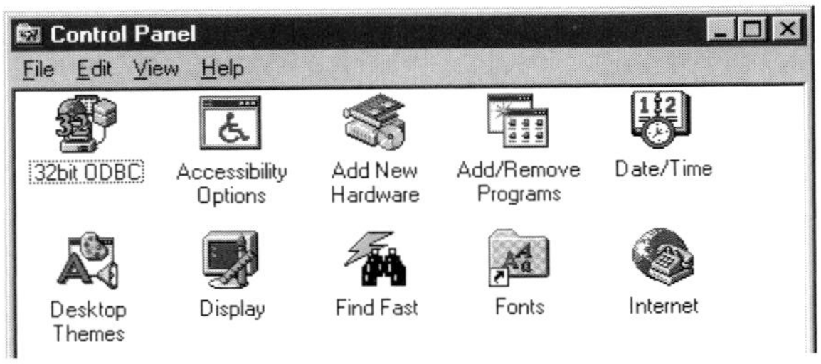

You'll need to consult online help and perhaps read a book like *Windows 95 for Busy People* (if you're using Windows 95) or *Widows NT for Busy People* (if you're using Windows NT) to learn more about the thousands of possible setting changes.

Find

Windows' Find feature can be an invaluable aid for digging up files that seem to be misplaced. To search for a file, choose Find from the Start menu and then choose Files or Folders. In the dialog box that appears, type a filename or part of one in the Named box and press ENTER or click on Find Now.

Help

Stuck? Not sure what to do? You can always consult Windows Help. To do so, choose Help from the Start menu. (If you're doing this for the first time, Windows will tell you that it's setting up Help.) In the Help Topics dialog box that appears (see Figure C.2), click on a topic from the expandable Contents list or click on the Index tab, type a key word in the first box, and choose a topic from the index list in the second box.

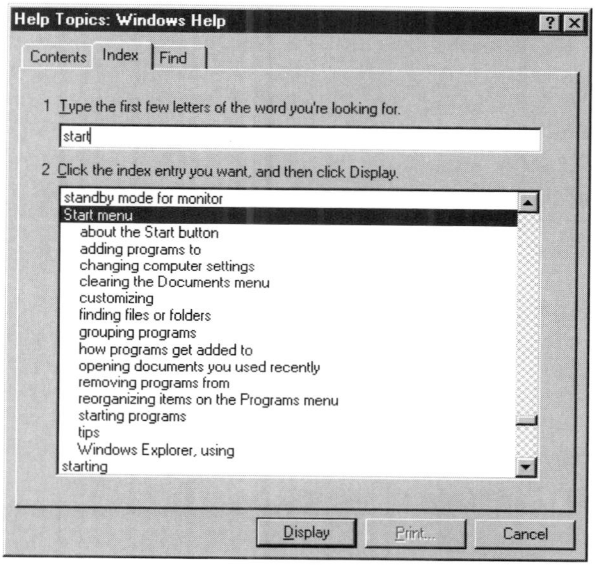

Figure C.2 Choose a topic or subtopic from the Help Topics dialog box

In most programs, if you're not sure what a button or other screen element does, you can hover the mouse pointer over it for a moment and a tool tip will appear, naming or explaining the object.

Also, in a dialog box, you can click on the What's This? button (a question mark) in the top-right corner and then click on the item about which you want more information in the dialog box. A brief explanation should pop up.

Run

Any time you know the name of a program file (although sometimes you also have to know the path of the folders that lead to the program on the hard disk), you can choose Run from the Start menu, type the name (or path and name) in the box, and press ENTER to run the program. It's usually easier, though, to start the program from the Start menu or one of its submenus.

Shut Down

When you want to turn off your computer, first shut down Windows. To do so, choose Shut Down from the Start menu. Click on Yes when asked if you want to shut down the computer. Wait until Windows tells you it's OK to turn off the computer.

Taskbar Tips

Every time you start a program or open or minimize some types of windows, the program or window gets its own button on the Taskbar.

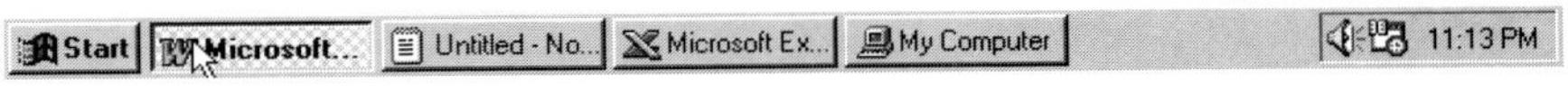

This makes it easy to switch to a program that is already running, to make a particular window active, or to maximize a window. All you have to do is click on the appropriate button on the Taskbar. When a button looks depressed (pushed in), it means that the task represented by the button is the active one, and its window will appear in front of the other windows.

If the Taskbar gets too crowded, you can point to its top edge and drag it so that it gets taller. You can also move the Taskbar to any side of the screen (top, bottom, left, or right) by clicking on any part of the Taskbar that is not a button and dragging. When the Taskbar is on the left or right side, you can drag its inner edge to set it to any width, up to half the width of the screen.

The My Computer Icon

One way to explore the files and programs on your computer is to double-click on the My Computer icon. In general, double-clicking on an icon opens it, runs the program it represents, or runs the program in which the document it represents was created. If the icon is a folder or a special icon such as My Computer, it will open into a window and display its contents, which will also appear as icons. Some of these icons might represent programs, and others might represent folders or other special icons.

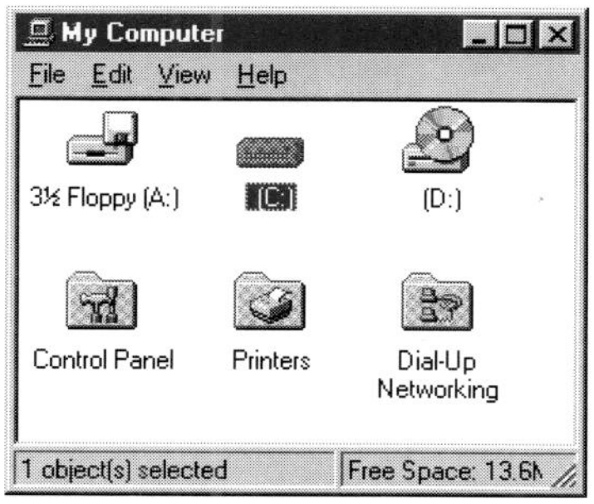

The My Computer window contains icons that represent your hard disk drive, floppy disk drives, and CD-ROM drive (if applicable), as well as icons for your printers, the Control Panel, and perhaps for dial-up networking.

Double-click on the hard disk drive icon to see the contents of the hard disk. The icon opens into a window that shows folders and other icons. Double-click on any folder to see its contents. Repeat as often as necessary. You can go back up a folder level by pressing BACKSPACE.

The Network Neighborhood Icon

If your computer is connected to a network, you will see a Network Neighborhood icon on the desktop. Double-clicking on it will show you a list of the remote computers, disk drives, and folders that you can access.

You might need to know the appropriate passwords to access some of the information on the network, and you might be limited in what you can do with files and folders on the network. For example, the owners of some files might let you read the files but not change them. When you have questions, contact your network administrator or help desk.

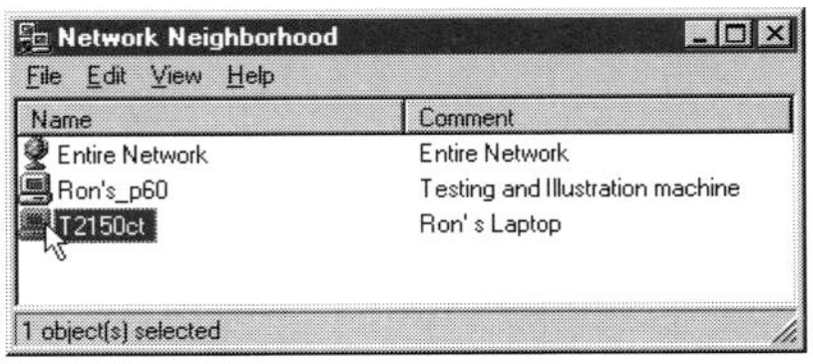

The Recycle Bin

When you delete files from your hard disk in Windows, they are not immediately erased. They are moved to the Recycle Bin. To recover an accidentally deleted file, double-click on the Recycle Bin icon and choose the item or items you wish to restore. Then choose Restore from the File menu in the Recycle Bin window (see Figure C.3).

As you add new files to the Recycle Bin, Windows will eventually start discarding the earliest deleted files left. If you want to free up space, right-click on the Recycle Bin and choose Empty Recycle Bin on the File menu.

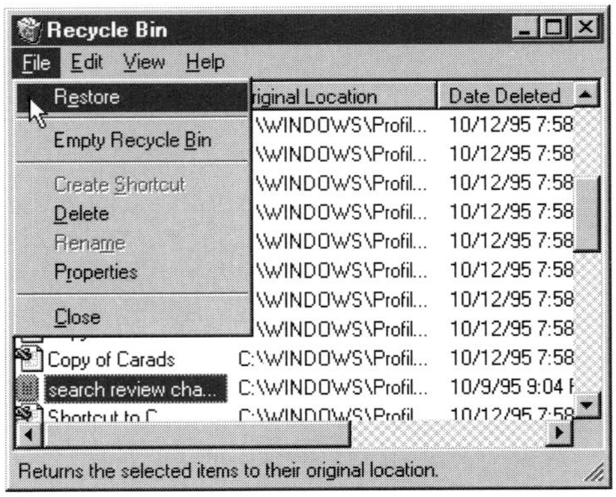

Figure C.3 The Recycle Bin gives you one more chance to "undelete" your files after trashing them

Folders

You and Windows can organize your files into folders, which are the equivalent of directories in oldspeak. You can place folders within folders, thereby creating what used to be called subdirectories. You can create a new folder at any point by right-clicking on the desktop or in a folder (or disk drive) window and choosing New | Folder. You can put a document or program in a folder by dragging its icon onto a folder icon or into an open folder window.

New Rules for Filenames

Windows allows you to use long filenames (up to 255 characters) that include spaces, if you want, so you can give your documents natural sounding names, instead of the pinched, cryptic filenames that DOS used to force on you. Now you can call that document Amortization Projections for 1997 instead of AMTPRJ97.

You might also notice that filename extensions seem to have pretty much disappeared. They're still there at the ends of filenames, but Windows hides all the extensions it recognizes. If you want to see the extensions associated with all filenames, choose Options from the View menu in the My Computer window, the Windows Explorer window, or any folder (or disk drive) window. Click on the View tab. Then uncheck Hide MS-DOS file extensions for file types that are registered. Click on OK. All extensions will appear. To hide most extensions again, repeat the same steps and check the box.

When you are sharing files with non-Windows users, and with programs that were sold prior to the release of Windows 95 or NT, filenames get shortened automatically. This can cause some confusion. Again, consult online help and Windows books for details.

Windows Explorer

Windows allows you to look through the folders on your computer in a single window, with the entire folder tree in a pane on the left side (sort of like the old File Manager). To do this, choose Programs from the Start menu and Windows Explorer (or Windows NT Explorer) from the Programs menu (or right-click on any folder and choose Explore from the menu that pops up). The Windows Explorer (or Windows NT Explorer) window will appear (see Figure C.4), with its folder tree in the left pane and the contents of the selected folder in the right pane.

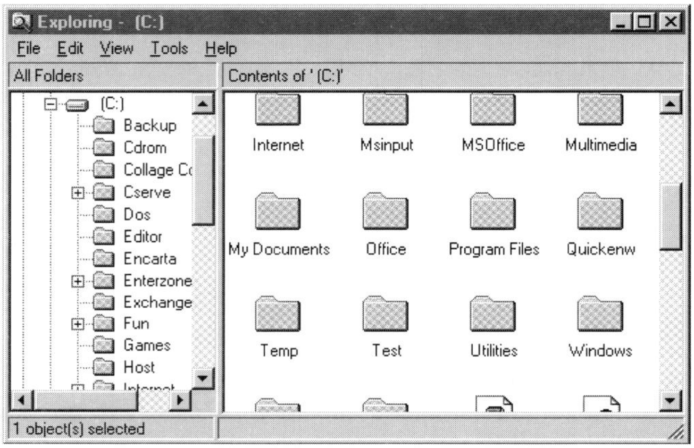

Figure C.4 The Explorer window shows a hierarchical view of the computer in its left pane. There you can thumb through your tree of folders without having to plow through separate folder windows

To see the contents of a folder, click on it in the left pane. To expand or collapse a folder's contents, double-click on the folder in the left pane (or click the little plus or minus icon in a box to the left of the folder). You can go up a folder level by pressing BACKSPACE, as you can in any such window.

Shortcut Icons

Windows allows you to create shortcut icons that point to a program, document, folder, or other Windows resource that you use regularly. This is particularly useful when something you use every day is buried in a folder within a folder. A popular place to keep shortcuts is on the desktop. That way, when you want to open your favorite folder, you just double-click on the shortcut icon on the desktop. Another place you can create a shortcut is on the Start menu, where it will look like a normal menu choice, not like a shortcut icon.

In general, the easiest way to create a shortcut is to right-click and drag a copy of the program's icon to the place where you want the shortcut. To do this, open the window that contains the program's original icon. Right-click on the icon and drag to a new location, such as another folder or the desktop. When you release the mouse button, a menu will pop up. Choose Create Shortcut(s) Here to make the shortcut. You'll probably want to rename the new shortcut icon. (Press F2, type a new name, and press ENTER.) If you drag an icon onto the Start button, even without first right-clicking, a shortcut to that icon will be placed on the Start menu.

That's the Short Course

Well, there you have a taste of Windows. Obviously, there's a lot more worth knowing. And the more you learn, the more productive you will become, so I encourage you to do some independent study, either by using Windows' online help or by cracking a good book or two.

db

Index

NOTE: Page numbers in *italics* refer to illustrations or charts.

C

D

E

F

G

H

T

U

V

W

X

Y

FAX
MEETING
IN
PROGRESS